LISTENING TO LAREDO

Listening to Laredo

A Border City in a Globalized Age

MEHNAAZ MOMEN

THE UNIVERSITY OF
ARIZONA PRESS
TUCSON

The University of Arizona Press
www.uapress.arizona.edu

We respectfully acknowledge the University of Arizona is on the land and territories of Indigenous peoples. Today, Arizona is home to twenty-two federally recognized tribes, with Tucson being home to the O'odham and the Yaqui. Committed to diversity and inclusion, the University strives to build sustainable relationships with sovereign Native Nations and Indigenous communities through education offerings, partnerships, and community service.

ISBN-13: 978-0-8165-5173-6 (hardcover)
ISBN-13: 978-0-8165-5172-9 (paperback)
ISBN-13: 978-0-8165-5175-0 (ebook)

Cover design by Leigh McDonald
Cover image adapted from photo of Laredo by halbergman/istockphoto.com
Typeset by Sara Thaxton in 10/14 Warnock Pro with Trade Gothic Next LT Pro

Publication of this book is made possible in part by support from the Office of the Dean and the Office of the Provost at Texas A&M International University.

Library of Congress Cataloging-in-Publication Data
Names: Momen, Mehnaaz, author.
Title: Listening to Laredo : a border city in a globalized age / Mehnaaz Momen.
Description: Tucson : The University of Arizona Press, 2023. | Includes bibliographical references and index.
Identifiers: LCCN 2022053797 (print) | LCCN 2022053798 (ebook) | ISBN 9780816551736 (hardcover) | ISBN 9780816551729 (paperback) | ISBN 9780816551750 (ebook)
Subjects: LCSH: Laredo (Tex.)—Economic conditions—21st century. | Laredo (Tex.)—Social life and customs—21st century. | Laredo (Tex.)—Social conditions—21st century. | Mexican-American Border Region.
Classification: LCC F394.L2 M66 2023 (print) | LCC F394.L2 (ebook) | DDC 976.4/462064—dc23/eng/20230104
LC record available at https://lccn.loc.gov/2022053797
LC ebook record available at https://lccn.loc.gov/2022053798

Printed in the United States of America
♾ This paper meets the requirements of ANSI/NISO Z39.48-1992 (Permanence of Paper).

Dedicated to the people of Laredo

Mary Louise,

Mehnaaz

Contents

Illustrations

FIGURES

MAPS

Foreword

When one reviews a book or is in negotiation with publishers, one is always pushed to explain who the audience of the proposed publication will be. Beyond a mere marketing tool, it is not such a bad question to ask. In her introduction, Professor Momen provides analysis and detailed examples of how Laredo appears in conventional cultural stereotypes. It is a complication of "what everyone knows" or, most likely, thinks, without thinking about it. If you find yourself there or even nod in recognition, then you are a potential reader.

Momen explores Laredo from within. By bringing together scholarly work, media reports, and local news and interviews, she produces an approach to understanding analogous to experiments with figure-ground interplay in the visual arts. To say this in another way, Jacques Rancière argues that analysis errs when it assumes to know from a distance. Traditions of "talking story," for example in Hawaii, stand in opposition to assumptions about abstract knowledge. In these modes, experiences are aired and circulate. What happens when an academic who is also an acute observer talks story with Laredo residents? The result is a rich combination of analysis and description in the fullest sense of the word. Residents' reflections follow and are sometimes interwoven with the historical and sociopolitical topics the author introduces. So, reading provides an immersive experience, a little like living there.

For example, this quiet researcher lets her conversation partners articulate their vision of a good society with the memories they construct and select to share with her and readers. The history of Laredo as a trade center is linked to a culture of coexistence, where family and community are primary conditions for relations of tolerance and harmony. Relations based on heterogeneity extend the traditions of intermarriage to welcoming newcomers.

Considering the components of a working community also leads Momen to further investigate spaces in which community is most clearly manifest. Examples that residents experience as space in which they have a place include the pre-NAFTA porous border and active aspects of downtown. One of the most illuminating presentations of unsolved contradictions in Laredo, which also has to do with constructing successful public spaces, is Momen's analysis of the annual Washington's Birthday Celebration (WBC). While the structure of language can mitigate against interest in heterogeneity, treasured ephemeral events such as WBC embody it. Urbanists can use this kind of case study to continue valuable research into how heterogeneity works. Momen suggests guidelines: a time of managed freedom (even including open border bridges before 1977), cultural space that brings together people from different worlds, and most important, time/spaces that highlight residents as actors in their own behalf.

In this study there is an accumulation of evidence for fluid categories. Most obviously, this includes "the border." But just as broad reaching is the repetition by example of loose applications of "identity." In census data and immigration policy, identity is inscribed in abstract, closed categories in service of a number of external agendas. In the vernacular of Laredo, the criteria are more volatile: the bond with the city instead of immigration status, for example. What is identity, after all, if not a place to hang your hat? Isn't that what the people of Laredo are about as they navigate among the economic, political, and cultural forces that condition the circumstances of their city?

Readers can thank Momen's energy and devotion to making the living Laredo visible.

—*Helen Liggett, Professor Emerita, Urban Studies*
Cleveland State University

Acknowledgments

The primary data for this book are my seventy-five interviews of Laredo residents. Without their time and support, this book would never have been written. I see my role as a narrator of local voices. My only goal has been to decipher and analyze the themes that emerge from the rich details of life in the border zones, something that is lacking from almost all political and national discourse over the border. I am thankful to Professor Helen Liggett for teaching me the theoretical tools to understand and experience urban transformation. I am grateful to Professors Daniel D. Arreola, Robert Lee Maril, Saskia Sassen, and Norma Elia Cantú for their insightful endorsements.

The maps used in this book are from the City of Laredo, Planning and Zoning Department, and Webb County Heritage Foundation (WCHF). The pictures in this book are from the Laredo Public Library, WCHF, Rio Grande International Study Center (RGISC), Washington's Birthday Celebration Association (WBCA), and Texas A&M International University (TAMIU). I am immensely grateful to Miguel Hernandez (City of Laredo), Margarita Araiza and Christina Davila-Villarreal (WCHF), Tricia Cortez (RGISC), Renée LaPerrière (Laredo Public Library), Celina Alvarado and Nino Cardenas (WBCA), and Steve Harmon (TAMIU).

I would also like to extend my thanks to the wonderful people at the University of Arizona Press: Kristen A. Buckles, Elizabeth Wilder, Amanda Krause, Abby S. Mogollón, Sara Thaxton, Leigh McDonald, and Carl Steven LaRue for their assistance and enthusiasm. As always, my colleagues (Jerry Thompson, Frances Bernat, and Lola Norris), my friends (Moniza, Laila,

Elora, Gemini, and Miti), and my family (my mother Humaira and my sister Nausheen) lent their ears and support all through the years I compiled the interviews and finished this project. Anis deserves special thanks for asking difficult questions and especially for his editing, which has enriched the quality of the book. I am, of course, responsible for any mistakes or omissions.

Historical Timeline of Laredo, Texas

1755	Don Tomás Sánchez de la Barrera y Garza establishes the Spanish colonial settlement of Villa de San Agustín de Laredo
1768	Laredo becomes an incorporated town after a city charter was granted
1840	Laredo becomes the capital of the Republic of the Rio Grande
1846	Texas Rangers occupy Laredo during the Mexican-American War
1847	First election held in Laredo as part of the United States
1848	Treaty of Guadalupe Hidalgo establishes the Rio Grande as the boundary and permanently divides the city. Nuevo Laredo is established as a city in Mexico
1849	Fort McIntosh established by the United States Army
1852	Laredo rechartered as a city
1861	Laredo emerges as a smuggling point during cotton times (Civil War)
1868	Downtown grid system established by Mayor Samuel Jarvis
1881	Railroad connects Laredo to Corpus Christi and San Antonio
1887	Railroad connects Laredo to Mexico City
1889	First bridge with footbridge and electric trolley is built on the Rio Grande
1894	U.S. Postal Service starts door-to-door mail in Laredo
1915	Laredo Chamber of Commerce established
1916	The first public school, Laredo High School (renamed Martin High School in 1937), established

1920   Laredo Rotary Club established

1932   Rio Grande floods

1935   Pan American Highway connects Laredo to Mexico City

1939   The headquarters of the Twenty-Third Customs Collection District established

1947   Laredo Junior College (Laredo College) founded at Fort McIntosh

1954   Rio Grande floods. First International Bridge (Gateway to Americas) starts operating

1957   Interstate 35 construction begins

1971   Interstate 35 construction ends

1976   Second International Bridge (Juárez–Lincoln) starts operating

1978   J. C. Martin indicted, ending patron system in Laredo

1992   Third International Bridge (Laredo–Colombia Solidarity) starts operating

1994   North American Free Trade Agreement (NAFTA) signed

1995   Texas A&M International University (TAMIU) established as the first four-year college in the city

2000   Fourth International Bridge (World Trade) starts operating

2004   Laredo College opens its south campus in the Cuatro Vientos neighborhood

2017   Viva Laredo adopted after two-year community engagement

2018   Farmers market begins in Laredo

2019   President Donald J. Trump declares emergency at the border. Laredo surpasses Los Angeles (temporarily) as the largest inland port of the nation

2020   Contract awarded to Customs and Border Protection (CBP) to construct a seventeen-mile contiguous border wall system in Laredo

2021   Border wall contract for Laredo and the Rio Grande Valley terminated

LISTENING TO LAREDO

Introduction

Laredo is not part of Texas or Mexico, or even America.
It is the Republic of Laredo.

THOMAS JEFFREY,[1] LAREDO RESIDENT

Laredo is semiarid desert, but then you have this green ribbon of life, this extraordinary river and its creek systems
that just save this place from being a total desert.

TRINA CASE, LAREDO RESIDENT

The border crossed us. We were already here. This was our
land and all of a sudden we became part of America.

ALEX MEAD, LAREDO RESIDENT

Profile of Laredo

The largest inland port of the United States along the U.S.-Mexico boundary is Laredo, which before the North American Free Trade Agreement
(NAFTA) used to be a dusty little border town with a quaint history. Nestled
between the U.S.-Mexico territory along the Rio Grande in Texas, the city
is older than the United States. Fueled by a dizzying spell of growth that occurred in the short span of three decades, Laredo surpassed Los Angeles to
become the largest port of any kind—sea, land, or air—in the United States
in 2019.[2] The aura of the bygone age surrounding its charming downtown
is now overshadowed by negative ordeals associated with trade and migration. The flocks of tourists and traders to the twin cities on both sides of the
Rio Grande—Laredo and Nuevo Laredo—are now memories of a departed
era. The same features of proximity to Mexico and ease of passage currently
spell disorder and chaos in the political discourse. The border of Laredo has
become synonymous with international trade to a greater extent than in the
past. Under this new iteration, the remarkable history of the rich culture,

economic success, and spatial evolution of Laredo is being buried. This book attempts to excavate the story of the city from the viewpoints and experiences of the people who actually live there to make sense of the concurrent drifts of being a historic city, a border city, and a global trade center.

Historic cities emphasize their glorious pasts; border cities are perceived as intermediate sites between nation-states, allowing clandestine activities; and global cities are centers of unmitigated growth. Historic cities are formed by the annals of antiquity, border cities are characterized by peripheral conflicts around boundaries, and global cities attempt to navigate national boundaries with the promise of economic boons. Laredo boasts of the distinct record of having been under seven flags (one as the capital of a short-lived republic), and its intricate history has served as a matter of pride for the people. The overwhelmingly Hispanic town relished its interdependent relationship with the people of Nuevo Laredo, which included family and business bonds going back several generations. Even though borders are contested sites for nation-states—and Laredo had been disputed terrain between Mexicans, Texans, and Americans—the umbilical cord between Laredo and Nuevo Laredo remained robust until Laredo evolved into a global port. Geography situated the coupled cities along a navigable river but detached from other metropolises, which strengthened their mutual dependence. Laredo has a long history of benign neglect by all the nation-states to which it belonged. The city flourished organically by taking advantage of its location and cultivating a socioeconomic hierarchy nuzzled in ethnic and cultural homogeneity.

An economic windfall came to Laredo during the Civil War when Laredo became a center for smuggling the cotton that funded the Confederate army. The city blossomed into a trade center by the turn of the twentieth century. Local folklore goes so far as to claim that by the 1950s, downtown Laredo was more prosperous than New York. The 1980s devaluation of the peso brought disaster to the retail economy heavily dependent on Mexican customers. Globalization ushered in a new meaning for border territories in the 1990s, as Laredo found itself perfectly situated to be a key locale in the postindustrial economy in the thriving Sunbelt, with an existing transportation network and abundant cheap labor on its periphery. The neoliberal growth rationale for border zones is based on transportation, consumption, and enhancement of the state apparatus with incessant surveillance, a notable deviation from the established pattern of the gradual progress of a city.

As the busiest land port,[3] Laredo functions as a major link in the expansive global trade web, which requires simultaneous speedy transit and strict policing of the nation-state's boundary. With its newfound international trade link, the codependency between Laredo and Nuevo Laredo has evaporated. Nuevo Laredo, the largest transportation nerve center in Mexico, fell under the power of the drug cartels as its location in the global network abetted narcotics transactions. In this new reality, the river, roads, and bridges are all under constant supervision, impairing the previous openness of the border. Only large freight trucks enjoy swift entrance from the south. The ceaseless flow of people across the border is a not-so-distant memory and is mourned by residents. Local concerns about preserving water quality and the riverbank or even investing in homegrown businesses have to compete with national or international trade and growth imperatives. The evolution of Laredo reveals both internal and external elements in the process of economic advancement and the formation of cultural identity in the border city.

The southern border was always the defining feature of Laredo. It has a 95 percent Hispanic population, the highest proportion for any border city. The overwhelming majority presence of this ethnic minority group, which was not shut off from power positions, nurtured a self-pride and cohesive identity among residents that is markedly different from other marginal groups that manifest in both racial and regional variations. Laredo is restricted on its southern periphery because of the Rio Grande and the border with Mexico, but it has hastened to include large expanses toward the north within city limits, owing mostly to lax zoning laws in Texas. Suburbs, which typify major cities in the United States and function to distance the prosperous from the poor, remain rare and novel in Laredo. Historically, wealthy neighborhoods were located near downtown but have now shifted to the emerging northern parts of town. Laredo is bisected between its northern and southern parts, and the separation of rich and poor neighborhoods in the physical landscape reflects particular policies and visions regarding the institutions, infrastructure, and imagined futures of the city. Although the city center followed the trend of falling into decay like most American cities, it is set apart by the fact that the downtown retains the most lucrative source of revenue through the four bridges that connect Laredo to Nuevo Laredo.

Laredo grew over time as an important junction for trade, its distance from nearby towns and proximity to river and road networks determining its destiny. The thrust for unprecedented growth and expansion came through

NAFTA, making Laredo one of the fastest-growing cities in the nation and elevating it as one of the major cities in Texas. In appearance, the historical downtown seems to have passed its heyday since it cannot compete with the new social and cultural centers that are developing in the growing northern sections of town. Efforts to revive the business and cultural ambience of downtown have recently been facing a new threat (evaded for now), namely, the political push for a border wall that would not only destroy the ancient plazas and buildings but also impede the flow of Mexican customers who remain a large part of Laredo's economy. This paradoxical turn in border discourse is rooted in the heated contest of local dynamics with intrusive national politics and expansive international trade.

Globalization generates strategic sites of production that are tied to new networks of trade that compete with established national and local political priorities. Saskia Sassen draws our attention to the processes of reterritorialization where such global networks create new socio-spatial orders by moving selective economic pursuits from the margin to the center of the production process. The new market order becomes localized, breeding inequality and manifesting cultural transformation.[4] The political implications of such economic alignments have been analyzed for larger cities such as Los Angeles, but smaller cities that are in the process of reconfiguration often stay beyond the radar of such scholarship. Laredo is now a site where locality and globality intersect as local stakeholders are deciding whether to resist or participate in the spatial and economic rearrangements following national and international recomposition. It is precisely this conjunction that provides a unique opportunity to examine local versus global conflicts of interest and to observe how the city is taking shape by addressing these somewhat mutually exclusive objectives. The conflict between local, national, and international preferences has also opened up the question of identity, both for the border region and for the Hispanic inhabitants who have been forced out of their comfort zones.

Laredo in Popular Culture

The phrase "streets of Laredo" reverberates in popular culture through literature, movies, and music. Most people are familiar with the song "Streets of Laredo" (1965) by Johnny Cash, about a cowboy who meets a violent death in the border town. The song was originally a traditional folk song, first pub-

FIGURE 1 San Agustín Church. Photo by author.

lished in 1910.[5] Numerous musicians (Pete Seeger, Don Gibson, The Kings-
ton Trio) have sung this famous number, often with a few variations in the
lyrics (the song is also known as the "Cowboy's Lament"). The song describes
a dying cowboy's plight and his last words as he is "wrapped in white linen"
and lies under the hot sun of Laredo. Knowing that he has very little time
left, the cowboy remembers the good days of his short life and pleads for a
merry funeral with "jolly cowboys," "dance-hall maidens," and "bunches of
roses" befitting his life. This is the image of Laredo, where the gap between
life and death is trifling, and the last rites can be as frivolous as life itself.
The cowboy's lament about his impending death under the scorching sun in
Laredo signifies the hostility and brutality of Laredo itself:

> The streets of Laredo grew cold as the clay.
> We took the young cowboy down to the green valley,
> And there stands his marker we made to this day.
> We beat the drum slowly and played the Fife lowly,
> Played the dead march as we carried him along.

Down in the green valley, laid the sod over him.
He was a young cowboy and he said he'd done wrong.[6]

This notion of Laredo as death or punishment is perpetuated in songs from different genres over and over. In Laredo, even passion is woven under the shadow of death. Warren Zevon sings of Ramona, the beautiful seductress who must be shot for her sin in "A Bullet for Ramona." Ramona here is as treacherous as Laredo; encounters with her end in humiliation, and the only honorable end seems to be death itself.[7] Passion in Laredo is always tinged with betrayal. Leonardo "Flaco" Jiménez sees Laredo as the land where promiscuity prevails and promises are broken. The dancer from Laredo swindles her lover and takes his money and car in "Ay te Dejo en San Antonio." He leaves her in San Antonio but cannot escape from her magic, much like the allure of Laredo.[8] Even in the deepest passion, the hints of crime and death are inescapable, as Bronco reminds us in "La hechicera."[9] The singer is looking for the sorceress who has bewitched him with her eyes. He wants to chain her to life imprisonment with him, returning her lustful kisses. Where else, but in Laredo, can he start his voyage of passion?

Laredo figures as a long punishment, like an ailment without recovery, in the cultural landscape. The city has its enticements, but death always eclipses the temptations. Laredo is not only associated with physical death but also the death of dreams and fantasies. Los Alegres de Terán speak of a prisoner, wrongfully detained, and worse, his lover walks out on him when he needs her the most. Laredo signifies the prison he is in for the crime of being in the wrong place with the wrong girl. So he can only voice his anguish in "Los pilares de la cárcel": "Through the streets of Laredo, after you saw that they put me in bars / You went back, to enjoy a new love."[10]

Laredo beckons a few hapless people traveling through the inhospitable southern territory and yearning for love or home. People who are victimized by the system, trapped in prison, or fleeing from prison for a crime they did not commit may have left their love back in Laredo. "Letter to Laredo" by Joe Ely is another familiar tale of a man running from the law for a crime he did not commit but who has kept his silence to shield his lover in Laredo.[11] Laredo is a place where a man who has never owned a gun ends up in a fight and kills a guy. Frankie Laine tells the story of a "Wanted Man," always on the run like a mountain cat. He is being hunted by the brother of the man he killed over a girl who has moved on with her life. He doubts whether the girl was even worth the fight, because she seems as careless and mercenary as her city.[12]

Laredo became part of the literary canon with Larry McMurtry's best-selling novel *Streets of Laredo* (1993), which was made into a much-publicized television series. The actual novel exhibits multilayered characters and storytelling from multiple perspectives. The choice of the lead characters, the ex-prostitute and the bounty hunter, is unusual and allows the story to be told from a nonelitist viewpoint. The transitions enveloping Texas, including the agrarian success of ranchers and the relative plight of cowboys, remain in the plotline to set up a powerful historical context of geography and spatial power.[13] In an earlier movie with the same name, Laredo is pictured with blood-oozing scenes of death, children being burnt alive, a pregnant woman being raped, and a gang on horseback riding over an old woman and crushing her to death quite nonchalantly. The television miniseries *Streets of Laredo* (1995) followed the format of the 1949 film rather than McMurtry's novel. The original story became transformed into the classic Western template of good versus evil framed in explicit violence.

Laredo's starkly violent iconography has been repeated on numerous television shows. These include the Western television series *Laredo* (NBC, 1965–67) and the series *Bordertown: Laredo* (A&E, 2011), both of which showcase the negative and brutal side of Laredo. Airing in the mid-sixties, *Laredo* adopted the style of the Western genre, even though it had comedic elements, while following the adventures of three Texas Rangers.[14] The portrayal of the town was more about Texas in the 1870s and not so much about Laredo at the time. The name of the city serves as a convenient backdrop for the Texas Rangers to valiantly seek out criminals while taking the opportunity to show off courteous Southern mannerisms, especially toward women. Although Laredo has always been overwhelmingly Hispanic, including its elites, the show was almost all white except for a few Hispanics as sidekicks. Running for fifty-six episodes, it introduced Laredo to a national audience with its dose of comedy toward the violence in the Wild West on the southern border.

Bordertown: Laredo, the recent reality series, evokes the same prism of disorder and crime to depict the city today. The storylines revolve around the dangerous assignments of the narcotics unit of the Laredo Police Department and its encounters with cartels and local drug dealers. The series is not based on any real incidents, but the style of journalistic narration makes it appear so. In this dystopian fantasy of Laredo, only the police and drug smugglers are visible while the residents are hardly ever present on the screen. This kind of myopic, even hysterical, presentation of Laredo is common in popular culture and has seeped into the national consciousness. It has mostly been drugs, violence, and illegal immigration that have constituted the storylines that depict Laredo. In April 2019, a Fox News reporter covered the immigration crisis from the very safe international bridge wearing a bulletproof vest.[15]

A noteworthy response to this stereotype of Laredo was penned by local writer Norma Elia Cantú in the form of her memoir, *Canícula*.[16] With care and compassion, Cantú describes her girlhood in *la frontera*, which was impoverished and yet filled with love and family alliances that spanned the border. Canícula describes the long summer months, known as the dog days by local people, and the stories contain snippets from her family, huddled together and exploring their home and beyond. As an autobiography with partly fictionalized characters, the nonlinear tales mirror the fluidity of the border, while the pictures of idyllic childhood reiterate the serene narrative arc. Cantú introduces us to a very different rhythm of the borderlands, relaxed and loving, nourishing and colorful, the stark opposite of the violence and brutality marking the received idea of the border regions. Her memories paint the border as a periphery of the American dream, where people thrive in their compact community, all but oblivious to wider political trends.

The political discourse about the border—chaos, crime, lawlessness, and the invasion of asylum seekers—is freely dispensed in popular culture, which has historically romanticized a similar lawless image of the frontier. Lone voices like Cantú's are inundated in the cacophony that emerges when the border is constructed from the outside. The Southwest often represents a place of refuge from the modern in our collective imagination. In the shared production of cultural memory, border town Laredo has been constructed as an exotic wild space, a heterotopia or even a dystopia, where the Native Americans, Spanish, Mexicans, Tejanos, and Anglos collided to subjugate the frontier.

What Makes Laredo Unique?

The city of Laredo has a distinct origin story as neither a fort funded by the king nor a mission empowered by the church. Without a benefactor, the city

BUSINESS DISTRICT, FLORES AVENUE, LOOKING NORTH. LAREDO, TEXAS.

FIGURE 2 Business district, Flores Avenue, Laredo. Webb County Heritage Foundation.

raised taxes to protect itself against Indian attacks. As one of the oldest cities west of the Mississippi, the historical roots that are still tangible in the kinship patterns and the connection with the land that extends to Nuevo Laredo are what make it unique. The residents of the sister cities were geographically and politically removed from their respective national terrains, which fostered a self-contained identity enclosed in the comfort of their homogeneous environment. Laredo lived and grew in the shade of studied indifference by Mexico City, Texas, and the United States. The city with seven flags flying over it started off with the Spanish Crown, and after a brief interlude with French colonists who never set foot in Laredo, it became Mexican territory. The independent and spirited strain in Laredo's identity is evident in its history when for a brief period of ten months it served as the capital of the Republic of the Rio Grande. The subsequent tug-of-war between the Republic of Texas, the Republic of the Rio Grande, the Confederacy, and the United States has deeply shaped Laredo's identity.

Geographic isolation nurtured and protected the character of the border city that was interdependent with its Mexican counterpart through economic, cultural, and family ties bridging generations. The intercultural homogeneity between twin cities along the U.S.-Mexico border is often a romantic myth,[17] but Laredo might be one of the few places where this myth is alive. One of the interviewees, *Rodrique Taylor*, firmly believes that what makes Laredo unique is the fact that "the city never lost its identity." This perception from the grassroots level is supported by scholars. As Robert Wood notes, "The Laredoans in many ways established their own little world which respected the supreme authority and even took advantage of it when necessary or possible, but they could also circumvent undesirable situations or regulations and survive or even thrive under different governments."[18]

The principal prism of understanding minority history in the American landscape is through oppression and subjugation. Mexican American natives in Laredo contest this dominant narrative by having held on to power in the city government since its inception. Although Laredo had a handful of Native Americans, and the inclusion in Texas and the United States made room for white settlers, there was almost no overt conflict over either land or power. The practice of intermarriage between Anglos and Mexicans created a racial harmony where people could claim bicultural heritage with pride and not face prejudice. The biggest difference in Laredo is that the record of white people is associated with positive history, unlike other Hispanic cities, such as San Antonio or El Paso, where Anglos dominated the ethnic minority. Intermarriage was common and allowed outsiders straddling different ethnicities to become part of the social structure. There was no cultural separation in family-oriented Laredo for interracial families. The Anglo population learned Spanish, went to the same churches, and intermingled with Mexican Americans. As was apt for a trade center, trespassers could set up homes or businesses and find themselves integrated into the community. Because of the Hispanic concentration, racism (though not classism or any other type of prejudice) was almost absent in any meaningful or even symbolic manner.

Local residents claim that the city has created a space for a third culture, namely border culture, by allowing the two cultures to blend and coexist. To its credit, Laredo has protected the bicultural environment for several generations, which is another distinct feature for a city located at a global crossroads. Laredo was commonly imagined as being located almost at the midpoint between Mexico City and New York in the transportation node, and yet distant (by 150 miles) from the nearest cities to the north (San Antonio), south (Monterrey), and east (Corpus Christi). These unusual features made it possible for the minority community to be on its own and avoid the discriminatory practices and policies that were customary nationwide. His-

FIGURE 3 Flag of the Republic of the Rio Grande. Webb County Heritage Foundation.

panic people in Laredo seldom experienced being treated as "others" as long as they remained inside the border city. These day-to-day living practices of a minority group acting as a majority are also quite distinctive in American political history.

Laredo in Border Studies Discourse

In intellectual circles Laredo has been explored through two distinct lenses. The historical and cultural significance of the border town has attracted historians, geographers, and urban theorists to chronicle the growth patterns, the plazas, or the economic interdependence of sister cities along the border. This prism of examining the border went through a discernible change in post-NAFTA scholarship on the border, which centered on trade, crime, and broader economic aspects. After the 1990s Laredo featured in scholarly pursuits as part of globalization studies that replaced the bicultural heritage with cultural ambiguity and equated the fluid periphery with chaos and criminality. The curiosity about the border through the medium of border studies deals either with broad abstract concepts connected to Hispanic identity or urgent crises pertaining to drugs, illegality, and the militarization of the border. The day-to-day lives of most people have become invisible in the bulk of this scholarship.

Gilberto Hinojosa has documented the early history of Laredo in *A Borderlands Town in Transition: Laredo, 1775–1870*, where he recounts the reasons for its demographic expansion, which mirrored the growth in trade and economic prosperity.[19] The city lost almost half its people when the Treaty of Guadalupe Hidalgo was ratified, as a substantial number of residents crossed the Rio Grande and resettled on its west bank, carving out a separate city, Nuevo Laredo, which had been part of Laredo.[20] The border has always been shaped by political upheaval in both the United States and Mexico. Whether it was the Mexican War of Independence, the Texas Revolution, or the Civil War, these occasions of bloodshed often dictated drastic demographic changes.[21] John Adams provides a more colorful history of the clashes in his *Conflict and Commerce on the Rio Grande: Laredo, 1775–1955.*[22] His chronicle of Laredo's growth follows the route of commerce in the transborder marketplace. Laredo was known as Zona Libre in the 1850s, allowing merchants to bypass regulations and tariffs, stratagems that would result in over five decades of rivalry between the United States and Mexico.[23] After political unrest in Mexico and Reconstruction policies in Texas dampened growth from trade,[24] it was the railroads that spurred the growth of markets and people in the 1870s, providing an outlet for agricultural and mining products.[25] History seems to have repeated itself with the cycle in black gold, first in the form of oil exploration in South Texas in the 1860s and more recently the fracking of natural gas in the 2000s in the same region. Laredo has a history of being a site of conflict, though it has a much stronger tradition as a center of commerce owing to its strategic location.[26]

Kathleen Da Camara records Laredo's agricultural past in her book *Laredo on the Rio Grande*, along with documentation of the city's cultural practices and architectural landmarks.[27] She mentions various churches in the downtown area as well as Fort McIntosh, all part of the historic district. Her recollections of Native American and Mexican festivals provide a noteworthy backdrop for an analysis of Laredo's most important monthlong cultural festivity, George Washington's Birthday Celebration (WBC). Robert Wood has complemented the work of historians with archival records and first-person accounts in his *Life in Laredo: A Documentary History from the Laredo Archives.*[28] While these narrations of Laredo's history convey the demographic and economic expansion by accentuating the city's strategic location, they do not set it apart from other border cities in any remarkable way. Milo Kearney and Anthony Knopp have documented the historical evolution of the relationships between twin cities on the U.S.-Mexico border, providing both historical and comparative perspectives to situate Laredo among its cohorts.[29]

Daniel Arreola and James Curtis seek to locate the personalities of cities in terms of their land-use practices, urban structures, and cultural heritage.[30] Arreola has collected and analyzed a vast array of postcards from the Río Bravo border as part of the visual history of the first half of the twentieth century. This historical geography of border towns illuminates several themes that often capture the stereotypes of border towns but also negate common labels by humanizing the subjects and objects portrayed in the postcards.[31] Setha Low examines the cultural meaning of plazas in border towns,[32] which is a valuable tool for any analysis of the Laredo landscape. Scholars agree that cultural policies can often determine the shape of urban forms and functions.[33] John Hannigan studies such policies and practices in various cities that strive to attract people by articulating their fantasies.[34] Amorphous desires and illusions inscribed in texts, images, and sounds can be extracted from metanarratives of the city.[35] All of these frameworks are relevant, and in some instances essential, to making sense of Laredo.

Borders are acknowledged as zones of transition, but the forces of globalization have redefined the territoriality of the border by simultaneously opening it up for more commerce yet also overseeing the very openings they have created to adhere to the parameters of the nation-state. This new phenomenon has been called "penumbral," as it is neither hard nor soft but shifting in its permeability.[36] In this vein the U.S.-Mexico border has attracted substantial scholarship on the process of deterritorialization and reterritorialization, especially with respect to NAFTA.[37] The hardening of the southern border in the United States is the result of the reorientation of the border as a security/economy nexus[38] that attempts to overwrite historical and cultural connections. The sociocultural impact of the redefinition of the border on identity formation has also garnered attention, although identity is usually premised on power relations between rival ethnic groups that extend across national boundaries.[39] There is an increasing recognition of the boundary as a narrative by itself, produced by its internal knowledge base and institutions,[40] perpetually organizing the space and its memory and thereby constantly participating in identity formation.

Border communities have been called a "thirdspace," an opaque no-man's-land, in sociocultural studies, even if in Laredo's case the stringent monitoring of the mobility of people has emerged along with physical boundaries following the upsurge in global trade unleashed by NAFTA. Scholars such as Edward Soja have provided us with new frameworks to question the growth and configuration of a city in relation to its geography and economy, especially in connection with globalization. Cities that are highly integrated into international networks of finance, trade, and production evolve into global cities as their position within a global urban hierarchy supersedes their relationship to territorial or national economies.[41] Laredo remains torn between local, national, and global interests. It escaped the painful transition from a typical industrial town to a postindustrial one as it was always a trade center, but as an emergent global node it reflects economic polarization and reshaped internal patterns of urban development that devalue the specific advantages of place and location.[42] Laredo has emerged as a perfect site to study the impact of the political economy of globalization on its physical landscape as well as its cultural manifestations. The economic restructuring of the city has generally sidestepped local preferences, but clashes between national and local political stakes have opened up new encounters focused on identity and claims to the city.

Fernando Romero calls the U.S.-Mexico border a "hyper-border," one of the busiest international borders encapsulating global concerns such as trade and migration as well as the age-old dilemmas of nationality and identity.[43] He discusses various global border regions and classifies their relationships from hostile to cooperative over a range of common problems extending from the political to the ethnic amid labor, trade, transportation, and environmental concerns. The U.S.-Mexico border divides a superpower from a developing nation, yet the two unequal partners are bound to each other through trade and migration along with illicit exchange of drugs and weapons.[44] Both security and fluidity are inherent characteristics of this border and intrinsic components of urban lives. The escalation of trade and migration after NAFTA disrupted the age-old pattern of the regular flow of people and merchandise that had been established through ancestral and cultural ties. While focusing on current ideas about the city, its public spaces, and its identity, I pay special attention to the historical implications of the border before it emerged as a hyper-border that has become an indispensable route for commerce with a nationwide impact.

Cities have historically been associated with fear. The oldest continuously inhabited city in the world, ancient Jericho, also has the distinction of being surrounded by the world's first known protective wall. Sophie Body-Gendrot links this old fear and insecurity with the new era of globalization across a number of global cities in *Globalization, Fear and Insecurity: The Challenges for Cities North and South.*[45] Globalization has inspired a number of scholars from many disciplines to look into the anatomy and psychology of the border. Cari Eastman draws our attention to civil society along the Arizona-Mexico border,[46] while Joseph Nevins examines the actual wall built on the same border.[47] Nevins's analysis connects the construction of the border wall with that of national identity, where illegal aliens are framed as the other. Sylvia Longmire offers another useful perspective by analyzing the border apparatus as a profit-making industry in *Border Insecurity: Why Big Money, Fences, and Drones Aren't Making Us Safer.*[48] Ronald Rael has recently supplemented academic interpretations of the border by introducing us to artistic and innovative subversions of the physical wall by border communities.[49]

Perhaps the most important recent work on the impending border wall in the Texas-Mexico region has been produced by Robert Maril. He has chronicled firsthand accounts of Border Patrol agents by incorporating their encounters and concerns in *Patrolling Chaos: The U.S. Border Patrol in Deep South Texas.*[50] In his most recent book, he presents stories of borderland residents in their own voices, sharing their knowledge to depict the diverse meanings of the wall, its nuances, and its consequences for their lives.[51] Personal accounts of experiences in border communities, often by Border Patrol agents, seem to have become a prevalent niche. Ray Maldonado has documented the vigilante movement on the Arizona-Mexico border, where he worked for the American Civil Liberties Union (ACLU).[52] His intimate experience of growing up in a border community and his professional expertise as a lawyer play a key role in a narrative that includes the perspectives of the most vulnerable characters, the actual border crossers, whose risks and dreams are fleshed out. In *Desert Duty: On the Line with the U.S. Border Patrol*, Bill Broyles and Mark Haynes have collected narratives from nineteen active-duty and retired agents who staffed the Arizona-Mexico border, allowing their challenges and frustrations to humanize them and loom over prevalent political narratives of border policies.[53] In *My Border Patrol Diary: Laredo, Texas*, Dale Squint has published his own diary over twenty-three years of working as a Border Patrol agent in Laredo, where he interprets the border from a law enforcement perspective.[54]

Border studies have flourished in the globalization era not only in volume but across disciplinary parameters, opening up new vistas to locate and re-imagine the border.[55] Emmanuel Brunet-Jailly has introduced local culture and popular control as key factors in border regions, adding to the existing common denominators of market forces and government actions, even if he considers the former elements to be ancillary and less powerful.[56] The systematic analysis of border regions continues to prioritize economic and structural changes, overlooking local characteristics. But the new concept of "glocalization" questions the hegemony of global power and shifts agency to existing local structures and networks and their forms of resistance.[57] A very interesting parable of glocalization is revealed in *Baseball on the Border: A Tale of Two Laredos*, which traces the story of Tecolotes de los Dos Laredos (The Owls of the Two Laredos), the only binational professional baseball team (1985–94), which called both Laredo and Nuevo Laredo its home base.[58] This team questioned the very construction of nationalism and its militant connection with sports, instead illuminating a coherent border identity that subverted the language of national identity. Perhaps it is not co-incidental that the team was dismantled in the mid-1990s, just when NAFTA

FIGURE 4 World Trade Bridge. Webb County Heritage Foundation.

intensified border trade but disconnected local economic interdependence between the two cities.

Rethinking the Border from Within

Laredo cherishes the memory of the open border, which was a way of life until the mid-1980s. During Washington's Birthday Celebration (WBC), the bridge would be open to let thousands of people come to Laredo. It was understood that not all were going to turn back to the south, and maybe a few would continue their northward journey, but this did not dampen the celebration. Everyone had a free pass, and no questions were asked at the checkpoints. One could not go past the twenty-six-mile marker, but no one needed a green card or any papers to come across. This practice of the open border is deeply inscribed in the living memory of older Laredoans. The argument about how the open border leads to chaos and disorder contradicts real lived experience. The fluidity of the border was deeper and more enduring than just the ceremonial symbolism. The concept of controlling the border is indeed a new notion for the locals. One of the residents, *Samantha Taft*, asks, "How do you control a highway? There is a flow, and you manage the flow. You manage the flow of people coming and going." *Matilda Roy*, who belongs to a much younger generation, claims that she grew up not noticing the border. It never existed for her as she could cross it daily, whenever she needed to. People become aware of the border not by living on the border but by hearing its definition on the news. As Roy points out, "The population of Laredo doubles on a daily basis because of the traffic from Nuevo Laredo. Is Laredo ready to give up this economic exchange?"

Urban scholar Mike Davis defines borders as surrealist landscapes where fear and surveillance reign and further amplify marginality,[59] but for the people of Laredo, the border has been nurturing. The language of "otherness," which stresses ethnic identity or immigration, also subverts the rights of residents in the border regions. This categorization falls flat in the heavily Hispanic city that unabashedly celebrates its Mexican roots. The current overtones of the border clash with the recollections and experiences of the people who live there. The discrepancy is not only rooted in time—namely, past versus present—but more tellingly in the perception of the border as abstract or concrete. Which narratives are accepted and projected shape who is in control of the border. In Laredo, the border serves as memory, space, and identity, concepts that can be defined from both inside the community as well as by outside forces. These different ways of looking at the border yield very different functions of the border. Past memories reveal the border as a form of kinship with Nuevo Laredo, but present turbulence in the Mexican city requires some level of control at the border. The border as an abstract concept allows life, business, and different forms of exchange to flow smoothly, but a concrete border is only as meaningful as its system of vigilance. The local narrative of a thriving community is quite simply at odds with the federal projection of the border being out of control.

The border that remained invisible to people in Laredo for generations only became palpable with economic policies that paradoxically were adopted to increase the volume of business. Historically, we have differentiated between legal and illegal trade. NAFTA raised the amount of trade as well as the stake in quick transactions. As a result, priority is accorded to the rapid movement of trucks carrying merchandise from Mexico rather than checking the vehicles for illegal drugs or merchandise. Most of the counterfeit materials including drugs enter the port of Laredo through legal channels. The aspect that gets the most scrutiny is the much smaller amount of smuggled drugs carried by people illegally crossing the border. It takes less than seven days for goods to reach Canada from Mexico via Laredo. Instead of disrupting the flow of trade with tools available to check for drugs, the emphasis has shifted to forbidden pathways rather than prohibited items of trade. As emphasized in this book, the border has always remained open for business. Law enforcement in Laredo has been vigilant to guard against the crime wave of Nuevo Laredo, but even the cartels have been careful not to affect the city of Laredo too much.

Laredo must remain a safe destination for the billions of dollars in both merchandise and drugs that pass through every single day. *Charles Vega*, who served in local government for several decades, emphasizes that almost all the human trafficking and drugs come over the bridges. Statistics show that most drugs enter through trucks rather than tunnels. Again, instead of monitoring drugs, the emphasis has shifted to monitoring the border. Only a tiny portion of tractor trailers is checked for drugs, as disruption of trade is not a real option. There are some programs where companies allow the government or law enforcement to visit warehouses that are opened up to reviews without being notified. These companies are given Fast Passes, allowing their trucks to proceed faster since they do not have to be screened because of their privileged status. It is not that difficult to carry drugs in a vehicle that has a Fast Pass and get away with it. The primary investment in the border has been in physical infrastructure such as roads and bridges for trade, but it has only been nominal with regard to human development capacity.

The border for Laredoans started as an abstract notion, which continues to dominate their own narrative until the present day. They appreciate the hard border that stops potential cartel violence from seeping into the city while also acknowledging that daily crossings have shrunk, dampening the local economy. Unlike the federal government, most of them do not want to turn the border into a concrete physical obstacle. Typical of the respondents for this book, *Theodore Valenti* defines the border as an arbitrary line drawn on a map. Having lived in the Middle East (Kuwait) and North Africa (Tunisia), he is acutely aware of the capricious processes of nation making where countries emerged or dissipated upon the whimsical stroke of the colonizer's pen, often ignoring historical or ethnic bonds. He could not tell the difference when going from Morocco to Algeria or Tunisia. He ponders, "The U.S.-Mexico border was supposed to reside on the Nueces River, but in the end the Rio Grande became the agreed-on point in the negotiations. I wonder how the history of Laredo would have been different if the agreement about the border had pinpointed the Nueces River."

Nevins calls the border a conduit above all, as economic transactions between the two nations have intensified since the 1960s and accelerated even more after NAFTA.[60] Increased patrolling of the border may seem paradoxical at a time of heightened transborder activities, but the extreme policing is an act of balance against the radical opening of the border for business. Urban areas along the border are densely populated and are experiencing rapid economic growth. Barriers like the fence or wall are about controlling the growth and nature of cross-border migration. In one sense, the constant flow of merchandise and money erases the national boundaries of economies, but then the nation-states reclaim justification for the boundaries by policing the people. We are used to thinking of border mechanisms along historical timelines, but more relevant is for whom or what the border remains accessible and for whom or what it has hardened.[61]

The border has become "highly charged as the repurposed barricade of the idea of America," according to *Jose Diaz*. He remembers going to Big Bend National Park after his graduation and meeting people from Mexico who had crossed over on the ferry without any check from the Border Patrol. He defines the border as "a line that was drawn in 1848 to separate two nations when they had not yet been separated." The border used to be a post but is now a shield against imagined enemies. All the vice moved beyond the Mexican border in the 1920s in the era of Prohibition, as prostitution, gaming, and vice districts opened on the Mexican side. In its new incarnation in the current period, the border is the fictional line that protects us from the flow of undocumented people, crime, and drugs. Patricia Price suggests that borders no longer mark off strict lines of separation but are fragmented and disjointed. In late modernity, borders do not function as lines of delineation, but instead they highlight the scars inflicted by the division of spaces and cultures.[62]

"The border is an imaginary line that no one can see, therefore it has to be recorded," *Thomas Jeffrey* declares. This, in essence, is the function of the border in the era of economic liberalization. Before NAFTA promoted the notion of the open border, the border was indeed porous in Laredo. Now with growth and transportation, there is almost a psychological need to visually assign a corporeal border. In the volatile environment of economic insecurity, racial anxiety, and nationalistic fervor, the issue of the permeable border has erupted as a campaign issue that invigorates a substantial number of people, mostly those not living in the border regions. The purpose of the border has become to demonstrate a concrete boundary without disturbing the actual amount of trade and even overlooking transgressions as long as the boundary is perceptible.

Conversing with Laredo

In this book I aim to explore Laredo from within, through the eyes of the people who have lived in the city and participated in its shifts. I set out from the beginning to study Laredo through its people, their memories, their voices, and their visions. I interviewed seventy-five residents of Laredo—old and young, natives and settlers—who have witnessed the metamorphosis of their hometown, the place they have chosen as their abode. I tried to incorporate people from key institutions and diverse occupations. I started out with a list of people I already knew who were familiar with Laredo's history, who wrote about Laredo (or the border), or who worked in crucial political or cultural institutions. As the interviews proceeded, I got a clearer picture of whom else I needed to talk to and accordingly reached out to more people.

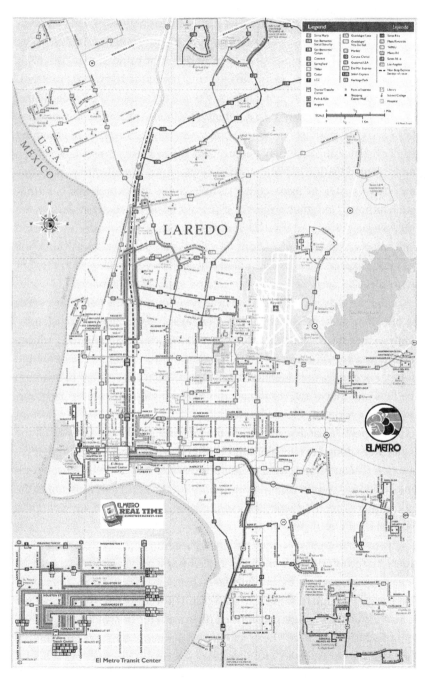

MAP 1 Map of Laredo. El Metro.

Asking interviewees for further contacts and information proved to be very helpful. I used the *tree and branch method* to identify potential interviewees.

I was careful to include people from different professions—teachers, administrators, lawyers, historians, elected representatives, nonprofit employees, community group members, city government staff, Border Patrol officers, people associated with detention centers, business owners, journalists, artists, activists, and blue-collar workers—as well as maintaining gender balance and including people from different age groups. I prepared a letter of introduction explaining my project, which I emailed to prospective interviewees after the initial contact. I followed up with a prepared questionnaire, although different probes or explorations occurred depending on the interviewee. I prepared myself by reading books of oral history and started with my own observations about Laredo. As an outsider, I was expecting questions expressing concerns about my eligibility to write on Laredo, but to my pleasant surprise I only encountered enthusiastic support.

Each interview was approximately an hour long, mostly held in my office or the office or home space of the interviewee. My focus was to listen intently to how the respondents connect with and analyze the city, so I seldom interrupted even if the conversation went off on a tangent. I had a limited number of probes, only fifteen to twenty, so it was relatively easy to maintain the flow and follow the conversation. I was not focusing on any particular traumatic events but rather those memories of Laredo that were important to the respective participants. With the exception of the border wall, all the issues were noncontroversial, and people were open and warm in their responses. The interviewees had the option not to answer questions, but no one decided to refrain from responding. With the written permission of the interviewees, the interviews were audiotaped. I did not take any notes and focused on the conversations.

The interviewees have been assigned pseudonyms to protect their identities. All the interviews were transcribed by first using software (transcribe .wreally.com) and then by carefully going over the original audio. I manually corrected incomplete sentences and grammatical errors. Then I read the transcription thoroughly, prepared summaries of the informants' views, and identified sections I could use in various chapters. Information from the interviews is interspersed with secondary information from relevant books. The names of the interviewees are in italics the first time they are mentioned in a passage.

I asked general questions about their recollections, their connections with the city, their perceptions of the border, and their visions of the city. Mostly I let them tell their own unvarnished story about the city of Laredo. In the end, I discerned several threads from their collective voices, storylines that confront and challenge accepted premises regarding border cities. These themes have clearly emerged from my interviews to complicate the theoretical discourse about border cities:

1. Border cities offer wholesome community experiences to their residents.
2. Border cities are porous in their peripheries but strictly controlled in their inner zones.
3. Border cities are torn between local versus global interests.
4. National and local clashes are restructuring border regions spatially and culturally.
5. The hidden portion of border cities is not the underworld but rather their successes.
6. Border identities are distinct from ethnic identities.

These themes are tied together by the basic insight that *border cities have always been defined from the outside, seldom by the people who live at the border.* I have examined the city from the eyes of its residents to weave a narrative of its metamorphosis that includes its history, geography, and economy along with cultural and community arrangements that have shaped the border identity of the people.

Overview of Chapters

Chapter 1, "Laredo Speaks! What Is a Border Town?" deals with the construction of life in the border town from insiders' perspectives. The chapter recounts Laredo's history and its residents' memories about life in Laredo. Geographically isolated Laredo cherishes a deeply interdependent connection with Nuevo Laredo, its Mexican counterpart. The interviewees reveal a profound sense of loss as they hold on to cultural bonds and increasingly feeble functional ties with the sister city. These narrations, ensuing from both history and personal exposure, contain the key characteristic of Laredo, the fact that residents never became marginal in their own land and managed to hold on to power, contrary to the experience of most minority groups in

U.S. history. The urban population also reveals a deep connection to ancestral land, the surrounding ranches having served as abodes and holding the keys to prosperity for earlier generations. Instead of bifurcation and confusion, the acceptance of the dual lineage along with the dual language persists across generations. The theme that emerges from interviews is that *border cities offer wholesome community experiences to their residents*, which refutes the common perception of the border as chaotic and disorderly.

Chapter 2, "Where Is the Border? The River/the Wall/the Checkpoints/ the Prisons/the Colonias," attempts to locate the edifices that limit the mobility of Laredo's residents. For the people of Laredo, the internal borders of poverty buttressed by the checkpoints are often more invasive and exclusive than the Rio Grande, which denotes connection rather than separation. The tangible border remains partially porous (selective toward trade) while the internal spaces of the border city are severely scrutinized. The permeability at the margins cannot be fundamentally disturbed as it would disrupt the economy. The expansion of private prisons and the encroachment of checkpoints deserve special attention in deciphering the relationships between order, space, and identity. Based on the daily experiences of the people of Laredo, it appears that *border cities are porous in their peripheries but strictly controlled in their inner zones*.

Chapter 3, "The Bazaar on the Border: How Did It Evolve?" chronicles the changing nature of trade in Laredo, transforming Laredo from a trade route to a community and back to being a global corridor after NAFTA. The erasure of local control over business has reshaped downtown and other commercial spaces within the city with far-reaching social and economic consequences. Laredo's residents remain nostalgic about their local entrepreneurs, the once-booming downtown, and the shared prosperity that circulated within the tight-knit community. As a node in the trade corridor, Laredo is a conduit for billions of dollars but can retain only a fraction of the huge wealth that flows through the city. The border is the ideal spot to examine transnational globality, territorial decentralization, and recentralization at the more local or regional scales. The hybridity at the border allows us to observe closely the dialectic shaping contemporary global dynamics. The recurrent issue in Laredo seems to be how *border cities are torn between local versus global interests*.

Chapter 4, "Public Spaces and Community Engagement: Claiming Laredo," delves into the history of the civic square and community activism in Laredo. Laredo has a rich history of local empowerment, but it is yet to be documented properly, let alone celebrated as a heritage. The physical architecture of Laredo, with its large number of plazas (now withered to a mere five), barely celebrates its Hispanic heritage other than in the downtown area. Laredo has traditionally been split along class lines, and in the new global order socioeconomic polarization is a necessary condition. The ongoing expansion of public spaces in Laredo is a response to residents' demands, documented in the ambitious new city plan, Viva Laredo. These public places and their usage have inspired a new Hispanic identity, which attempts to make liaisons with minority communities across the nation while remaining aware and proud of border roots. Laredo's residents welcome the money flowing in from global trade but resent that policies regarding their city are increasingly being formulated in the nation's capital. As *national and local clashes are restructuring border regions spatially and culturally*, many of these conflicts take place in the articulation and claiming of public spaces in Laredo.

Chapter 5, "Visions of the City: Institutions and Infrastructure," examines the contradictory themes of discord and opportunity that originate from the national and local perspectives respectively and their impact on the planning and prospects of the city. The people of Laredo value their city for creating and expanding opportunities, yet in the national profile Laredo remains a space that needs to be controlled and consistently brought back to normalcy. The efforts and proposed budgets to revive the city center reflect the contradictions of these competing visions for Laredo. Downtown remains a space for cultural pride and architectural marvels, but economically its importance has shifted to revenues earned from bridge tolls, which constitute roughly 70 percent of the city budget. What surfaces from the conflicting national and local narratives is that *the hidden portion of border cities is not the underworld but rather their successes.*

Chapter 6, "Border Identity: Remains of the Day," centers around the historical construction of border identity and how it is evolving to accommodate and confront national and global challenges. People in Laredo do not demonstrate much conflict in their identity and belonging; historically, they have embraced border identity, which overlaps with ethnic identity but is distinct in its self-assertion and its relation to national identity. One key feature of Laredo's identity paradox is the grand monthlong celebration of George Washington's Birthday, the most spectacular one in the nation. Laredo's residents do not deny past division along class lines, yet it is also true that inclusive spaces existed around the city center that allowed everyone to lay claim to the city. The recent thrust toward revitalization of public spaces has clearly led to new forms of civic engagement and reclamation of border identity. The people of Laredo eloquently and proudly claim that *border identities are distinct from ethnic identities.*

The conclusion attempts to figure out where Laredo is headed. The increasing demand for urban land by multinational corporations and affluent residents often collides with the needs of existing residents and users of urban space. Laredo's residents present not only conflicting visions about the future but images that can often be mutually exclusive. A natural habitat for winter birds can flourish without much human intervention, while strict regulation is essential to maintain a trade hub. These conflicts over space, memory, and identity undergird the path forward for Laredo. As a nexus of global trade, a locale of the border wall, and a community energized by new avenues of opportunity, Laredo serves as an appropriate site to examine the conflict of interests between local, national, and global stakeholders. Will it retain its image of a "gateway city" or evolve into a "destination city"? Will it cherish its past glories or be content to be a "hub of globalization"? Can it offer any lessons to other border cities in terms of resilience, growth, and ownership of the future?

Laredo offers a rich resource to study and to make meaning out of several interrelated paradoxical phenomena. The narrations of the city of Laredo have followed the threads of its historical and economic growth patterns, often acknowledging the uniqueness of the border city. However, there is yet to be a full body of work that ties together the different aspects of this border city and endeavors to analyze where the spatial and cultural theories intersect and where they take off on tangents. It is about time to capture the transitions of Laredo and expand the framework of urban theory to understand, analyze, and predict the transitions of border cities. My focus on the clash of local, national, and global concerns in Laredo and how these shape the physical landscape, the strong cultural core, and the contours of border identity provides a lens to understand both border and global cities from within. The voices of local people in defining their cities, their past, and their ongoing direction deserve a legitimate footing and a tangible presence in political processes. If the community is not placed at the heart of future planning, our border cities will regress to cogs in the superhighway of the worldwide trade network, losing their distinctive appeals and thoroughly disregarding the concerns of the people who populate these vital spaces.

CHAPTER 1

Laredo Speaks!

What Is a Border Town?

> We have always been on to ourselves since the colonizers
> came from Spain to settle along the Rio Grande. I still equate
> the city to the original idea of settlement. We are a settle-
> ment as was true then, and even though we are grown-up
> with this large land port, we are still trying to find our way.
>
> *FELIX RIVERA*, LAREDO RESIDENT

> Laredo is a little insidious. No city is perfect. My life is per-
> fect in an imperfect city.
>
> *VIVIANA CORTEZ*, LAREDO RESIDENT

What is a border city? People who actually live in border cities know that
their definitions rarely dominate the national conversation. This chapter analyzes the viewpoints of the residents of Laredo, the oldest crossing point
along the U.S.-Mexico international divide, which is also one of the oldest
cities in the nation. Laredoans have a deep appreciation for their history
and a sense of identity that overlaps with their ethnic heritage but more
importantly highlights their connection with the land and living practices
in the borderlands. With a soaring 95 percent of people claiming Hispanic
ethnicity, Laredo demonstrates more homogeneity than any other border
city. For the people of Laredo, their experience of living on the border includes close relations with their sister city, Nuevo Laredo, across the bridge
in Mexico. Laredo has gone through different waves of transition that have
changed the city from a wild frontier to an orderly boundary as well as from
the interdependent economy of a twin city to the busiest inland port in the
nation.[1] Throughout these transitions, the people of Laredo have striven to
portray a distinctive personality rooted in the history, territory, language,
and culture of their own lived experiences.

Laredo is proud of its ancestry of seven nations—Spain, France, Mexico, the Republic of Texas, the Confederate States of America, the Republic of the Rio Grande, and finally the United States of America. Even after it had become part of the United States, for a long time it functioned as a no-man's-land where laws could be circumvented, yet strong norms remained woven throughout its economic and political structures. While the Rio Grande historically served as the border, the border itself remained easily navigable like the river. The two bridges constructed in 1889 and 1921 along with the Pan American Highway in 1935 connected the city to Mexico and supplemented the gateway function of Laredo.[2] The boundary aspects of Laredo first became tangible with the construction of Interstate 35, the federal interstate highway, which severed neighborhoods and provided a more concrete sense of perimeter than the river. The globalized neoliberal economy facilitates commerce across nation-states but requires hard borders to maintain and monitor the exchange of both goods and people. Finally, with NAFTA, Laredo's prosperous economy has ruptured most of its connections to its adjoining sibling, as Nuevo Laredo has struggled to curtail its drug trafficking network. The border, rife with new physical infrastructure, technological intelligence, and armed human surveillance, now truly divides an unsafe Nuevo Laredo from the secure port of entry in Laredo. Crime statistics attest that the city of Laredo and its citizens are well protected from the carnage of Nuevo Laredo. The interdependency between the sister cities continues to this day, albeit in a highly abridged functional version.

Frontier to Boundary

Laredo is the oldest independent settlement in Texas, founded in 1755 and preceding the American Revolution and the formation of the nation. It was an exception from the beginning, established almost casually without a strong mission of Christianization or as a garrison for the colonizers.[3] The land grant from Governor José de Escandón, the most successful colonizer of South Texas, to Don Tomás Sánchez de la Barrera y Garza, a Spanish nobleman, led to the hurried establishment of a new settlement on the arid lands by the Rio Grande.[4] Three families followed Don Sánchez and established a twenty-five-mile territory spanning the northeast from Dolores, one of the very first Spanish settlements. It was named San Agustín de Laredo, after the town of Laredo in Santander, Spain. In 1768 Laredo was granted a

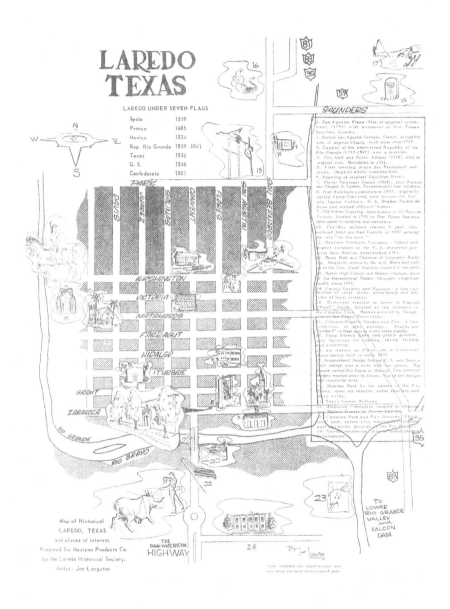

MAP 2 Old map of downtown Laredo. Webb County Heritage Foundation.

city charter, electing city officials and becoming an incorporated town. Laredo remained poor and small despite steady population growth. Trade grew steadily after the Texas Revolution, while the city remained within Mexico and served as the frontier where occasional squabbles took place between the Mexican and Texan armies.

The expansion of Spanish colonies disrupted the way of life of the Indigenous population, and conflicts between the colonizers and the Apache and Comanche tribes erupted regularly.[5] By 1773, now a town with a couple of hundred people, Laredo was assigned a permanent garrison or presidio, which elevated its status and contributed to further growth.[6] The attacks of the Indians turned the new city into a frontier. For a long time in the land of Mexicans the "others" were Indians. Oscar Martínez has elaborately discussed how the identity of Native Americans in the border region was constructed as a "problem."[7] It is also important to note that in Laredo, true to its frontier characteristics, between such attacks there were peaceful phases of coexistence. The 1788 census documents twenty "Indian" families and five unmarried males as Laredo residents, although they were all baptized and given the new name de la Cruz.[8]

As a border town Laredo inevitably experienced territorial brawls, but what shaped the loyalty of Laredoans was the issue of survival. Laredo was the only border town that supported Santa Ana, as it had no important trade relations with America. In 1835 the Centralista army confiscated the horses of residents.[9] Laredo was loyal to the Spanish Crown during the Mexican Independence War as the Spanish garrison protected the city from Native American attacks.[10] After one such attack in 1790, Lipan Apaches celebrated their war dance at San Agustín Plaza.[11] Even with the presence of presidios, whenever there was a larger threat, such as from the Spaniards in Tampico in 1829 or from the French in Veracruz in 1838, soldiers left the town unguarded to fight more important battles. Laredo had to learn to fend for itself.[12] Native American onslaughts remained a constant threat until U.S. troops finally vanquished the tribes when Laredo became part of America.

Laredo had the reputation of being an uninhabitable chaparral desert with a hot and dry climate, having ample vegetation for cattle along a few streams. With its desert soil, Laredo had almost nothing to offer compared to the rich moisture and soil of McAllen, Carrizo Springs, or Crystal City. The valley along the Rio Grande, and even Corpus Christi, had rich black loamy soil, whereas it rained little in Laredo. *Richard Andrew*, a native of Laredo, narrates the past history of his hometown as a place ideally situated as a frontier because life was arduous and challenging. It served as a hinterland where people could battle out differences to gain access to land that would be their destination. While the nearby settlements of Revilla and Dolores grew into more prosperous colonies, the significance of Laredo's location was secondary to the abundant grazing lands found in the area, which were deemed to be its only advantage for decades. The concentration of land and horses in the hands of a few families seemed to be the natural order of society. Laredo in its founding period was viewed more as Don Sánchez's personal acquisition of a hacienda with plentiful grasslands to graze animals rather than an important colonial outpost.[13]

Laredo was not part of Texas when the latter revolted. The presidio troops located in Laredo actually fought the Texan rebels. Native American raids were more of a problem for Laredo than the Texas Revolution. While the Nueces Strip emerged as contested territory, Laredo remained part of Mexico. What shifted Laredo's loyalty from the Mexican Centralists toward the Federalists was loss of the right to gather wild horses, the economic crash after the war along with rapid emigration, and the Mexican government's neglect of the frontier to address escalating Indian attacks. In short, Laredo started its existence as a true frontier, caught between wars, Indian raids, and economic downturns. It was ransacked by both the Texans and the Mexican army as the city mostly sided with the former. Like Laredo, Nuevo Laredo was also burned by the Huertista troops in 1914, which triggered another burst of migrants to Laredo along with the escapees of the Mexican Revolution.[14]

Political battles outside Laredo have always shaped its fate. The revolt against the Federalists in Mexico in 1839 had a novel culmination for Laredo as insurgents formed an independent nation between Texas and Mexico. For a glorious ten-month period in 1840, Laredo emerged as the capital of a new country, the Republic of the Rio Grande. The new republic might have had a short span, but it has lived long in the psyche of Laredoans. Laredo often found itself caught in the crosshairs between the Federalists and the Centralists in Mexico, between Texas and Mexico, and between the Confederacy and the United States, with the Republic of the Rio Grande standing out as a rebellious moment of forging its own destiny. The downtown still maintains its capitol building as a museum to show off this eccentric identity. This dramatic act of rebellion is entirely characteristic of the frontier, where anything is theoretically possible. Laredo's allegiance to different geopolitical powers was carved out of the necessity of survival, with the Republic of the Rio Grande embodying a grand gesture of forever being at the crossroads of danger while signifying fidelity.[15]

Laredo was formally included in the United States after the Treaty of Guadalupe Hidalgo forced the Mexican government to secede more land between the Nueces River and the Rio Grande. Webb County was formed to absorb Laredo into U.S. territory in 1848. After Texas joined the Union, General Lamar occupied Laredo and held an election to formally bring the city under United States jurisdiction. The first election in Laredo as part of Texas was held in 1847 with forty votes cast in a city of 1,891 people.[16] At the time, Laredo was a relatively small city, mostly dry and barren with only a few cattle ranches. Historically, residents owned land on both sides of the river, and ranchland across the river functioned as part of the city. Robert Wood discusses how the conflict between the elites in Laredo in its formative days acquired a spatial manifestation when the opponents of Captain Sánchez, who were often called the renegades, settled on the south side of the river and were threatened with fines and prison terms.[17] Many residents established homes on that side to escape the dominance of Don Sánchez as the altercations between the two factions continued.[18] While Nuevo Laredo was formally constituted almost a full century after Laredo's establishment—the former in 1848 and the latter in 1755[19]—its existence as a counter to the power elite can be traced back to the early days of Laredo. Despite separate national identities, landholding in both countries would continue for generations. Even when Nuevo Laredo emerged as an independent municipality in Mexico, it remained conjoined to its older twin.

Laredo functioned as a frontier or in-between space in its formative days. Even when it became part of a nation-state, its boundary aspects remained ambiguous for a long stretch of time. Frontiers denote the opening of territories while boundaries denote their limits. The modern state is legally defined and restricted to specific areas by boundaries, while frontiers are an outward-oriented delineation that cannot be brought under control. Frontiers imply defensive and strategic locations, and although subordinate to the state, they always remain out of bounds. Frontiers are spaces of transition and therefore in a condition of constant flux and ambiguity. Boundaries are about separation, whereas frontiers are meeting places.[20] Nevins correlates the term *la frontera* with daily interactions and the concept of the boundary or *la linea* with a hard edge that actually subverts such interactions.[21] Laredo started out as a frontier but was turned into a boundary, though the frontier aspect has never completely been eliminated from its cultural landscape.

The frontier features are etched in the architecture of downtown buildings, observes *Richard Andrew*, who has lived in Laredo all his life. He points to the historic buildings around San Agustín Plaza, most of which have a flat design instead of arches. The colonial architecture, including many churches, had flat roofs from where it was possible to keep an eye on possible attackers. Most of the historical buildings were built to protect themselves from Native American attacks. This is also the reason why in that era of timber, buildings were made of concrete rather than wood. Indians used arrows with fire, which could burn down structures. In its architecture, downtown Laredo still feels like a frontier to Andrew. A lawyer by profession, who often deals with asylum cases, he believes, "For asylum seekers Laredo is still very much a frontier. Laredo never belonged to Indians or Spaniards. Each group fought over Laredo, but their conflicts were never really settled. This is the ultimate characteristic of a frontier, a land that belongs to no one and defies all authority." Only a few decades ago, Laredo was the less sophisticated passage to Nuevo Laredo, the cosmopolitan world of rich Mexicans with their live music and drinks and cultural energy. Now the tables have turned completely. Such an abrupt transition is also a quality of the frontier. For a large number of people, Laredo still functions as a frontier even as its meaning keeps changing.

The frontier characteristics are even more apparent to outsiders who step into its unique landscape. *Felix Rivera*, who migrated to Laredo from the East Coast three decades ago, recollects, "I felt as if I had stepped into the Wild Wild West. As an architect, I was watching the eclectic buildings in awe, and right in front of me, a little boy was walking a goat through the downtown streets." This surreal image, the contrast of the mundane with magnificent structures, still upholds what Laredo means to him, an opening for various sorts of lifestyles that can cohabit without onerous conflict. Laredo represents the first footstep into the country for many immigrants seeking a better life. Rivera describes how his wife's family emigrated from Mexico even though her mother was Turkish and her father was Polish. They ended up in Mexico City, then came to the border, and finally prospered by making a living in Laredo. He believes that Laredo continues to display the idiosyncrasies of a frontier.

The raw lawlessness of Laredo is reflected in how animals were treated by residents. *Justin Taylor* remembers the poor homeless dogs and cats on the streets in the 1960s and 1970s. As he recounts with horror, "Once a week the city would gather homeless dogs and take them in a van out to the highway. The city never had enough money to feed the poor creatures nor for bullets to shoot them, so they would throw the animals in there and a man would go with a baseball club and clobber them to death. I began working on the weekends with the Laredo Animal Protective Society started by a friend." This kind of brutality was casually accepted by residents for a long time until the organization was established. Scandals of animal abuse continue to plague the city.[22] While this violence does not seem to be out of place for a frontier, in some sections of the city animals are treated very differently. True to the temperament of a frontier where paradoxes prevail, there is a contrasting narration of the coexistence of humans and animals inside churches. *Elena Cruz* remembers going to the beautiful San Francisco Javier church in downtown, where it was always cool despite the lack of air-conditioning. Even on the hottest days the church was cold, inviting dogs, cats, and even peacocks to wander around while the priest delivered his sermon. The church was tiny, with just a few pews, but its large wooden doors were left ajar to permit pets and peacocks to roam in and out freely.

The frontier flavor of Laredo never completely evaporated from its land-use patterns either. Unlike most American cities, where proximity to the river represents more desired land that is occupied by the wealthy, in Laredo it is the poor barrios that are located along the riverbank. It was common for people to live on ranches on the outskirts of town even during the heyday of the downtown area. *Max Green* grew up on the periphery of Laredo on a ranch and had negligible connections to the city in his youth. He appreciates how he spent time outdoors, fishing and hunting, while mostly avoiding the city only twenty to thirty minutes away. The churches were the only attraction Laredo had to offer. Entertainment consisted in staying outside and relaxing by Lake Casa Blanca, eating barbecue, or camping. It was possible for him to live a life of tranquility amid the companionship of animals until the 1970s. He rode bulls for a living and participated in rodeos for six years. Now he lives in a gated community in the Mines Road area, which is the farthest location on the city's perimeter that contains the familiar chaparral—namely, the shrubs and bushes evocative of the ranches.

Another interesting part of Laredo's history is that outsiders were allowed to play key roles in the city's governance. *Richard Andrew* describes Laredo's mayor Samuel M. Jarvis (1868), who planned the downtown grid system and was selected only because he was not a local. Jarvis was a graduate of Columbia University working for a British mining company as an engineer in Mexico during the Mexican War. He settled in Monterrey with his Mexican wife and children and remained there during the Civil War. After the war he moved to Laredo with his family and happened to be the only elite person in town who had not served in the Confederate army. He became the mayor by default because nobody else qualified politically. This tradition of outsiders playing seminal roles in Laredo continued into the 1970s until the well-established patron system was challenged and defeated by another out-of-town figure, Mayor Aldo J. Tatangelo, who made Laredo his home and pushed the city toward progress. Frontiers often embody such hierarchical ambiguities, allowing outsiders to assume pivotal positions.

Historically and functionally, it was the river that served as the border for Laredo. Rivers are open and tend to connect rather than divide. The Rio Grande never functioned as a boundary to set the two cities or countries apart. Severing the umbilical cord with Nuevo Laredo has changed the frontier drift of Laredo and transformed it into more of a boundary. A frontier may exist between two border towns, but a boundary divides two countries. While the Pan American Highway, the first paved highway dating back to 1935, connected Laredo to Mexico City and facilitated commerce, I-35 was designed to cut through the city's densest neighborhoods, destroying unique districts. Just as with the railroad, the highway scarred existing prosperous neighborhoods, turning dense and rich urban locales into poor and broken ones. *Alex Mead,* a scholar of urban studies, traces Laredo's maturation as a city to the growth of its burgeoning road network, viewing the construction of McPherson Road within the city along with I-35 as major points of transformation toward becoming a modern commercial center.

This story of the torn urban fabric is not unique to Laredo. *Rodrique Taylor* turns to this history when describing the horrific communal impact of I-35, especially in the mid-1970s when additional construction to widen the interstate and add new bridges was undertaken. All of these developments seized a significant portion of historical properties from downtown residential neighborhoods under the powers of eminent domain. The interstate now snakes through downtown and has essentially killed the once thriving El Azteca neighborhood because of the highway and border station limiting growth on its western side. All the historical buildings along this corridor were demolished, and the neighborhood never regained its stature in postinterstate Laredo. The pedestrian and residential component of the city became divided by the interstate, with huge trucks streaming along all the time. It became unsafe to cross the road to attend church or buy groceries. Small shops started closing, and church membership thinned in El Azteca.

Much of Laredo's recent growth has mimicked the expansion of interstate commerce. Laredo's population has grown fourfold since the construction of I-35, from around seventy-five thousand in 1971 to around three hundred thousand in 2020. By the time construction ended in 1971, I-35 had ruined several working-class neighborhoods in the central city. Most Laredoans were willing to pay the price as the warehouses and transportation facilities located along the highway were a result of the road networks and commercial zones that brought unprecedented business and revenue to the city. Today 40 percent of Mexican imports cross the city along I-35 to reach the rest of the United States. An alternative NAFTA superhighway was planned to directly connect Mexico and Canada via Laredo,[23] but it has now been scaled back as Interstate 69. Part of the existing Highway 59 has already been expanded and upgraded to I-69. After the school districts and the Border Patrol, the freight industry is now the third-largest employer in town.

The interstate erected the first physical boundary between the two cities, although cultural and economic exchanges continued and even escalated for a short period after construction. Both commerce and the apparatus of controlling the border ramped up even as the centrality of the interstate and the presence of the Border Patrol solidified the border.[24] Globalization might connect countries, but it also disconnects them through particular mechanisms, because regulating the boundaries of the global network is deemed essential to the process. The flexible frontier of Laredo was made suitable for global transactions after NAFTA, which transformed Laredo from a frontier into a boundary. This boundary acts as both a barrier and a conduit facilitating interaction between national spaces. NAFTA is a perfect example of how integration and policing go hand in hand and are both necessary to maintain and justify national boundaries.[25] In the post-NAFTA era, fewer people cross the transnational boundary because the relationship with the boundary is official and functional as opposed to a transborder frontier where it is much easier to lay claim by dint of presence.

Distinguishing between this region's cultural geography (the transborder) and political demarcation (the transnational), David Danelo explains,

FIGURE 5 International Bridge and horse carriage. Webb County Heritage Foundation.

"The latter is the boundary of sand, water, and steel. The former is the filter somewhere north of the line; the place where you no longer smell fajitas grilling at a stand, see signs for discounts at an open-air *mercado*, or hear the sounds of the *mariachis* at midday. The U.S.-Mexican border blends amiably in San Antonio, but crackles divisively in Houston."[26] The border may be fragmented and disjointed as Patricia Price suggests,[27] but despite the continuous movement of vehicles and people, it denotes a strict line of separation between the two countries. Michael Smith argues that the distinction between the local and the global is difficult to maintain in the postmodern era,[28] but Laredo demonstrates a clash of interests between local and global stakeholders, as discussed in depth in chapter 3. Laredo essentially consisted of dual hinterlands and was caught in the crossfire when political borders kept shifting. After the border was politically stabilized, in economic, cultural, and even social terms it continued to function as a frontier. However, it was the global resurgence of trade that transformed Laredo into a boundary whose connection with Nuevo Laredo was severed, as Laredo became the edge of the country rather than an opening to new vistas.

A Tranquil Community

One of the major characteristics of the border is assumed to be instability. Border towns carry the stigma of being unsafe, erratic, and unpredictable. But people in Laredo view their city very differently. Almost everyone describes Laredo as a wholesome entity that has offered peace and prosperity to its inhabitants. Even when people recount their individual poverty, in the collective memory Laredo is enshrined as the space that allowed everyone to coexist and prosper enough to raise the living standards of most of the population. The stories of the elite, the poor, and the new entrants to the community all exhibit the theme of a deprived but peaceful body politic that was seldom sullied by the disarray of the border. It should be noted that although the aggregate size of the regional economy has grown manifold, Webb County is still one of the poorest counties in the country with a third of the people living below the poverty line, a statistic that remains almost unchanged despite major developments and the overall rise in prosperity.

The story of the tranquil town is immersed in memories of idyllic childhoods, though not necessarily aligned with affluence. *Bianca Frey* is a native of Laredo who has held important positions in the city and retains a strong institutional memory of Laredo's growth. Her family lived on San Eduardo Avenue, where they raised lambs and had an outhouse. She and her brother spent a lot of time on trees, throwing sour oranges at passersby. As she recounts, "Once the lambs were grown they would disappear, and my father told us elaborate stories about how they ran away or somebody stole them. Being the eldest, I always had the suspicion that something was going on. Sure enough, after a lamb disappeared, all of a sudden we had meat on our plate." She saw her first swimming pool at a neighbor's house on Clark Boulevard, which was considered an upscale section of the Heights. She remembers the neighbor, a local shoe store owner, adding a pair of shoes to what they bought from his store. This was a nice gesture to his less prosperous neighbors, though she grew up never realizing they were poor. As a child, she was grateful to have a roof over her head and food on the table. Once a week, her father and mother made a roast so they could all have meat, along with Kool-Aid to drink on the special day. Except for a few memories of being disciplined, she recalls her childhood as filled with the fun and games that her family and community made possible.

Life has always been easy for *Cesar Villarreal*, even though he grew up in an impoverished neighborhood in downtown. In his words, "I still live in my family house after retirement. I can walk into the bank or hospital and everyone knows my name. I like the service and courtesy as well as the sense of community in Laredo, where people lend a hand to change a flat tire. You can feel the warmth of the community everywhere, in rich and poor neighborhoods. This, to me, is the essence of Laredo." He laments that the violence in Nuevo Laredo has gotten out of hand and split his home in half. He grew up in a poor and dense part of town, the Colonia Guadalupe Federal Housing Project, in a resilient barrio, even if people were careful to chain the barbecue grill to a post to prevent theft. He remembers, "I grew up watching the city's water trucks chasing the clouds of dust from our dirt streets. Everyone blamed the dust from the unpaved streets for the high rate of tuberculosis. Only the interstate highway system had paved roads that were put in place after the Second World War to expedite the movement of troops and portable guided missiles. Most of Laredo's streets were *caliche* [unpaved] until the seventies. There were a lot of small cantinas in the old downtown area where my father took me." The main struggle in his childhood in the early 1960s was finding an appropriate space to play football that had grass and was free of broken beer bottle shards. The neighborhood children would walk for blocks to play at the Martin High School football field on actual grass until the groundskeepers would yell and chase them off. For baseball, they had to walk a mile and a half to play at Fort McIntosh, where Laredo College is located today. There were some vacant areas belonging to the city inside the fort where they played barehanded with shared bats and balls to their heart's content. Despite growing up in the poorest part of downtown, Villarreal ended up having a successful professional career in his hometown.

The memories of the affluent also follow the themes of intimate family ties, culinary adventures, and amusements in the beloved city. For *Rebecca Park*, growing up in Laredo meant a dream childhood, an American story but with a bit of spice thrown in. She learned Spanish and English simultaneously and claims both as her first language. Her supportive family structure was filled with joyous occasions, and almost all relatives lived nearby. Thanksgiving took place at her Aunt Josephine's house for thirty consecutive years, where she laid a formal table for scores of people with crystal, silverware, cloth napkins, colorful tablecloths, and centerpieces she herself knitted. The Christmas Eve parties easily consisted of more than a hundred people. Park's great-grandfather on her mother's side was French while her other ancestors were Mexican. Music ran in the family (her mother taught guitar lessons), so the gatherings would be saturated with music from the 1940s or 1950s or Mexican boleros popular in the cantinas. She fondly remembers musical numbers from *Cabaret* to *The Sound of Music* released when she was young during the 1960s and 1970s. Going to Lake Casa Blanca for fishing and hunting with her father was a common pastime. All of this port city was once open land, constituting a vast playground for younger residents. *Gary Bell* remembers riding his bike everywhere on the unpaved streets and playing basketball, baseball, and football in different neighborhoods and even soccer with his cousins in Nuevo Laredo in the 1960s. Apart from school, his entire childhood was spent outdoors—schoolyards and neighborhood parks—and inside the gym only when the heat became intolerable. Growing up without air-conditioning and playing outside on the dirt streets was a common occurrence in Laredo.

Residents claim that life was much sweeter and simpler without drugs or other anxieties, whether they lived in the elite Heights enclave or the poor barrios. *Jake Ruiz* remembers that most of the residential neighborhoods were agricultural fields when he was in his teens, less than four decades ago. Cattle farms and ranches existed very near the air force base, sandwiched between the older and newer parts of the city. He reminisces about working in the fields to pick melons along with his friends. They would all pile into his 1952 Chevy truck and leave for the fields along Highway 83 early in the morning. They stood in the relief line (before food stamps) on Santa Maria Avenue by the railroad tracks for a duffel bag filled with cartons of milk, fresh vegetables, and cans of food. There were almost no paved roads, just mud or *caliche* roads, which would turn into swimming pools with rain. Swimming in the Rio Grande—swinging from pillars on the bridge and jumping into the river to swim between the United States and Mexico—was a typical recreation of his youth, with no Border Patrol to guard any border. His grandfather, a white army officer, was stationed at Fort McIntosh when he met and fell in love with a Mexican girl whose family had fled to Laredo because of the Mexican Revolution. They did not know each other's language when they got married.

Whether it was Fort McIntosh in the 1940s or Laredo Air Force Base in the 1950s, military officers were the only "others" in the Hispanic town for a long time. The economic success of Laredo was crowned with the much-coveted air force base in the 1950s, which brought large amounts of federal money along with jobs and diversity. The base served as both an economic and cultural lifeline for Laredo. Air Force officers would get trained there before heading over to Korea or Vietnam. Many officers got married to local women and settled in Laredo, and it was commonplace for the wives of officers from the base to teach in the schools. *Gary Bell* learned good English at school from those teachers. His family mostly spoke Spanish at home because it was the only language his mother spoke. He had to learn to carry on a conversation in two different languages simultaneously when he was speaking to both his parents. Another interviewee, *John Allen*, recounts, "My first experience of living in an air-conditioned home was in a duplex at the base. I was so thrilled. The base was a fabulous place to live as Uncle Sam took care of everything. I was in my school parade when President Nixon visited the base."

The base closed in 1973, within months after Nixon's visit to Laredo during his campaign when he was anointed Mr. South Texas.[29] According to quite a few of the interviewees, when Nixon visited Laredo, the very powerful Mayor Martin did not show up at the airport to receive him. On top of this insult, Webb County was the only one in Texas that did not vote for him. The base fell victim to the chopping block in the next budget because of the political vendetta, as local stories allege. The dire economic shock Laredo faced when the base shut down cannot be exaggerated. But Laredo learned to diversify and enhance trade and transport to sustain itself. It was not only the resilience of city leaders but the cash flow from Nuevo Laredo that helped to sustain the economy. Former bank employee *Bianca Frey* recollects, "My husband and I both worked at the bank and we know those times were hard, but there were Mexicans walking in with suitcases of cash and wanting to open accounts. At that time nobody worried about illegal money or anything like that. In most cases we knew the customer well and would travel and visit with them in Mexico, especially the larger customers." The business development aspect of the banks required persuading Mexican customers from elite families to invest in Laredo. For the people of Laredo, recounting the days of prosperity almost invariably goes back to the days when downtown flourished on the backs of local business owners.

The historical coincidence of the base closure and Mexico's protectionist industrial policy proved opportune for Laredo. By the 1960s the flourishing downtown had become the economic and cultural epicenter. Narrations of daily life in Laredo between the past and the present revolve around the spatial significance of the downtown area. *Elena Cruz* remembers that weekends were for roaming around the endless downtown stores and little *placitas*. The era of prosperity was derailed with the construction of Mall del Norte in the 1970s, which not only brought in national stores to compete with homegrown businesses but also emerged as the fashionable place to hang out for youngsters. *Grace Terry*, who was forced to relocate to Laredo as a teenager after her mother's divorce, remembers the mall as the only place she could visit with her friends. Older people also preferred to stroll in the cold corridors of the mall rather than the heat outside.

The path for outsiders to Laredo has typically been through leading institutions. *Justin Taylor* came to Laredo for a teaching job, but the city became his home. He has lived for more than five decades in Laredo, doing extensive research on South Texas history. He offers valuable insights about Laredo as both an outsider and insider. He recalls his first impression of Laredo in 1968 as one of horror at both the heat and the unpaved streets:

> Only two streets in Laredo were paved in 1968, San Bernardo and Corpus. The cars on the streets would kick up so much dust they would create a cloud above the city. Some of the medical doctors told me that emphysema here was several times the national average because people were inhaling all the dust. It was a common sight to see people come out in the morning with garden hoses and sprinkle down the areas in front of their houses to prevent the dust from getting all over everything. I even heard that there were leper colonies in Nuevo Laredo in the late 1930s. One of the biggest accomplishments in my lifetime was the paving of the streets. I came to a very poor and impoverished Laredo that was ruled by a well-to-do oligarchy. One could not get a job with the city, the school district, or the county unless one had a list of people, ten names of relatives or friends one could bring to the polls on election day.

Nuevo Laredo was a destination not only for discos and nightclubs but also for taking classes in sewing, swimming, painting, or Mexican folk dances. *Ruth Solomon* remembers that neighbors were part of daily life, as together they would visit Nuevo Laredo for restaurants, dances, the orchestra, and the fantastic balls during quinceañeras. She fears that the younger generation is growing up in quite a different Laredo. *Nina Vargas* recalls the deep familial and neighborly bonds of the "talkative" Hispanic culture that seem to be frayed nowadays. *Katie Brown* laments that her daughter will never experience the childhood she had, living in the same city. She grew up on a cul-de-sac, knew all her neighbors, watched fireworks on New Year's Eve, and enjoyed barbecues with her friends. She was always playing outside or riding her bike. Her daughter, or even her much younger sister, led secluded childhoods with little neighborly interaction. She remembers chain-link fences enabling everyone to peek into everyone else's yards, but now everyone has cinder block fences which cut off communication from one another. These changes are not unique to Laredo but are corollaries of heightened individualism, protective childrearing norms, and upward economic mobility, all of which have occurred in quick succession since the 1990s.

Laredo is still a family town where strong clannish ties have served as the safety net. Regardless of social status, for most people life revolved around family and church. Many people inhabited the vicinity of their extended families, often within a two to three-block radius of the same locale. *Arthur Bailey* grew up in a poor neighborhood on the south side with no proper restroom (only an outhouse he was scared to go to) and a kitchen with a mud floor. He remembers, "My grandfather got an old-style barrel washer and my grandmother began crying with joy. It was such a big deal." His memories are centered around family gatherings and delicious food. It did not have to be Thanksgiving—every week could be like Thanksgiving even with just beans and rice. Weekend cookouts with carne asada were the norm for Laredo. His grandmother used to say, "Poor people's food is the richest food, it kills your hunger and humbles your soul." He still resides near his childhood home, and his neighborhood remains one of the poorest in the city. Bailey notices a strong work ethic, akin to the Japanese, prevalent in Laredo. This is the work ethic of the poor taking pride in their labor, though he believes that the stereotype of the lazy Mexican also thrives in this Hispanic town.

The serenity of community bonds is challenged when the memories of noncitizens are included, charged with agony over their illegal status. *Sara Calderon* grew up in the poorer part of town but has happy recollections of social life, enjoying barbecues with neighbors, sharing food, lending tools, and fixing each other's cars. The gift of a radio from a neighbor was a prized possession in the family. She and her sisters got rides to school with a neighbor, and her mother offered to drive another child to school when the neighbor was afraid to drive because she lacked immigration status and a driver's license. While she felt secure in her immediate vicinity, her remembrances of growing up in Laredo are shot through with fear because of her undocumented status. She is able to work and live by herself as a DACA (Deferred Action for Childhood Arrivals) recipient now, but it always feels like a temporary reprieve, so that unlike most people in Laredo, she doesn't regard the entire city as her home. As she explains, "I don't feel comfortable with everyone. I see myself as a member of the undocumented community. Home, to me, are the people who are always there for me. Why don't people come out in droves to join the DACA protests? Why do people from San Antonio and Austin have to come here to organize the protests? Where is the community when we need it?" She chooses three words to describe her relationship with Laredo: community, clash, and change.

Los Dos Laredos

Laredo has been cut off from other border cities, so naturally its relationship with Nuevo Laredo has been tightly intertwined. Border towns are supposed to be at the crossroads historically and spatially, connecting different spheres in functional terms yet embodying inconsistencies on the folds and edges of these connections. Although Laredo is geographically positioned as an ideal trade route, it has always been isolated within its own region. People who have grown up in Laredo and who have then gone on to live elsewhere agree that Laredo is secluded compared to other border cities in the Rio Grande Valley, which amount to a cluster of smaller towns. *Roxana Peel* believes that an alternative way of thinking about the border is in terms of unification rather than division. The story of Laredo thus begins with connectedness, spatial and cultural, not only among different segments of people but also between Laredo and Nuevo Laredo.

Older residents remember the rapid transition of their hometown within the interval of a single generation and do not view all the changes as having been positive. Laredo in the twentieth century was not only conjoined with Nuevo Laredo but also became well connected with the rest of the country through trains. People in Laredo remember taking daylong rides to travel to Chicago to take vacations. *Elena Cruz*, who grew up in Laredo and now works in downtown, narrates that her father was a conductor for Union Pacific Railroad, enabling them to ride on the train for holidays. *Richard*

FIGURE 6 San Agustín Cathedral. Webb County Heritage Foundation.

Andrew remembers the passenger rail service going from Chicago on one end to Mexico City on the other well into his adolescence, when people from Laredo traveled both north and south with equal ease. After the privatization of the service, it was deemed less profitable and closed down. The link between Laredo and the rest of the world that predates Laredo's transformation into a trade nexus in the 1990s was actually disrupted during the economic downturn of the 1980s.

Although the Rio Grande flowed between the two cities as the boundary between two nations, *Erin Arroyo* never paid much attention to this boundary because it could be crossed at any time. Her nanny escorted her to the park across the river, where she looked forward to the bus rides and still remembers the taste of delicious caramel candy and the sensation of mango dripping from her mouth. The concept of sister cities to express the relationship between Laredo and Nuevo Laredo was not just a ploy to connect disparate cities but was rooted in historical affinity. Laredo and Nuevo Laredo are 150 miles from both Monterrey and San Antonio, the nearest cosmopolitan centers in either country. In the Rio Grande Valley, the nearest city of McAllen is also 150 miles away. Oscar Martínez has introduced a model of dependency in the borderlands ranging from alienated (conflict prone) to coexistent (manageable hostility), interdependent (stable cooperation), and integrated (mutually beneficial relations).[30] Daniel Arreola and James Curtis cite the example of cardboard boxes for merchandise in Laredo regularly being supplied to Nuevo Laredo's downtown recycling factory in the 1980s.[31] These types of transborder commercial relations are now obscured by the massive volume of trade that passes through the transportation corridor but is not necessarily unloaded in either city. However, family relations, cooperation between local government agencies, and interdependencies between each other's health and education sectors continue to persist.[32] Laredo and Nuevo Laredo started out with integrated interactions in Martínez's terms, but this relationship has been relegated to interdependence in the aftermath of NAFTA.

People in Laredo unanimously mention family and community as the center of their lives. Perhaps it was the relative isolation that turned the society inward. Nuevo Laredo is often included in this definition for Laredo's residents, especially those who are older. People refer to their innocent childhood in Laredo as pleasant but boring, whereas Nuevo Laredo offered more excitement. Nightlife and parties were always alluring beyond the river, when the culture of violence was absent from both cities. In the eyes of *Samantha Taft*, Nuevo Laredo was the "other side" frequently visited for a night out. She was on the dance team, and after the recital her father would take her to have dinner at some nice restaurant. Across the river was an alternate world of fantasy and pleasure. It was a place to get Mexican candies and ride little buggies. *Jonathan Everett* remembers being able to buy cheaper and better quality beef across the border, although avocados were not allowed to be brought back. *Charles Fox* reminisces, "My Nuevo Laredo was a very wonderful place to be as there was danger lurking around every corner. It was exciting, and that was part of what made it fun." *Bianca Frey* believes that margaritas on this side do not taste the same. Still, she has stopped accepting invitations to parties in Nuevo Laredo because of safety concerns.

When *Rebecca Park* was a child, her family got up early every Saturday or Sunday to go to Nuevo Laredo. She remembers buying corn on a stick with chili and lemon mayonnaise or mango on a stick. They brought back legally permissible fruits and vegetables and sometimes even the illegal avocado. Laredo had no nightlife until about twenty-five years ago. All the buzz was in Nuevo Laredo, so people would go across for entertainment. But Laredo gave her a good education and bilingual skills, preparing her for the world. *Richard Andrew* remembers an adventurous childhood stretching across both cities as he and his friends would swim and boat in the river. They often took the boat to the other side, camped over there, and returned without trouble. It was a commonplace practice that was treasured and to him an ethereal experience. Until the 1990s going across the river was as easy as crossing the street in Laredo. Though the Border Patrol might throw out random questions such as "What is the capital of the U.S.?" Andrew feels that the border was not only flexible but more humane. One could show up at the bridge and claim, "My sister is on her deathbed. Here's a letter from her doctor that says she's not going to last and I haven't seen her in twenty years." Such stories did not end in jail but with the mundane practice of a twenty-four-hour visa.

The constant reciprocal flow between Laredo and Nuevo Laredo included casual strolls to pick up a pastry or have a meal in a restaurant. Only recently has the border become such a big issue that people are afraid to traverse it. As a high school student with limited pocket money, it was enjoyable for *Ria Sandoval* to shop at the Nuevo Laredo mercado for jewelry. She remembers small groceries and local businesses along with museums and galleries filled with visitors all the time. Her mother used to teach at St. Peter's Memorial Catholic School in Laredo, and many of her students would cross every day. Sandoval, who now runs an art center in downtown Laredo, used to go to art exhibits and museum openings in Nuevo Laredo in her professional role. The last time she collaborated on an art exhibit with the Mexican consulate, she had to get a caravan from the consulate to safely transport the Laredo artist and be back before the 9:00 p.m. curfew enforced in Nuevo Laredo. When an artist from New York was visiting, she booked a room on the other side but had to return the very next day because of a dangerous incident.

Another account of easy crossovers is narrated by *John Allen*, who describes growing up in a large household where both parents were employed and the maids were not working legally. Families in Laredo needed nannies while women in Nuevo Laredo needed work. This simple equation eclipsed the structural barriers to the legal process of working. People devised ways to send money home and even occasionally visit there and be back to their places of work on time. This interdependency might have been illegal, but it was tolerated as an unremarkable violation. What bothers some people now is the pressure on education and medical services when people from

Nuevo Laredo send their children to school in Laredo, often using a relative's address to fulfill the residency requirement, or visit doctors and hospitals for treatment.

Laredo's commercial prosperity is often contrasted with the cultural superiority of Nuevo Laredo. Laredo was the cheaper functional zone while Nuevo Laredo was the elite cultural hotbed, although the roles were somewhat reversed in the 1990s. Young men who came of age at the time, like *Alex Mead*, have no recollection of a robust Laredo downtown because by then it was reduced to a shell of its former self while Nuevo Laredo was still a focus of Laredo's inner life. Nuevo Laredo has more than double Laredo's population, but its growth rate is roughly half of Laredo's. Together the cities form the nucleus of a transportation hub, the major factor influencing their rapid growth. Nuevo Laredo happens to be Mexico's largest inland port as well, but urban growth in Laredo is more dispersed compared to Nuevo Laredo.[33] It is important to remember when and how these interdependencies changed.

The two cities have flipped as centers of prosperity versus poverty. When *John Allen* was growing up, people of means who lived on the other side traveled the world, kept servants and nannies, and sent their children to boarding schools in Switzerland. Laredo was then a dusty little town like Roma or at best McAllen in the Valley. Allen believes, "Border culture has made me more sophisticated. When I returned to Laredo after living on the West Coast for two decades, I was shocked to find the schools packed. I am still astonished to see the number of Mexican license plates on the roads of Laredo as I remember how rare it was to see such cars when I was growing up in the 1960s. Now it feels like half of Laredo's schools cater to children from Nuevo Laredo. All the schools are overcrowded, this is outrageous."

Allen clarifies that he does not resent the people who actually live here using these services as they are part of the society. When Laredoans complain about the onerous burden on services, the focus is not on nationality—who is American or Mexican—but rather on spatial connection, meaning who lives in Laredo and who uses these services from Nuevo Laredo. Néstor Canclini notes that in the border cities of El Paso and Tijuana, the immigrant-citizen divide or even ethnic classifications are futile; local vernacular develops to gauge the authenticity of the fluid identities.[34] In Laredo the yardstick to measure who belongs to "us" is the depth of the ties to the city. It is generally accepted that people who live in Laredo—if they pay taxes and participate in the local economy, notwithstanding their immigration status—are thought to have earned the right to the services. But some residents are upset at people who live in Nuevo Laredo yet share the services. The practice of kidnapping children for ransom by cartels has also pushed affluent Mexican families to relocate or to move their children to Laredo's schools. To complicate matters, many American citizens continue to live in Nuevo Laredo for family, business, or economic reasons.

The tendency is to focus on Nuevo Laredo's dependency on Laredo, ignoring how Laredoans remain reliant on different services from Nuevo Laredo. People without health insurance and even people with health insurance (those who are unable to afford high copays and deductibles) utilize medical and dental professionals over the border where not only treatment but medicine is much cheaper as well. Laredo keeps a record of people who seek medical treatment, but Nuevo Laredo lacks similar documentation. *Rebecca Park* tells the story of her mother who is in poor health. Even though she worked in the school system for forty years and has an excellent retirement plan, it will not pay for the care she needs. A woman from Monclova, Mexico, provides the daily assistance they can afford. Binational cooperation between the medical fraternities in Laredo and Nuevo Laredo plays an essential role in the health of residents on both sides of the border.[35] The number of residents who cross from Nuevo Laredo daily to work as maids or gardeners in Laredo remains hidden mostly because of lack of proper statistics. Neither the authorities nor the residents have any vested interest in documenting this essential labor exchange or to label the providers as transgressors.

Border life contains a range of services and engagements that cannot be abruptly cut off, argues *Paul Sergio*: "I see the river simply flowing between the cities, with an American side and a Mexican side." *Gill Taylor*, an American citizen, grew up in Nuevo Laredo and still comes to work in Laredo every day by crossing the bridge, just as she went to school earlier in her life. She notes that many businesses from Nuevo Laredo have moved to Laredo. For the first time, many of her neighbors have also started moving to Laredo for a safe place to stay even as they continue to work in Nuevo Laredo. They have rented out their houses while they live in Laredo, hoping that their move is temporary and that they can return when the violence subsides. The nature and degree of interdependency between the two cities has changed across generations. *Elena Cruz* fondly remembers spending weekends with her grandparents in Nuevo Laredo. She laments that her son never developed such a connection with either downtown or Nuevo Laredo.

The collaboration between the city governments also has a long history and continues despite the negative narrative afflicting the border. *Charles Vega* is a native of Laredo who has lived here all his life and held important positions in the county and the city, retaining institutional memory of Laredo and its backstories. In forty-four years of professional experience, the project he is proudest of and the one he believes has substantially improved the water quality of the Rio Grande is the sewage treatment plant improvement built in Nuevo Laredo through the International Boundary and Water Commission. *Kayla Hall*, a city government employee, claims that economic development in both cities remains interlinked. She asserts, "Without Nuevo Laredo, there would be no Laredo." It would be impossible to play the role she does without comprehending both languages and cultures.

While Laredo historically functioned as one border city with two centers, it has now been reduced to one. *Charles Fox* mourns that Laredo has ceased to be a border town as the linkages with Nuevo Laredo have shrunk. Even as economic growth accelerates in Laredo, cultural growth has all but petered out in Nuevo Laredo, leading some people to miss the old reciprocity. The new generation has never experienced dual life on the border, having a different exposure to the border town that may not be too different from other cities in America. But transborder interdependence has always been a common feature for twin cities along the U.S.-Mexico border. The close economic and cultural associations encompass generations and can be traced through both family histories and the spatial features of the cities.[36] Before the violence in Mexico erupted on a large scale, it used to be standard practice on a Friday or Saturday night for couples and city folks to either walk or drive over the bridge to enjoy a good meal and camaraderie with friends.

Laredo and Nuevo Laredo are excellent examples of how one city, Laredo, became bigger, better, and even safer following NAFTA, while the other, Nuevo Laredo, fell under the sway of drug lords. Neoliberal policies destroyed the umbilical cord between the two cities. Laredo's close symbiosis with Nuevo Laredo was severed in the 1990s, when instead of persisting as cultural and economic counterparts, the two cities began to function as boundaries within a global network, mere corridors between Mexico and the United States. *Bianca Frey* observes, "Drugs and illegal operations have always existed in Laredo but were never as deadly as they became after the 1990s. Businesses existed on both sides of the river, and the flow of money was never affected by the side hustle that went on in both cities. But after the 1990s, the cartels no longer cared about remaining in the shadows, and their power grab against the Mexican government became so transparent that it became a security risk for Americans to do business in Nuevo Laredo."

The dominance of Spanish in all walks of life is a testament to the seamless flow of everyday life in the two cities. One of the interviewees, *Giselle Lamar*, shared her story of encountering Spanish in an elementary school in Laredo when her mother returned to the city after getting divorced. She was enrolled in kindergarten at Lyendecker Elementary School close to Martin High School. She would go to school and come home weeping, telling her mother that she did not like it. Her mother consoled her and persuaded her to try the school for a week. At last, she showed up at school to find out what was wrong and was aghast to learn that little Giselle had been placed in an exclusively Spanish-speaking class when she did not know Spanish. The little girl thought that was how the school worked and was confused and miserable because she could neither understand anything nor respond to her teachers. When her mother asked, "Why didn't you tell me they were all speaking Spanish?" she answered, "I didn't know they were speaking in Spanish. They were just speaking and I had no idea what was going on." In contrast to many cities in the 1970s where children were punished for speaking in Spanish, Laredo's schools accepted Spanish as the first language.

The bicultural flavor of Laredo manifests in the use of quirky language. *Rebecca Park* treasures the fact that Laredo incorporates both languages to enrich the lives of the people. People often use Spanish phrases in unaccustomed ways to alter their meaning. "I think it's a beautiful thing to have two languages to choose from when expressing yourself," she claims. "Words that talk about love and beauty are so much more beautiful in Spanish than English. I think if we can blend in colorful language that is good. I don't think there is a problem speaking two languages and mixing them up if the receiver also understands the sentiment behind it. There is nothing more beautiful than Mexican love songs. Why doesn't someone write them in English? They can't." Some residents, however, point to the problem of code-switching where people can be asked a question in one language and respond in another. *Martina Russo* laments that her son is no longer proficient in Spanish whereas the children of her European and Mexican friends can speak three or four languages. While she is not even sure which is her own predominant language, by the time her son grew up, English and Spanish were arranged in a strict hierarchy rather than allowing him the opportunity to be organically attuned to two languages. Neither of the languages is taught now in the lower grades the way it used to be, which has influenced the younger generation negatively.

Even with its heavily Hispanic population, it was (and is) possible to grow up in Laredo without Spanish-language proficiency. The difference lies in the status of the languages. Not knowing English denotes inferior class origins, but not knowing Spanish, though inconvenient, is not attached with serious stigma. *Katie Brown* grew up speaking English in her home despite having a Hispanic parent. Her family teased her by talking about her in Spanish. She relearned it in high school and later as a professional working in the theater. Not only do theaters in Laredo put on Spanish-language plays, but they often have actors from Nuevo Laredo and coordinate shows or galas with them. There are many more monolingual Spanish speakers in Laredo than people who know only English.

More than either English or Spanish, what is common is the confluence of English and Spanish and the creative substitutions people find in everyday discourse to incorporate Spanish. *Karla Garcia* explains, "When I speak, when I communicate, I always mix languages. I think language on the border is a very interesting phenomenon. To see how languages mix is to feel how cultures perpetuate new worlds." *Cesar Villarreal*, who is a professional translator at American and Mexican universities, jests that he is not bilingual in the typical sense, as he pretty much destroys both languages. Border language is different than in other parts of Texas or Mexico. Border culture used to be considered peripheral, but because of rapid population growth it may not be so peripheral anymore.

If we apply the phrase "Los Dos Laredos" within the city, we decipher another duality: the landowner class enjoying all the privileges and the working poor struggling to make ends meet. Class divisions in Laredo manifested in spatial partition from the very beginning of the settlement. *Charles Fox* views Laredo as one city that got split. But instead of two Laredos, he points to multiple Laredos: the Laredo of landowners, the Laredo of professionals, the Laredo of the working poor, and the Laredo of the have-nots. *Steve Griffin*, a longtime resident who settled in Laredo in his early youth, concedes that Laredo was always fractionalized between barrios and neighborhoods. This division only became more pronounced and visible over time. With the exception of Washington's Birthday Celebration or the Little Theater, social activities and sports were confined to particular neighborhoods. The city became more circumscribed after losing the air force base, which had made for a more varied population. In some ways Texas A&M International University now serves as a pipeline between outsiders and the city. Although the small town became a vibrant city, it carried its class-centered cultural and spatial divisions to the new iteration. The big difference is the absence of the downtown as a cultural axis providing the central public space for all of Laredo's people.

Laredo was considered the poorest community per capita in all of the United States when the war on poverty was launched in the 1960s. A large number of residents were reliant on a program called surplus commodities,[37] similar to food stamps, which helped out farmers by buying excess food and distributing it directly to needy families. It was a common habit for farmers to head to the northern states with their entire families during the summer to harvest crops. Many students never got to finish school owing to continuous interruptions because they would return after September when school had already started. *Felipe Calderon* worked on farms with his parents in the summertime all the way up in Minnesota and Wisconsin throughout the 1970s. They would harvest sugar beets in Minnesota, then cucumbers for pickling in Wisconsin, and then on to North Dakota, which offered better wages. He started traveling with his parents when he was eight or nine and was working when he was twelve. Whether by car or train, families traveled together. Although it was hard work, it was a respite from the hot summer, and generous wages made good food affordable in the new locations. As he remembers, "I never had a bad day working in the agricultural fields. Instead, it was a humbling experience working alongside my parents. I visited games and museums, and later at school wrote essays about my adventures, omitting the part about working in the fields. One summer, I visited the Museum of Natural History in Chicago. I watched the Detroit Tigers play at Tiger Stadium. None of this would have been possible without the farm work in the north."

The economic division in Laredo was always present, but it has crystallized with the spatial dismemberment of the poorer quarters. *Arthur Bailey*, a struggling artist living in his poverty-ridden childhood barrio in south Laredo, complains that all the interesting places for entertainment are located far from the poor neighborhoods. People are tired after a long day of work, and driving to another part of town to relax becomes a chore rather than a pleasure. The walkable section of Laredo has been enlarged with pavements, but the barrios remain severed by the interstate. In the south-side neighborhood where he grew up, there are no movie theaters, art galleries, fancy restaurants, good stores, or even proper grocery stores. The neighborhood has been split apart by I-35 and is adjacent to Sacred Heart Children's Home, an institution for abandoned and abused children.

Urban planning has diverted resources from particular neighborhoods and made the poor invisible, observes *Eric Owen*, a pastor who serves at two churches in south Laredo. He has witnessed the growth of the city resulting in billions of dollars flowing through the bridges. The poverty in the neighborhoods where he works as chaplain remains unchanged despite the city having transitioned to such a prominent port. He wonders why a portion of the bridge revenues cannot be invested in eradicating poverty. Owen works at a small forty-five-year-old Hispanic church in the older part of the city on McPherson Road and an even smaller church in the new neighborhood of Cuatro Vientos. The churches each feed 150 families twice a week from supplies provided by the local food bank. Interestingly, while Laredo prospers, the demand for food continues increasing. The poor in Laredo have remained untouched by prosperity. Instead of federal, state, or even local government, about a hundred Catholic churches and their pastors serve as community leaders dealing with food and housing insecurity. Although access to education has been enhanced, Owen feels that supporting cultural programs such as proper parenting or access to gyms that can equip poor children with social skills needed in the job market remain missing. A free recreation center in poor neighborhoods where children congregate, play, and learn together could help fulfill some of the needs that the churches are unable to deliver.

Conclusion

Laredo's residents define their city in terms of history and heritage, the self-definition that is undermined and invisible in the national discourse over the border, where trade and crime overshadow all other integral features of the border. The geographic or economic advantages of the border may dominate the broader conversation about the region, but the people who live in the territory have preserved the history of their land, language, and culture in their day-to-day lives, and it is their voices that defy the current connotations of the border. When *Ariana Raymond* moved to Laredo from Mexico City,

FIGURE 7 Promotional flyer for Noche Mexicana. Webb County Heritage Foundation.

she was surprised not only by the bicultural traits of the city but by the way the two cultures have blended, allowing each to coexist and thereby create a third culture. Laredo is a combination of Mexican and American cultures, but it also embodies a different border culture, as explained in detail in chapter 6. *Rodrique Taylor* reiterates that local people often claim that Washington, D.C., or Mexico City do not understand what happens on the border. He notes, "Laredo was once under the seven flags and very closely tied to Nuevo Laredo. Politics and policies have changed a lot, but they have not been able to transform cultural roots. In a meeting place of cultures and languages, it is the continuous collisions that make the place interesting."

Despite its frontier features, Laredo has remained a cherished and chosen home for its residents for generations. This attachment to ancestral land and history is indeed deep rooted. *Nina Vargas* remembers, "My grandfather told me stories of bones being dug up from graves and taken over to Nuevo Laredo after Laredo was included in the U.S. I have worked as a teacher and homeschooled my special needs child. All of the textbooks start with the thirteen colonies while indigenous history, the story of this land, is never part of the founding narrative." The Hispanic history that has remained outside the nationhood narrative was intrinsically woven in everyday life in Laredo. For *Giselle Lamar*, "The city is home not only because I chose to raise my family here but also because it is my ancestors' land. My family was on this land before it was Texas or Mexico or the U.S. My parents are Hispanic, my grandparents are Mexican, and one great-grandmother was Comanche." She has a sense of belongingness and direct affiliation with the land, which is not necessarily present in other metropolitan areas. She even wonders how many "illegal immigrants" have Native American blood from tribes in North America rather than Central America and therefore have more of a claim to this land. United States authorities would dismiss any such ancestral claims to territory, but land and blood relations have a deeper history than the existence of the United States. In a city where the first mayor's great-great-granddaughter serves today as assistant city manager, land and lineage are intertwined in living memory.

Compared to many other border towns, Laredo has protected the bicultural environment for several generations, which is what makes Laredo unique. *Ben Tristan*, who moved to Laredo from his hometown of Corpus Christi, finds Laredo much more attuned to Mexican culture compared to other border cities in South Texas. *Cecily D. Vega* notes the difference between McAllen and Laredo. What strikes her is that in McAllen people state their name as Rodriguez, a sign of having been Anglicized, not José Rodriguez as they do in Laredo. *Charles Fox* compares Laredo with El Paso, where he grew up and was part of the "others." While Hispanics elsewhere took pride in legends of the Mexican Revolution and Pancho Villa, many residents in Laredo identified with the Mexican Federalists, the elite rather than the revolutionaries. In Laredo, there has never been a need to dig up ethnic history or ancestry for a demographic that has been dominant in number and power.

The fraternal bond between Laredo and Nuevo Laredo is definitely a distinguishing feature of this border town where residents grew up enjoying the amenities of both cities and nurturing loyalty for both of their hometowns. The usages *going across* or *el otro lado* (the other side) belong to Laredo. Even people from El Paso or other border cities in the Valley need an explanation of these phrases. It means so much more than literally crossing the bridge and meeting people. *Charles Vega* thinks it is the visual presence of the river that makes it possible to embrace the two cultures in harmony. He compares the more Anglicized culture of McAllen by noting that McAllen is ten miles away from the river. He recalls testifying in Congress and being asked what kind of programs were needed in Laredo for minorities. He responded, "Sir, where I am from, you are the minority!" He believes that in Laredo the twin streaks of allegiance to this country and pride in Mexican heritage run parallel and seldom collide.

Laredo was once the capital of its own country, which is why the museum at the Republic of the Rio Grande capitol building is considered the most important historic landmark in town. *Millie Allen* believes this independent and stubborn spirit has maintained its hold on the population over time, having been protected by the insular geography. Laredo has had to provision for itself from the very beginning of its existence, always having to rely on its own resources for survival. Whether it was the weather or war, outside assistance was scarce. The isolation that drove Laredo to be autonomous and self-driven may still be true geographically, but politically and economically Laredo is now an integral part of the global transportation network.

CHAPTER 2

Where Is the Border?

The River/the Wall/the Checkpoints/ the Prisons/the Colonias

If you are looking through bars, it does not matter which side you are on, there is a jail. It does not matter which side you are on, it is certainly not inviting.

THOMAS JEFFREY, LAREDO RESIDENT

You cannot hold up money. You have got to let it move.

BEN TRISTAN, RETIRED BORDER PATROL
OFFICER AND LAREDO RESIDENT

Laredo started out as a frontier where Native Americans and Mexicans fought to control land, Mexico and Texas sought to establish political authority, the Republic of the Rio Grande instilled temporary sovereignty, and finally the United States incorporated the strategic location in its nation-building enterprise. Historically, the Rio Grande was the agreed-on border between Mexico and the United States but the river never functioned as a boundary to keep outsiders away. Rather, the river joined the people living on either bank and eased their seamless cultural and economic interactions both at the individual and collective level. The political boundary of Laredo became tangible with new infrastructure like Interstate 35, although road networks also enabled more people and vehicles to travel back and forth. Openness, as opposed to fear, was inscribed in much of the landscape and commercial dealings. Interestingly, it was NAFTA that prompted anxiety about the porous border and made it possible to invest massive resources to erect physical structures and deploy large numbers of people to guard it. The plan to block the Rio Grande with a wall has been on and off the national priority list for a while and aims to convert the border into a physical and tangible deterrence.

This chapter is about locating the border in Laredo by way of identifying the real barriers that obstruct the mobility of different groups of people and are located in various parts of the city. Throughout Laredo's history, there has been little fear about outsiders (with the exception of Indian attacks); rather, the Rio Grande has always remained open and inviting for trade. The people of Laredo take pride in subverting the meaning of the political boundary with their daily activities across the river. Yet they also appreciate the border when the sounds of gunshots by the drug cartels reverberate across the Rio Grande. Much of the infrastructure of fear, in the form of checkpoints and prisons, is situated inside the city, not necessarily on the transnational border. Citizens from Laredo have to submit to official inspection when they drive northward within the United States. Similarly, the private prison industry has flourished all over South Texas because of the militarization of the border. Moreover, there exist zones of isolation for the poor, namely the colonias, residential neighborhoods that are near the city but never included in it, where the poor (mostly the undocumented) can afford cheap land prices while often subsisting without basic amenities such as water, electricity, sewage, hospitals, and fire stations. These different formations—the river, the wall, the checkpoints, the detention centers, and the colonias—all tell very different stories about the purpose and function of the border in Laredo.

The River (the Unborder)

A legal treaty between the United States and Mexico created the political boundary between the two nations in the middle of the Rio Grande.[1] For geographically isolated Laredo, its cultural ties with the sister city of Nuevo Laredo remained unbroken and actually became strengthened because of economic interdependence despite territorial separation. Laredo was always conveniently located on the trade route from New York City to Mexico City. The easy-to-navigate waters of the Rio Grande further enhanced the significance of Laredo's setting as a commercial axis. The river has historically marked off the political boundary separating the two countries, but economically and culturally it always joined Laredo to Nuevo Laredo.

Because Laredo was founded on both sides of the river, the settlement spread back and forth, points out *Millie Allen*, adding that the Rio Grande functions like the Colorado River running through Austin. The river evolved into a political and legal construct only after 1848, following the Treaty of

WASHING CLOTHES IN RIO GRANDE, LAREDO, TEXAS.

FIGURE 8 Washing clothes on the Rio Grande. Webb County Heritage Foundation.

Guadalupe Hidalgo. Even after it became a boundary, people were able to cross it easily several times a day without much scrutiny. Allen notes how during Washington's Birthday Celebration (WBC), the bridge used to be open on the day of the parade, allowing people to cross without paying or showing papers. The rest of the time people from Laredo went across to buy groceries, be entertained, or catch a cheap flight. Nuevo Laredo had the nightlife and attracted teenagers who would dance and drink on weekends. People rarely carried their passports on them, and even money on the border was interchangeable as both pesos and dollars were accepted as valid currency on either side of the border for a long time.

The twin cities along the Rio Grande have historically functioned as unified economic and social bodies. The ethnic, cultural, and often familial bonds have proven more resilient than the international boundary line.[2] Although people in Laredo almost unanimously agree that the Rio Grande is their border, its meaning has hardly been constraining to them. Instead of a hard political boundary, the river was not only symbolically but literally the easily navigable and transparent line setting an abstract demarcation that could be breached any time one wished to by going across. The very phrase "going across," as explained in the previous chapter, is Laredo vernacular that subverts the national narrative of the border as a fixed boundary. The tradition of getting married on the river on a boat for couples belonging to two nations continues in the middle of the bridge today. The Rio Grande is not only Laredo's boundary but also its only source of drinking water and a precious natural resource shared with Nuevo Laredo.

Memories revolving around the Rio Grande serve as a constant reminder that as a people Hispanics have always been on this land. *Larry Sanchez,* who served as president of Texas A&M International University (TAMIU), narrates his wife's family history of owning land on both sides of the river. In the founding days, the Spaniards and later the Mexican government granted land to settlers in the Rio Grande region. People used to keep homes in well-connected Laredo and ranches in the relatively fertile lands of Nuevo Laredo. After Laredo became part of the United States, families divided their properties and often decided to settle on the side where they had land. There are still a handful of people who own ancestral property on the other side, although it is becoming harder to take care of it. The Rio Grande was never any kind of deterrent for the people of Laredo, or for that matter the people of Nuevo Laredo.

People have been able to navigate back and forth and maintain family ties despite belonging to two different countries. Residents on both sides drink the water of the Rio Grande, which translates into a strong relationship. As a teenager, *Viviana Cortez* would spend the night with her cousins in Nuevo Laredo over the weekend and go to school in Laredo on Monday. This is how easy and persistent the connection has been between the two settlements. She does not go across as regularly as she used to, but she tries to make up for it through social media. The border is literally a bridge for *Gill Taylor,* who lives in Nuevo Laredo and works in Laredo. *Martina Russo* sees the border as a uniting force, creating harmony. To her the fluidity of the river is a metaphor for the relationship between Laredo and Nuevo Laredo. She adds, "If the people on the other side [as is true of most Canadians] spoke English, none of the issues would arise. Fences divide, but borders do not have to divide."

Without much fuss the Rio Grande parted people on either bank and was viewed more as a source of water, recreation, and fishing than any binding delimitation. A major concern that arose in the 1970s and 1980s was the contamination of the river and its safety. *Jonathan Everett* moved to Laredo in 1967 and stayed away from the river because he saw it as filthy and unsafe, even forbidding his daughter to take a canoe trip. Instead of trying to keep the riverbank vacant, if today the government would subsidize repopulating it with goats, sheep, and donkeys, it would be a natural haven for the animals that would also protect the river. Everett worries, "The federal government is destroying the environment along with the animal habitat. The water is being poisoned with chemicals and toxins meant to kill giant invasive cane. Look at what is going on in Flint. Many water sources have been tarnished by the government."

The jurisdictional limit of Laredo has always been the river. *Michael Factor* invokes his legal training, which stresses that the border is established by law, to specify over which jurisdiction the state has control and authority, but in Laredo the border has been the river, which can easily be crossed back and forth. The change that most stands out to him is how the water that once was the source of recreation, namely swimming and fishing, has become so befouled. *Gary Bell*, a career politician, has always viewed the river as the yoking of two cultures. He has never perceived it as any line of separation, even if he values the sovereignty of both nations. He believes that laws and regulations should be reciprocal, and citizens of both countries should enjoy some rights in each other's domains. Regardless of legal and political constraints, the two cultures have always been coupled by the river. It carries the memories of old traditions for both peoples, which is not going to change. No matter what new twist immigration policy or border security unveils, the symbiotic relationship between the two partner jurisdictions cannot entirely be vanquished.

Although the border has been referred to as an edge by scholars,[3] the river never epitomizes an endpoint. Especially when people are catching fish on either bank, it is visually difficult to imagine any estrangement even when one is aware of the reality. *Rachel Lawrence* views the division between Laredo and Nuevo Laredo as a geopolitical, not necessarily a geographical, border. When she moved to Laredo she was excited to live on the edge of the country, but with time she came to realize how artificial the boundary is. The militarization of the border, particularly the checkpoints, seems creepy to her, a sharp contrast to actual life in the border city. She experienced the change in the meaning of the border personally when a Border Patrol officer pulled a gun on her while she was jogging on a trail by the river. Although it turned out to have been a mistake, the use of the riverfront lost its charm for her after the experience.

The recent undertones of the river pose a stark contrast to memories honored by residents. *Felipe Calderon* remembers that in the 1960s his grandfather used to get water from the river in large vessels mounted on horse-drawn carriages for his garden. Instead of flower shops, people relied on farmers like his grandfather, especially from September to December during the peak of religious festivities. Flowers from the family garden were sold as far away as Monterrey as well as to local residents who stopped on their way to the cemetery. Calderon remembers watching the river flow, which for him means a deep-rooted link with history, the memories having instilled a sense of pride in him and formed his identity of being from a border town. *Rodrique Taylor* values the memory of walking with his grandmother as a child down the street and lounging on the rocks by the river. The simple act of walking along the river and watching it flow has become obsolete now. The river was not a boundary but an integral part of daily experience not too long ago.

The Rio Grande has always unified lives on opposite banks in Laredo. In contrast, in El Paso the river is so dry that the view from one side of the fence does not trigger similar robust bonds. While the presence of the river for the inhabitants has been tranquil, the federal government has made numerous attempts to control the land adjacent to the river to monitor illegal border crossers. Complaining that high-rising cane shielded trespassers, the Border Patrol has mowed it down several times. In 1990 the Border Patrol cleared brush along the Rio Grande near downtown. The Texas National Guard aided the Border Patrol with logistical support in the form of electronics and equipment as well as labor while abstaining from direct immigration enforcement functions.[4] Controlling the border by slashing the cane on the banks became a recurrent action and a point of contention between the Border Patrol and residents. Rio Grande International Study Center (RGISC) had to initiate a lawsuit against the Border Patrol to stop it from spraying pesticides and weed killers from the air to clean up the riverbank as far as sixteen miles into the interior of the city. The federal government wastes a lot of money by harming the fish upstream and then trying to replenish the river downstream in repetitive cycles.

The story of the Rio Grande from an ecological perspective captures the incongruities between political and natural boundaries. *Theodore Valenti*, a biologist from Laredo, recounts his canoe trip with a colleague in 2010. They started out looking for mussels in the river along with the goal of comparing the amount of harmful cane on the U.S. versus the Mexican side. Based on visual observation, they concluded that on the U.S. side, from Eagle Pass to Laredo, somewhere between 90 to 95 percent of the banks were invaded by the cane, while it was only 2 to 5 percent on the Mexican side. The management of land on the two riverbanks was drastically different. The Mexicans let their animals—cows, sheep, goats, and horses—all the way down to the river, which has controlled the cane. On the U.S. side, mainly because of cattle tick fever, ranchers have kept animals away from the river, so there is nothing to stop the growth of cane. On that trip, they always slept on the Mexican side, as the U.S. side was inaccessible because of overgrown cane. This is how Valenti explains the Border Patrol's combat against the cane in the early 2000s, which was driven by brute power and lacked expert knowledge or proper planning:

> Cane reproduces by way of rhizomes, which lie underground and therefore cannot be terminated with mowing. The Border Patrol continuously mowed aboveground, leaving the nodes alone, so that new shoots came up within a few weeks. To stop the cane from growing, there needs to be a restoration process with native vegetation. Otherwise, the energy remains below the ground in the rhizomes and starts new life. Using heavy equipment, the Border Patrol dug the rhizomes out of half the land at the bend of the river and dumped it in the landfill. They mowed the other half of the land, used herbicides to control the growth of cane, and planted a pallet of native vegetation in a particular spaced-out pattern. The plants needed a lot of water, but without the water rights from the river they had to use very expensive city water for the drip irrigation system. The flood of 2010 washed away all the plants, the irrigation system, even the topsoil. All that remained were big mats of rhizomes in a portion of the control area. The contractor who was responsible for planting and revegetating could not meet the standard for the percentage of surviving plants. By this time, the Border Patrol did not have money for additional irrigation. The result is that the area is now densely overgrown with all kinds of trees and shrubs that are much more difficult to control than cane.

Valenti summarizes his perception of the Border Patrol with the punchline, "Not very bright!"

The river only turned into the state line because of the presence and actions of the Border Patrol. Border crossings changed dramatically after it became difficult to cross back and forth. *Cesar Villarreal* grew up seeing Mexican men walking right to the campus of Laredo Community College, still dripping wet from swimming the river, while people glanced the other way. He remembers calling them *mojados* because they swam across the river. They worked hard and repatriated as much as 80 percent of their income to their families in Mexico. When Valenti first started working on the banks of the river four decades ago, he would see piles of clothing along the U.S. side, left there by illegal entrants. Initially he says it was 99 percent male attire, belonging to migrants who were usually already working in the United States and going back and forth without proper papers. When security became tighter, the men stopped going back and tried to get their families into the United States. In Mexican villages, young men are rare and women and children dominate the population. Female and children's clothing now surpasses male outfits in the heaps of clothes. When he used to paddle in the river twenty years ago, Valenti would notice as many as eight or ten people crossing the river during the daytime. They used inflated big-truck inner tubes, which they discarded on the banks. This was a regular mode of transportation and some people even commuted daily on the river. The Border Patrol started puncturing holes in the tubes, and now that tires are tubeless anyway, life jackets have replaced inner tubes as a means of transportation.

The dynamics of the strict supervision of the river have had a drastic impact. *Sara Calderon* grew up in Laredo and was always conscious of her undocumented status. The river was never a border for her but a place of peace. She explains, "I hike regularly at the Paso del Indio Nature Trail, which is my respite. One time, the Border Patrol stopped me hiking on the trail and asked about my status. I told them I was a student and a DACA recipient. One of the Border Patrol agents responded that he himself had a brother and sister who were DACA recipients. I never feared the river, only the check-points. But I got really scared when the military put the barbed wire along the trail. I touched the wire, it was so sharp."

The river continues to carry different meanings to different groups of people. *Trina Case* points out that there are so many ways to look at the river when reflecting about the border: "It unites and it divides, and it is beautiful and it is polluted as well. There is so much illegal activity there, and then there is recreational activity." She embraces the contradictions and tries to minimize the negative aspects and push for change that might promote

FIGURE 9 Escobares Ferry. Laredo Public Library.

the positive side of things. She is deeply saddened by the violence that has marred the kind of natural flow and interchange that used to exist in the past. She explains, "There are security issues, and there is drug trafficking. However, the bulk of the drugs comes through legal ports of entry by way of trucks and vehicles on bridges." American consumption of drugs drives the turmoil south of the border with a distorted political and security system. Ideally, there would be controls at the border to prevent the flow of cash and goods that travel southbound to perpetuate the cycles of violence. For Case, the problems are deep rooted, because the United States abides by free trade agreements that create gross inequality in Mexico and Central America, pushing many people to despair and economic misery.

The Checkpoints (Strong Border)

While the Rio Grande may have provided a soft and weak boundary for Laredo, forms of impenetrable infrastructure have been constructed inside the city. There are seven checkpoints on the major highways (and the airport) in the Laredo Sector, where the Border Patrol has a permanent presence and the authority to stop all vehicles to question people about citizenship status, purpose of visit, and merchandise in the vehicle. These inspection stations were established to prevent human and drug trafficking, although after 9/11 deterrence of terrorism has been added as a major objective. The checkpoints are supposed to be the last layer of control after passage through the initial border. For all practical purposes, these checkpoints function as deterrents that are as important and real as any boundary for the nation because anyone traveling farther into the United States has to undergo their scrutiny.

United States law allows checkpoints to be set within a hundred miles of the border, although in reality most checkpoints are located not so far inland. As a point of comparison, the checkpoints in San Diego, the whitest border city, are so close to the actual border that residents do not have to go through them unless they are traveling from Mexico toward the city. The locations of checkpoints are based on maximum coverage and traffic patterns to make sure that every back road is included and no one can escape scrutiny. Laredo used to have the main checkpoint on Interstate 35 at mile marker 13, but because of increased traffic it was shifted to mile marker 29. The checkpoint on Highway 59 is about forty miles away from the city center. The federal government has sole authority over their management.

At the checkpoints, each vehicle leaving Laredo is stopped, photographed, and inspected before being allowed to leave. Citizens and legal residents undergo scrutiny that can range from a few polite questions to hours-long inquiries including vehicle and in-person searches. *Roger Gordon* argues that if checkpoints are located closer to the city, there are more ways to get around, whereas it is harder to avoid them if they are set farther out. Texas has too many country roads, which might be the reason why most Texas cities have checkpoints farther out compared to California or Arizona. The efficiency of these checkpoints is measured by the number of drug traffickers and illegal entrants that are stopped.

The major problem in the Laredo Sector has always been the relative shortfall of needed officials despite the steady growth of the number of Border Patrol officials in Laredo.[5] When *Derek Perez* joined the Border Patrol in 1978, there were sixty-five agents, but by 2007 he was supervising four hundred agents. Starting from two checkpoints, the Laredo Sector now has seven checkpoints: north, west, south, Zapata, Freer, Cotulla, and Hebbronville. Perez constantly faced problems with turnover at all of these stations. He was aware that spouses and families did not want to live in Laredo. Often the agent would face the option of resignation or divorce. When training new recruits, Perez was honest with his men: "Discuss this with your family. Tell them about Laredo, tell them to research it, because if you go to the academy and graduate and then you come here and leave, then you are wasting [government] money." Nevertheless, it kept happening. Officers who transferred from bigger cities like Fort Worth or St. Louis had a terrible time adjusting. Perez believes that along with the natural barrier of the river, logistical and infrastructural impediments such as all-weather back roads, cameras, and sensor equipment would go a long distance toward monitoring the border. Yet the only way all the infrastructural and technological advances can be used efficiently is with enhanced manpower, a core problem that has never been fully addressed in Laredo.

Another retired Border Patrol agent, *Ben Tristan*, stresses the importance of the coverage area to include the outer roads so that no one can circumvent the checkpoints. They have no authority to go beyond the hundred miles, but twenty-five to thirty-five miles seems a reasonable perimeter to him. He recounts his experience at the Canadian border when he was stationed in Montana for training. The checkpoint was deserted and the lone agent worked from nine to five. Anyone who crossed the checkpoint after hours was supposed to sign the clipboard hanging by the checkpoint. It was quite a contrast to the way checkpoints operate in Texas. Canadians were trusted to get out of their vehicles and provide the needed information, while anyone coming from Laredo (and obviously Mexico) is perceived to be untrustworthy.

Tristan's rotation training in Montana was an eye-opening experience in contrast to the southern border. Instead of checkpoints busy all twenty-four hours, he performed the night shift at checkpoints that looked abandoned. All they caught was a religious group (Mennonites) who were trying to smuggle cigarettes into the United States and take back some insecticides that were banned in Canada. He felt it was pretty harmless compared to the smuggling that takes place every day on the southern border. In Montana there were a number of Chinese and Mexican workers in the ten thousand acres of surrounding farmland who might not have had their papers in order, but the small communities were reluctant to report their asparagus farmers and strawberry pickers. If an agent caught someone, he had to drive to the nearest town with the prisoner. The long commute, especially during winter nights, was torturous for the officer, but the little Montana towns that had prisons earned seventy-five to eighty dollars a night for each prisoner, which was a bit of a moneymaker.

Tristan also mentions high turnover as a huge problem for the Laredo Sector. Many people join the Border Patrol in the first place just to move up in the federal government. He explains, "This is a blue-collar law enforcement job which involves running and crawling through dirt, while FBI positions require a suit and tie. People often join the Border Patrol, acquire a degree, and ascend the career ladder. After the Iraq and Afghanistan wars, ex-military officials have signed up to be Border Patrol agents in significant numbers." More narcotics are being caught, even if marijuana has lost its allure. One can get it legally in many states, so why take a risk carrying a bulky item? As Tristan narrates, "It is all cocaine and methamphetamine, it is all in small packages, and we need to step up our game. I believe it all comes through eighteen-wheelers at the ports." But Tristan agrees that 90 percent of trucks cannot be stopped without causing major delays in commerce.

People from older generations, such as *Michael Factor*, remember well when there were no checkpoints in Laredo. Factor calls the Border Patrol "an army of occupation" focused on searches and seizures. He elaborates, "These officers also commit crimes and abuses, but often get away because of their status. The checkpoints, the control mechanisms, and the dogs all seem reminiscent of Nazi Germany, with soldiers parading around with guns and German shepherds." He finds the whole production offensive. Patricia Price echoes these concerns when she writes, "The border checkpoints strung along the U.S.-Mexican border function as pores, distilling meaning from the vast bereftness of the desert southwest."[6] *Felipe Calderon* resents waiting in long lines trying to get through the checkpoint and the Border Patrol interrogation. He feels that everyone from Laredo is perceived as an illegal entrant to the United States. He and his family have been on the land for generations, and yet he has to go through the checkpoint to travel anywhere: "People in other parts of the country don't understand how it can actually be demeaning to somebody, and I wish they would put Border Patrol checkpoints in Washington, D.C."

Along with exponentially increased federal funding, the mission and composition of the Border Patrol have undergone drastic changes. *Giselle Lamar* believes that the Border Patrol used to have a lot more discretion when it was staffed with local people. They operated under the notion of keeping the border safe and could decide to send people back without filing charges. In the aftermath of the war on terror, when the southern border was redefined as a national security concern, the discretion regarding voluntary return that a field level Border Patrol officer could exercise was revoked. The number of agents multiplied rapidly with added funding for the war on terror, and new officers who came to guard the southern border outnumbered local applicants. Lamar believes that once veterans from the Iraq and Afghanistan wars started joining the agency, the patriotic element in the Border Patrol acquired a heightened anti-immigrant fervor. The Border Patrol in Laredo now has a lot more agents, files more cases, and pursues the mission to stop illegal immigration; it's no longer about just keeping everybody safe. There is an implicit push for higher numbers of detainees, so the figures have gone up dramatically.

Checkpoints are typically designed to oppress, intimidate, and terrorize people. *Russell Garray* narrates his experience of driving on the public roads along the border in the Valley with a group of attorneys from Earthjustice. They were in the van with the director of the National Butterfly Center when the Border Patrol in two unmarked cars started following them. They were driving slowly, at twenty miles an hour, but the Border Patrol cars encircled them. The director of the Butterfly Center, Marina Trevino Wright, took out her phone and started recording what was happening. The Border Patrol just looked at them and laughed, making everyone nervous. They did not ask for any identification or pose any questions. When they saw the people in the van, who were all professionals but mostly Hispanic, they backed off. To Garray, "This was an act of racial profiling and intimidation. It is against American values and yet officially thrives in the border region. This intimidation affects everyone living on the border, citizens and non-citizens alike."

Not everyone associates the checkpoints with fear; for some they are a mere inconvenience. *Justin Taylor* jokes that all he needs to do at a checkpoint is to take off his sunglasses so they can see his blue eyes for him to be waved through. He is certain about the prevalence of profiling at the checkpoints. *Cesar Villarreal* also feels that the border has changed over the years with the growth of aggressive law enforcement. The border is now fully militarized, and law enforcement is one of the biggest employers in the city. A sizable contingent of DEA, ATF, and FBI officers are now part of the Laredo landscape. To counter insulting queries about citizenship status at the airport and checkpoints, Villarreal often wears a T-shirt proclaiming

"I only look illegal!" *Cristopher Cartin* cannot help thinking of Checkpoint Charlie in Berlin, when he expresses his doubts: "Can any wall truly contain immigration and drugs? World history shows that walls do not work. The comparison with concentration camps is hard to ignore with children being imprisoned." The framing of border issues also seems eerily reminiscent to him of South African apartheid days.

Border Patrol agents are not only part of the security apparatus, but their sheer number also adds substantially to the local consumer base. *Roger Gordon*, who works for the Border Patrol, claims an overall positive influence for his organization, which is now the second-largest employer in the city. *Derek Perez* feels that his former employer has good rapport with the residents, updating ranchers who in turn allow the agency access to their lands. Local law enforcement officer *Jake Ruiz*, however, feels that he has seen better days. He mourns, "There are a lot of rogue Border Patrol officers. Everybody fears and hates police officers, especially when crimes committed by them come to light." The sensational serial killings of a number of prostitutes in Laredo were actually committed by a Border Patrol agent.[7]

The checkpoints set clear limits for two young Laredoans who grew up in Laredo undocumented. *Sara Calderon* stepped outside Laredo only after she got her DACA approval and became really nervous at the checkpoint. She was traveling on Greyhound and was ready with her Texas ID and DACA card. Border Patrol agents regularly step onto buses to interrogate travelers. They started checking people's bags randomly but spared her. She noticed, "People with darker complexion were more subject to scrutiny. I have heard this kind of profiling is fairly common at checkpoints." *Sebastian Fabian* also had a nerve-wracking experience the first time he passed the checkpoint. He had grown up with a trapped feeling all his life as he could never leave Laredo to explore life like his friends. He had never attended an out-of-town concert before his DACA approval. Despite having proper documentation, he felt shaken at the prospect of finally crossing the city limits. He was also amazed at how normal the procedure appeared to other people. Everyone seemed calm whereas it was one of the most intense moments of his life. American citizens like *Gill Taylor* who opt to stay in Nuevo Laredo cross the international bridge without any fear every single day. All through her school years, which involved a daily commute, the only problem she encountered was with traffic and having to stay back for extracurricular activities, which made it a long day at school.

FIGURE 10 Pontoon Bridge. Webb County Heritage Foundation.

The whole city was in effect a prison for *Sara Calderon*, who has lived in Laredo since she was a toddler. She remembers, "I was not able to drive or work, always alert to the Border Patrol. As a child, I was scared of green trucks and helicopters [regular sights on Laredo streets and in the sky] even before I understood about my status. My sisters, all of them American, had no such fear." The first time she left the city and went to San Antonio was after getting the DACA permit as an adult. She had accepted uncertainty as part of her life, but only after acquiring her DACA status did she realize that living with fear is not normal. Glancing at a helicopter in the skies of San Antonio, she had to remind herself, "Relax, it's not Border Patrol." When Calderon received her DACA approval, she felt like she was the luckiest person alive as she was finally free to travel beyond city limits.

The Detention Centers (Lines of Deterrence)

Texas has become a big penal colony, asserts *Justin Taylor*, calling the phenomenon prison for profit. *Charles Vega*, a former city government employee, also laments that prisons have turned into lucrative moneymakers. Campaign contributions flow toward the behemoth CoreCivic (formerly

Corrections Corporation of America) or the GEO Group (formerly Wacken-hut Corrections Corporation), and there seems no way to stop the growth. Vega remembers the days when the county used to get federal contracts: "There were so many regulations they had to follow, but I do not know whether private prisons have to go through the intense scrutiny that the county did." The lack of an effective court system and the prioritizing of punishment pushes the entire society toward an abyss, argues *Giselle Lamar*, who works as a prosecutor in the federal court system. She explains, "The punishment of individual crimes by prison sentences penalizes the whole community. People take jobs to move drugs or people illegally mostly out of desperation. A lot of people in jail have mental health issues." Laredo is seriously deficient in mental health treatment capacity. There is no psychi-atrist for children in the entire city. Laredo has a center for mental health problems, Border Region Behavioral Health Center,[8] but no doctors. Ex-pressing her frustration, Lamar says, "Outside doctors evaluate a child based on twenty-minute video screen time. Children with anger issues do not get help and may turn violent later in life. Small individual problems are not ad-dressed and become larger social issues. I would like to see more resources directed toward kids who can be steered in the right direction."

Judges in the federal criminal court system have to follow sentencing guidelines. For a number of years, they had little discretion because in the Bush era the guidelines were interpreted as mandatory, but now they are deemed to be advisory. Even with the discretion, however, there are implicit norms. For instance, judges are frowned upon now when they grant anyone asylum. When an illegal border crosser is caught, the Bureau of Prisons de-cides the person's fate based on established criteria. Those who are going to be deported are usually kept in the border region to save money. If they are part of a gang, then safety measures with regard to placing them in certain prisons are observed. People caught by the Border Patrol are placed in the growing number of private detention centers that can now be found all over Laredo and South Texas. The County Detention Center only holds people for four days and does not process immigration cases. If it is a federal case, they are sent to a private detention center. Private detention centers were initially established because of the presence of the federal courthouse in Laredo. Prisoners are held for thirty days until being deported. If they are caught again, then they serve an enhanced sentence for sixty to ninety days before being sent back to their home country.

The GEO Group has built one of the largest private prisons to hold federal prisoners in Webb County, situated between the colonias of Rio Bravo and El Cenizo. Despite its record of egregious ill treatment of prisoners, it obtained a lucrative contract, with a state senator's husband acting as one of its attorneys.[9] In Del Rio, there were protests against GEO over the suicide of a prisoner after she was allegedly raped and humiliated by cellmates and prison guards. Nicholas Hudson notes that South Texas has been very active in profiting from major immigration incarceration and has allowed private prisons all along the border to capture nonviolent border crossers who bring in the highest federal per diem rates.[10] Budgetary allocation to different sectors in turn shapes immigration enforcement policy. Timothy Dunn describes how the Lower Rio Grande Valley became a detention zone for Central American refugees in the 1980s because of budgetary constraints. Fair treatment and due process in immigration cases took the back seat, and more pressing concerns about financial resources led to inconsistent bail bond rates in Texas, including the Laredo Sector.[11]

As a result of the controversy, GEO's proposed 2,800 beds were reduced to 1,500, but it remains one of the largest private prisons to hold federal prisoners. It was the fourth private detention center to be built within fifty miles of the federal courthouse in Laredo. CoreCivic operates two private prisons, one in Laredo with a 350-bed capacity and one in Webb County with a 500-bed capacity. In nearby La Salle County, Emerald Correctional Management opened another 540-bed detention center,[12] which is now run by LaSalle Corrections after Emerald went bankrupt.[13] Private prisons became a huge profit-making industry after touting cost reduction and employment generation for localities. In reality, the handful of low-paid jobs have negligible impact on local economies as high-salaried corporate positions are rarely filled by local applicants. Instead of cities economically profiting from prisons, it is prison corporations that end up with enormous profits. CoreCivic's stock price doubled between 2002 and 2004, and by 2015 it was holding 51 percent of federal prisoners in its facilities, emerging as the second-largest private prison company.[14] Texas politicians, both Republicans and Democrats, receive major campaign donations from such corporations and are more than willing to protect them.

The private detention centers employ chaplains from local churches to address the pervasive problem of the inmates' depression. *Eric Owen*, who serves as a priest and counselor, explains, "I mainly listen to their stories and motivate them to pray and stay positive. I offer them Bibles for their spiritual health. I am the person responsible for the mental health of the prisoners. They have a good medical system. Officers are trained to treat prisoners well. I have not seen many complaints or grievances. They have programs for prisoners to go outside and exercise or play for two hours every day." On the other hand, as part of Mercy Ministry, *Rosalie Wright* believes that serious human rights violations occur in the detention centers. She met a woman from Angola who saw ten of her family members killed in front of her. During her nearly yearlong stay at the detention center, Wright was her only visitor.

The plight of border crossers has become worse just as the difficulty of crossing has heightened. Owen observes, "Now it has become harder and more expensive as cartels are claiming their share. Still, more people continue to come, because the conditions in their own countries compel them to risk their lives." One of his most striking memories has to do with a fifty-four-year-old man from Colombia who lost his seventeen-year-old son in the Rio Grande. His only thought was how to recover the body of his son. When his wife got the news of her only son's death, she killed herself. As a pastor, it was difficult for him to give courage to the man who had lost his whole family. As he ponders, "I talk to people at their lowest point in life. They are scared to be in prison, but just as scared to go back to the war zones they have escaped from. Often they prefer death rather than going back and losing all their money. All they are looking for is often a job, a decent opportunity in life." He wonders why a smart country like the United States cannot use its resources wisely and help people in need instead of making immense investments to imprison them. After the recent practice of family separation, women became overwhelmed with locating children. Owen cannot believe that the U.S. government has lost track of so many children and does not understand the rationale behind it. Breaking up a family seems to him like going against God's will. It has become expensive to hold them in prison, but it is also expensive to deport them. Detention centers in Laredo have the capacity to hold as many as four thousand people, but when prisons run out of capacity they push for deportation.

The federal government recently built a migrant processing center using shipping containers in the most picturesque part of downtown overlooking the river. Asylum seekers faced judges on a video screen in this building, where they were allowed to set their first foot in America. *Jill Webb* of the local newspaper reported her surreal experience in the virtual courtrooms.

Someone in authority might be sitting in San Antonio hearing a petitioner's story and making snap decisions. To watch the proceedings as a member of the media, Webb had to show up at the migration processing center at the border at three in the morning and then drive to San Antonio. She sat in front of the judge in real life while watching asylum seekers on the electronic interface. None of the cases was resolved that day, which meant that all the asylum seekers had to return to Mexico and wait for a couple more months for another court date. The process makes it very difficult for the media to talk to asylum seekers.

Detention centers are filled with people coming from Guatemala, El Salvador, Venezuela, Honduras, and Nicaragua. Meanwhile, people from Mexico bring their whole families because of the escalation of gang violence in Mexico. The refugee crisis is the result of a proactive foreign policy that has affected the countries negatively for generations so that refugees are compelled to leave them. *Rodrique Taylor* points to U.S. policies that contribute to, if not create, the refugee disaster. The different arms of the U.S. government have failed to accord enough importance not only to Mexico but also to the rest of Latin America. *Alex Mead* wonders, "When we call Mexico or Latin American countries dangerous places, why do we not mention more than a century of American military intervention in Central America?"

FIGURE 11 Courthouse and Jail. Webb County Heritage Foundation.

The Colonias (the Invisible Border)

The strategies of exclusion in the border city reach beyond the highly visible checkpoints and detention centers. The Border Patrol has the authority to open up temporary checkpoints for tactical reasons. One very popular location of such a tactical checkpoint is on U.S. Route 83, the road to the El Cenizo and Rio Bravo colonias.[15] Colonias are unincorporated communities whose strategic location in the migration corridor often makes them temporary or permanent havens for undocumented immigrants.[16] Private property owners develop their land into substandard residential units without adequate public benefits, taking advantage of the lack of zoning in Texas, and spur colonias on city perimeters. The poor and working classes in the colonias are usually unable to raise any hue and cry for better services. Robert Maril notes that residents of the colonias in the border regions have always been invisible and overlooked for local, state, and federal amenities.[17] Most colonias areas overwhelmingly lack basic water and sanitation services.[18]

Webb County lists forty-one colonias in its territory,[19] but it is difficult to get accurate statistics for the number of people living in these areas. *Rosalie Wright*, who works with underprivileged people, estimates that close to twenty thousand people live in the colonias. *Ishmael Reyes* explains how Webb County continues to brazenly approve the formation of colonias along Highway 59, knowing that residents will lack basic conveniences. The high poverty rate of the Texas-Mexico border zone is disproportionately concentrated in the colonias.[20] Peter Ward has studied the Webb County colonias and remarks that while El Cenizo and Rio Bravo have paved access roads to Laredo and regular service through a private bus company (El Aguilar), the bulk of the roads inside the colonias are unpaved, and both settlements lack garbage trucks and regular trash collection.[21] They have to rely on meager county resources for essential services such as ambulances and fire engines.

El Cenizo is seventeen miles from the Laredo city center and considered rural, but many colonias lie much closer to city precincts. Many people live there who are unable to find affordable housing within the confines of the city. The Texas State Affordable Housing Corporation (TSAHC), a nonprofit agency, purchased the majority of the lots and resold them to property owners at below-market interest rates after the developer D&A Realty never fulfilled its promise of providing adequate infrastructure. Also the El Cenizo Infrastructure Corporation (ECIC) was created for street paving and sewage lines. These changes only took place because of adamant residents who were willing to go to court to fight for their rights.[22] Instead of government, NGOs try to negotiate for better living conditions. Along with imparting important information, advising on policies, and delivering some services, NGOs focus on capacity building and public participation. Gente Aliada para Mejorar El Cenizo (People Allied to Improve El Cenizo), for example, emphasizes youth development.[23]

Colonias have been referred to as buffers or safety valves, which function as suburbs for the poor. They lie close enough to urban communities to supply low-income labor and yet conveniently outside the urban periphery to hide questionable issues of poverty and legality.[24] The residents of colonias face constant monitoring by immigration and law enforcement officers. A climate of distrust and fear prevails in these impoverished communities. Sudden immigration raids and even unpredictable checkpoints are part of life for these residents, many of whom are actually American citizens.[25] The heavy presence of the Border Patrol and its entitlements have created new conflicts with the community.

In 1999 El Cenizo drew national and international attention for its "predominant language act," which allowed city council proceedings in Spanish, and its "safe haven act," which permitted local officers not to report undocumented residents to the Border Patrol.[26] While El Cenizo was the first city to adopt Spanish as an official language and receive its share of both admiration and criticism, the response to its second resolution had a more momentous impact on the life of its residents.[27] The Border Patrol retaliated by setting up a temporary checkpoint on the Zapata Highway (State Highway 83), which connects the colonias to Laredo. Every morning and evening, cars and buses were stopped for lengthy inspections, making students late for class and adults late for work, causing some to lose their jobs. Residents were required to carry birth certificates as proof of citizenship.

This collective punishment continued for several months until people banded together, and a local chapter of the Human Rights Commission was formed. The commission held a public forum and presented documentation of over a hundred instances of civil rights violations. The Border Patrol then adopted a conciliatory policy and attempted to appease the complainants with various youth outreach initiatives.[28] A pioneer program of public relations was introduced in the Laredo Sector whereby the Border Patrol sponsored youth groups such as explorer scouts or soccer leagues. Although at first the effort was meant to connect the Border Patrol with the community, the methodology of involving the youth (fifteen to twenty-one years old) in line watch, clerical support work, and provision of uniforms and badges soon evolved into a recruiting mechanism.[29]

Ben Tristan, a Border Patrol officer, remembers the El Cenizo incident well. In his words,

> I was there in the middle of it, and it was worrisome. For better or worse it seemed like we were targeting them, and not just El Cenizo but all of the South Laredo and colonias areas. We did not go knocking on people's doors or anything like that. We still respected homes, but we started checking public transportation. We asked people for papers. But in those days, people were just sent back to Mexico. There was no record of any biographical data, it was not around in those days.

The Border Patrol couldn't care less about the predominant language ordinance but was triggered by the prospect of noncooperation heralded by the safe haven act. Over the years the mission of the Border Patrol has changed from overall safety to protection against crimes. At the same time, in recent years being undocumented has been elevated to a federal crime on par with smuggling or other violent behavior. Tristan found it onerous to sneak around and catch residents who were living and working in the colonias without being involved in any criminal activity. To him they were residents within the community, not resident aliens. Before the current militarization of the border, his job was easy and uncomplicated, mostly catching and sending anyone without proper visas back to Mexico rather than putting them in jail.

In contrast, people who live in the northern part of Laredo only encounter the Border Patrol at checkpoints or as their neighbors. The relationship between Border Patrol agents and private property owners in rural areas, however, has a history of bad blood. As Tristan notes, "We can easily ruin a relationship. We have to be really cautious because we constantly get new recruits in, so they have to understand that this is all private property and we can do so much more harm than the groups of people who cross through their property. We go in there chasing them and do more damage with our vehicles on wet or muddy roads than a hundred aliens passing through there if they're not cutting fences." The relationship with ranchers improved after the Border Patrol started training out-of-state agents to have local sensitivities and focused on community outreach. Especially in the impoverished colonias of Rio Bravo or El Cenizo, people's frustration with constant intrusions needed to be addressed.

Duncan Earle identifies colonias as marginal settlements that may be spatially located inside national boundaries but are socially positioned as the in-between spaces of two cultures. Texas is constantly trying to normalize the presence of these colonias by restriction, regularization, and infrastructure construction.[30] The colonias sprouted in rural Texas where land was cheap but labor demand was high in adjacent urban settlements. The lack of zoning and land development policies made it profitable for landowners to build shanty houses in the middle of nowhere and rent them out. This is how Nunez and Klamminger summarize the conundrum: "The colonia residents' relationship to migrants in Mexico and their links to immigrants in other regions of the United States make these individuals and these communities critical in the share of information and resources involving more profitable and sustainable labor opportunities."[31]

The majority of respondents agree that the most important border in Laredo consists of economic divisions. There is a constant influx of immigrants, and 90 percent of them are from the lower economic scale, many of whom will live in barrios and never get access to the real Laredo, *Derek Perez* claims from his experience. As a Border Patrol official, *Roger Gordon* views the relationship between his agency and the affected folks as peaceful and positive. This assertion is at variance with the El Cenizo experience where the Border Patrol and the colonias at one point found themselves at loggerheads. At the end of the standoff, the Border Patrol changed its stance and started cultivating a new relationship with residents. The elite neighborhoods have Border Patrol agents as neighbors, but their presence in the poorer neighborhoods is associated with fear and anxiety. The most important fact about the Border Patrol is that it is the second-largest employer in the city. It has easy access to all the schools and universities, and it has capitalized on its presence with various youth programs that double as recruitment and public relations efforts.

There is more support in the colonias areas like Rio Bravo and El Cenizo for the border wall. The reason lies in the harsh reality for small localities where drugs and crimes are ubiquitous without the countervailing presence of law enforcement. The concept of the wall is not only tinged with a sense of security but also filled with promises of resources and reinforcement.[32] *Jesus*

FIGURE 12 Grocery store at El Cenizo. Photo by author.

Castillo grew up in Rio Bravo and complains of excessive illegal crossings, feeling that the border wall sends a timely message to illegal encroachers. Protecting the local economy, the relationship with Mexico, the parks that lie along the river, the wetlands and wildlife, and the image of the city are not so meaningful to impoverished communities only twenty or thirty miles from Laredo. In May 2016, when agents shot and killed an illegal entrant on the streets of Rio Bravo, it turned out to be Claudia Gómez González, a twenty-year-old unarmed girl from Guatemala,[33] not the drug trafficker or cartel member everyone is afraid of.

The Wall (the Tangible Border)

The ongoing discourse over the border wall is not only an attempt to make the invisible border in Laredo tangible but also to solidify many forms of marginalization as permanent ways of life. The proposed wall would enclose the city, divide its historic downtown, and cause irreversible damage to the river and the environment. The Biden administration paused the impending construction of the wall after winning the election and by October 2021 had canceled the bulk of the existing contracts in and around Webb County. The militarization of the border precedes the construction of the wall, which is only the most material part of the entire project of making the border impenetrable for people (though not necessarily for trade). The wall is a transition from *la frontera* to *la linea*, with a palpable structure that stands tall as a symbol of nationalism at best and racism at worst, but it is not intended to address actual problems. As the borderless economy flourishes, the need for a concrete visual structure denoting exactly the opposite message deepens.[34]

Peter Andreas argues that borders are essentially military structures, mired in the history of territorial conquest, acquisition, and proclamation.[35] The militarization of the southern border started in the 1970s with the simultaneous presence of the Border Patrol, the National Guard, immigration law enforcement, and various joint task forces along the border.[36] In a sign of the times to come, in 1990 the Border Patrol along with the U.S. Marines deployed a high-tech drone along an eighty-mile stretch to the west of Laredo. In three weeks, 1,009 pounds of marijuana and 372 undocumented people were apprehended.[37] Scholars generally agree that the process of globalization on the southern border has accelerated security concerns related to trade, transportation, communication, and all types of cross-border linkages. The pliancy and blurring of the border have been countered by extreme scrutiny and data collection.[38] Laredo displays this paradox by investing in surveillance of the river and the ranches, areas categorized as susceptible to border crossers, while sanctioning smooth and unbridled passage to the trucks coming over the bridges and highways because they are associated with commerce. It is common knowledge that narcotics typically enter the country across the bridge on a legal thoroughfare, not necessarily surreptitiously across the river. The labeling of legal and illegal routes is hardly based on a rational examination of which kind of transit routes actually process drugs. Instead it is a superficial but easily implemented separation between trade and counterfeiting.

The fear of the open border was renewed with vigor as soon as economic activity exploded after the onset of NAFTA. The Clinton administration initiated the concept of a virtual wall while the succeeding Bush administration opted for a visible physical barrier. The Secure Fence Act of 2006 (H.R. 6061) identified Laredo as a priority area, making its seventy-eight miles of pedestrian fencing and fifty-seven miles of low vehicle barriers eligible for

reinforced fencing of two layers and installation of additional physical ob-
structions as well as new roads, lighting, cameras, and sensors because of the
elevated classification.[39] This solidified Operation Linebacker,[40] which had
started in 2005 as a second line of defense in Texas.[41] When Hidalgo County
judge J. D. Salinas III pleaded with Senator John Cornyn (R-TX) that the Rio
Grande Valley did not need any levee-fence enforcement as per the Secure
Fence Act, Homeland Security chief Michael Chertoff agreed that what was
needed in Arizona or New Mexico might not be required on the Rio Grande.[42]
The Obama administration continued both the low- and high-tech components that categorize the border as a low-intensity crisis zone.[43] A large chunk
of the border wall in South Texas was constructed during the Obama presidency. In 2012, Customs and Border Protection (CBP) Laredo field office
director Eugenio "Gene" Garza testified in Congress that violent crimes on
the border had dropped by 40 percent and were the lowest in the nation,
making these regions some of the safest in America. Incidentally, Garza was
transferred to the Canadian border after the process of building the border
wall intensified in the Trump era, as he did not support it. The decrease in
crimes occurred even when drug-related violence escalated in Mexico.[44]

Always vigilant about their land, private property owners in Texas have
taken the federal government to court to stop eighty-five miles of fencing and
alternative barriers. Former Laredo mayor Raul Salinas has called it "a wall
of shame" and instead pushed for measures such as paved roads, stadium
lighting, and better enforcement to deal with border security.[45] The only
property owners who received what could be considered fair compensation
were those who hired big-name lawyers and had the courage to fight it all
the way. There are variations ranging from four thousand to four hundred
thousand dollars for adjacent properties of roughly similar worth, which are
supposed to go by appraised values. There are also concerns about impact
to the remaining properties, depreciated values, and water rights. Eminent
domain normally implies a public benefit, but the national emergency declaration (2019)[46] was an attempt to articulate and justify benefits flowing from
the wall to national security, working around the normal appropriations process and further militarizing the border by shifting funds from the Pentagon.

Border militarization is usually debated in the context of crime, rarely on
the grounds of how it creates opportunities for huge profits for construction
companies. Local residents are better situated to note the disbursement of
taxpayer funds to large corporations, essentially favors that are paid back

through campaign contributions. *Mother Jones* reports that Fisher Sand & Gravel, a North Dakota construction company, procured a $1.28 billion contract for forty-two miles of the wall in Arizona with President Trump's son-in-law Jared Kushner as an (informal) lobbyist.[47] For the Laredo Sector, Caddell—an Alabama-based construction company that was once barred from federal government work because of its fraudulent record[48]—was awarded a $275 million contract for fourteen miles of the wall in Webb County.[49]

As mentioned above, Trump escalated the border wall project, his most outspoken campaign promise, with his declaration of the National Emergency Concerning the Southern Border of the United States in February 2019. After failing to convince the Republican-controlled Congress, it was this proclamation that allowed him to switch part of the military budget to the border wall. *Russell Garray* concedes that the southern border has been militarized by many administrations in the past, but the projects of the Trump administration radically altered the natural and human habitats for the worse. Trump reframed the border as lawless and compared it to a war zone, thereby erasing vibrant local cultures and economic viabilities. As Garray notes,

> With the emergency declaration, they [the federal government] can come and do construction without any hearings about environmental laws. They can pollute the water further and they do not have to answer to anyone so they can devastate the river. They can change the water flow. If they had an accident during construction or if they diverted the river or significantly polluted the river, no one would have any way to repair it. There would be no laws that could be applied in order to sue the government or whoever was responsible for it.

The International Boundary and Water Commission (founded 1889) is bilateral but presumably has little power to hold the U.S. government accountable over water safety issues. With the waiver of forty relevant environmental and safety laws, which have not been reinstated by the Biden administration, the security and well-being of residents of the borderlands are in peril. It is interesting to note that the justifications of these waivers are rooted in the 2005 Real ID Act and the 2001 Patriot Act.

One of the historic cemeteries that was to be destroyed in the Rio Grande Valley by the construction of the border wall was that of the Eli Jackson family. The Jackson family occupies a special place in South Texas history.

The matriarch of the family, a runaway slave named Matilda Hicks—often called the Harriet Tubman of Texas—married Nathaniel Jackson, the white son of a plantation owner from Alabama. They settled in the Rio Grande Valley in 1857 and paved the way for intermarriages and harmony in Hidalgo County.[50] The Eli Jackson cemetery also carries the graves of veterans. One of them is no more than six feet away from the levee, which is where the wall would have been built, tearing up the cemetery and desecrating the graves. Earthjustice, an environmental advocacy group, is representing the family as well as the Carrizo/Comecrudo tribe, one of the Indigenous groups settled in the Lower Rio Grande Valley.

The Biden administration's cancellation of all the existing contracts for the border wall in the Laredo Sector has been a hard-fought victory for the #NoBorderWall Coalition, the local community organization, which joined Earthjustice's lawsuit against the Trump administration. *Erica Hall* is one of those who has sued the federal government along with the #NoBorderWall Coalition and Earthjustice. The Laredo City Council also voted in favor of joining the lawsuit. The long process of fighting such a powerful adversary involved flying to Washington, D.C., and presenting the case. As daunting as the process has been, Hall felt she had no choice but to fight, as her small three-acre ranch would lie partially or even fully on the other side of the wall. She has many unanswered questions, such as, "How is that going to work? I am going to be outside. We are going to be in no-man's-land. They promised a gate at every mile. What about emergencies like fire or ambulance? It is like a big prison. I will be a second-class citizen in my own country. I will be a prisoner in my own home."

The construction of the border wall started in adjacent counties during the last year of the Trump administration. Starr County was negotiating with the federal government about the latter's security needs, but as soon as the administration secured military funds, all discussion was halted, and surveyors were brought in. Without securing permits from private property owners, land was surveyed and construction started. While city and county governments struggled to have their voices heard during the Trump presidency, a private group like We Build the Wall,[51] which relied on GoFundMe, actually built a few miles of the border wall without any formal coordination with the federal government in the nearby city of Mission as well as the more distant El Paso.[52]

As stated so frequently by respondents in this book, for *Jake Ruiz* the border used to be a line marking different countries without having much impact on lived reality. But the terror of a border wall that can turn vital communities along the southern border into forbidden ground has now become ubiquitous. *Sophia Brown* feels that invisible barriers have slowly been erected in the last decade as people have stopped going across. Whereas she used to spend nearly all her weekends in Nuevo Laredo, her grandson only visits there under protection. Focus on the perceived and real risks associated with border crossing often shifts attention away from the horribly broken immigration system. As of 2019, even before the chaos of COVID-19, eight hundred thousand people were waiting in line to be heard in immigration court. This horrendous backlog has developed because funding has not been approved for immigration judges for sites like Laredo. Compared to other border regions, the total number of apprehensions is still low, but alarmingly the ratio of deaths to apprehensions is the highest in the southern sector.[53] *Mike Smith*, who manages a nonprofit with a $33,000 annual budget, laments the utter waste of resources. He believes that instead of an unnecessary and ugly physical impediment, what is needed is proper immigration reform. *Rebecca Park* echoes the sentiment, calling the proposed wall "an atrocity, an insult to my city and sister city Nuevo Laredo, as well as to the people of Mexico." She feels it is a stupid solution to illegal immigration that is unlikely to work, as sawing through the wall or digging under it or climbing over it seem like no-brainers.

The concept of the border wall is not merely political or ideological for the people of Laredo. The city has escaped being enclosed (except for Laredo College) even as partial walls have been mounted along the Rio Grande. Along with damage to natural and cultural spaces, a number of basic institutions—such as The Outlet Shoppes, neighborhood schools like George Washington Middle School, and the Sacred Heart orphanage—are situated right along the river. The initial plan placed these on the other side of the wall. *Jake Ruiz* is concerned about the flooding potential of the Rio Grande, which will certainly be amplified by the wall. The risks of rerouting the river, drowning the Mexican side, and losing activities like fishing or viewing the night lights from the bridges are not part of any equation for those who make such plans. *Travis Mace* argues,

> Laredo has a naturally beautiful barrier, which is now saturated with electronics—drones, airboats, and all-terrain vehicles. The Border Patrol already has enough sensors and personnel to control the border. Laredo

College already has a fence, the only one in the Laredo Sector that has placed almost a hundred acres of land on the other side. Rare animals like jaguars and ocelots as well as javelinas, foxes, and raccoons roam along the river-bank, a habitat under great duress ever since the fence was erected.

What started as an outlandish campaign promise can end up submerging Nuevo Laredo, fears *Charles Vega*. As he explains, "We are in violation be-cause we have a treaty monitored by the International Boundary and Water Commission that does not allow any structure impeding the flow of water on one side if it affects the other side." Residents in Hidalgo and Starr counties already worry that the levee walls will cause flooding during heavy rains. Knowing that people in Laredo have always been self-reliant with a strong identity, Vega believes that they can band together against the wall and suc-ceed. The border wall is almost certain to displace all the businesses and people who have built their lives around the downtown area. *Erin Arroyo* also stresses, "The idea of the wall is ludicrous, we have enough technology to protect the border without going back to cavemen days. The city already has a budget deficit because fewer people are coming, resulting in lower bridge tolls and lower motel and hotel revenue."

Josiah Heyman points to the existence of a virtual border wall that stretches from ports of entry to checkpoints, encompassing streets, buildings, and internal roads in the borderlands. All U.S. commercial and noncommercial vehicles, as well as pedestrians, have to go through the invisible wall via proper inspection. Aircraft and helicopters in the sky also form important parts of the virtual wall from above. The use of advanced technology and rigorous documentation has made this process both efficient and lengthy. To bypass prolonged scrutiny, companies can pay substantial fees, go through background checks, and follow prescribed security procedures in order to acquire the "trusted" designation and pass through faster transit lanes with-out much examination.[54] Taking an all too optimistic view, Heyman believes that "the virtual wall will reduce the ambiance of illegality and disorder, and renew the sense of protection and control."[55] The Border Patrol already de-ploys X-ray and gamma-ray systems along with personal detectors, portal monitors, and isotope identifiers that use radiation.[56] But despite immense investments in technology and personnel, success in deterring either drugs or people remains far from satisfactory.

As retired Border Patrol agent *Derek Perez* explains,

> The major challenge is retention because Laredo has always been a low-ranking sector. There are five levels of security threats and Laredo has never reached above level two. There has never been vicious criminal activity in Laredo, compared to El Paso or even Brownsville. That is why Laredo was considered safe, so the only fence exists at the perimeter of Laredo College. Now the cartels in Nuevo Laredo have elevated the status of Laredo and put it on the map.

Roger Gordon, another Border Patrol agent, disagrees. He believes that Laredo needs a wall, not necessarily as a deterrent to illegal immigration but as a surveillance measure to address the lack of manpower in the Laredo Sector. He agrees that aesthetically it would be devastating for downtown but feels that a sovereign nation has the right to control its border. He cautions,

> It will not be a one-stop solution, only a tool to ease the task of Border Patrol agents. The Border Patrol cannot succeed without an efficient immigration policy. They do not have the resources to stop and check the hundreds of semitrucks that cross the border and carry illegal items. They do not want to slow down business either. They have to balance safety issues with trade priorities. Along with their canine aides, they use their judgment by examining the behavior of drivers, their willingness to cooperate, and their body language, all of which are part of their training.

Until the 1990s Mexico was a tourist attraction, and people went over there without concern for safety. The cartels have destroyed the tourism industry in Nuevo Laredo, which used to be as vibrant as San Antonio's. Now shoot-outs and high explosives can be heard from Laredo. Despite the terrible conditions in Nuevo Laredo, there have only been a handful of incidents related to the cartels that have taken place in Laredo. Based on his experience as a Border Patrol agent, *Ben Tristan* imagines that violence in Laredo would be bad for the cartels' business and bring too much unwanted attention: "They have enough trouble fighting each other over there, they do not want to bring it across." Narco-traffickers want to keep the American side safe and clean for business. The militarized border is not much of an obstacle for them, but they do not want the American military in their own territory.[57]

Tristan is more worried about local relationships being ruined by the wall. Technology can be useful in detecting human presence in trailers. However, caravans of people have to be addressed through proper immigration and asylum processes. It is unfair to shift the burden to the Border Patrol, which is not trained to deal with such people. He remembers that when the first caravan came through in 2000, they had to set up little facilities at the old air force base. Families were kept together, but it is also true that the numbers were much lower then. It was difficult to judge who was being persecuted and who was lying. Asylum seekers face appalling conditions in Mexico, yet the bulk of them were sent back after conclusion of the migrant protection protocols. After they were deported, the cartels got hold of them and extorted them or pursued their relatives for money.

The border has now become synonymous with illegal presence and crimes. A former mayor of Laredo, *Bianca Frey*, recounts the story of a hundred migrants who were going to be released on the streets of Laredo in 2005: "There was no space in Dallas, where they usually sent such detainees. I took the initiative to reach out to the detainees and found that almost everyone had a relative or friend somewhere in the U.S. I arranged for phone calls and all but one detainee received bus tickets from their respective families." Unfortunately, the recent erasure between drug dealer and asylum seeker dooms the asylum process. Frey regrets that immigration has been reframed as a security issue after 9/11. As soon as terrorism was attached to immigration and the border, public support for stricter immigration and border control escalated, and building barriers became acceptable rather than controversial.[58] As for drugs, she believes, "We need to address the demand side of the market that persists in the U.S., but the whole focus of the drug enforcement industry is on the seller, not the buyer." Drugs are a huge business with so many tiers that people at the topmost ranks actually hold high positions in society. Peter Andreas categorizes border policing as coercive as well as ceremonial, aimed to accentuate the differences at the border rather than keeping it safe. The flow of merchandise along the border has been undeterred; the only question is whether the state or market forces dominate the control of such transactions.[59]

As a federal government employee, *Giselle Lamar* has come across people who believe that Laredo is a violent city when factually San Antonio has much more violent crime than Laredo. The drug trade by nature is brutal and cash driven, with desperate people committing senseless crimes. She does not see how a wall or fence could prevent any drugs from getting through, although it would give people a false sense of security. The cost projection of $24 million per mile sounds like an outrageous amount to her, as she quips, "We need to make connections and build bridges as opposed to building dividers. I think we need the other side of the border and they need us." Lamar does not see any separation from the people who live on the other side. She knows that her office will have to deal with any number of private property owners with gripes and is thankful that she will not have to be personally involved with the predictable litigation.

The border wall proposition is not without its supporters among people I interviewed. *John Allen* defines the wall as "a fence with gates" and sees no problem with it. While recognizing that the two countries share a culture, having a barrier and requiring permission to enter each other's territory seems respectful and peaceful enough to him. He also points to the lengthy and cumbersome process of emigration to Mexico and the shoddy treatment of illegal people there. *Ruth Solomon* views asylum seekers as a huge problem for Mexico as well. She asserts, "Immigrants take advantage of America by having too many children. One day we will face a situation like Germany today with tons of people barging in. The government should help its own citizens before taking in more asylum seekers. The number of people who want to come to this country is so high and a lot of them in Laredo are unwilling to learn English." This view, from a well-respected artist, is echoed in different strata of society. *Max Green*, a handyman, does not think that the border wall will affect him because he lives on the right side of the border. Now that the common practice of visiting Nuevo Laredo has diminished, he does not care as much about the border or the downtown. He also feels that the wall can protect the ranches, where smuggling is easier. It should be stressed that these perceptions about Nuevo Laredo and the border wall are infrequent, and in general people in Laredo are empathetic to their own ethnic group, who are often literally part of the family. Historically, people from Nuevo Laredo moved to Laredo in search of better economic opportunities, but now cartel violence has pushed people from Nuevo Laredo to the American side in search of safety. Instead of the back-and-forth movement typical of the past, in the last two decades people have bought houses, sent their children to Laredo schools, and settled on this side of the border. Recent immigrants to Laredo from Nuevo Laredo tend to be from the affluent section, evident in the escalating number of restaurants and businesses that have moved to Laredo.

Jesse Knight, who does research on the border, feels that we need to keep it open for commerce while using more efficient technologies such as X-rays to check trucks for illegitimate drugs. It would be cost efficient to build more lanes and thereby process people and trucks quicker. But he doubts whether politicians have any incentive to actually resolve the problem and crush the multibillion-dollar drug industry. He sees a tap dance between talking about the dangers of the border to one audience and the importance of efficient trade at the port to another. He mentions a documentary filmmaker from Northern Ireland who approached him when she was doing a film on the drug trade in Laredo. He took her to the train bridge (the Texas Mexican International Railway Bridge) and showed her about forty trains crossing in quick succession. This is how he summarized the issue to her:

> Let's go find ten kilos of cocaine today. Tell me which boxcar in which train are you going to stop and search, knowing perfectly well that as soon as you stop the train, all the other goods do not get to Detroit in a timely manner. It costs us a few million dollars to check a little corner. Which little car? Is it worth it? Secondly, recognize that there is a heck of a lot more legal goods traveling across, many more good people that are coming to make a living or spend money rather than trying to cause serious harm. How much do you want to clamp down on the good people? What percentage of good people do you turn away?

He discusses signal detection theory in order to compare the situation with a cancerous tumor: "How much does a doctor want to treat you with chemotherapy? How much do you want to cut it? And sometimes you are cutting the good cells and spreading it all over the body. So it's always a risk when you intervene to treat and how much you want to let things go." He proposes relying on technology to impede the drug trade, as time is incredibly valuable: "We can develop little chips that let people pass back and forth, and we've got these great ultrasound scanners for trucks and trains. The only thing that makes sense is investing in technology that can protect the border efficiently without harming trade."

FIGURE 13 #NoBorderWall protest. Rio Grande International Study Center.

Conclusion

The national boundary along the Rio Grande has never been much of an obstacle to people or commerce in Laredo. Although crossing the border has become cumbersome for Mexican civilians, it has become more open than ever for commerce. Laredo residents, conversely, face scrutiny by law enforcement within the city at internal checkpoints. While I-35 is open for traffic that can be either legal or illegal, strict monitoring occurs for individuals crossing the checkpoints. The safety measures in the border city include a growing number of private prisons and segregation of areas where the poor (possibly undocumented) residents live. The river was the historically accessible boundary and never a deterrent; the interstate, however, expanded the flow of commerce while narrowing the mobility of Laredo residents, especially those who lived in poor neighborhoods. The border has to be both hospitable and controlled; what needs to be understood is for whom it remains open and for whom it is being closed.

Borrowing from socialist ideology, *Alex Mead* defines the purpose of the border politically: borders are imaginary lines drawn on a map to establish hegemony and meaningful mainly for the allocation of power. *Charles Fox*, coming from a different political perspective, similarly envisions a significant change in the border from an abstract concept to necessary law enforcement to a vital political construct. The abstract line started hardening in the 1990s. Regardless of political and economic shifts, the border has always been its own place, defying definition. Growing up in central Mexico, *Ariana Raymond* gave little thought to the border, but her definition of it altered when she started living in Laredo. To her, "The border was a line without any association of apprehension or fear. Now I work in downtown and can actually see the river from my office. My work often involves meetings in Nuevo Laredo, and I simply walk to them. I had never imagined that crossing a national boundary could be as easy as crossing the street." The border now feels surreal to her, as she has come to terms with how abstract the concept is. The line is concrete in many people's minds, but people who live in Laredo comprehend it as an abstraction. The country does not end at a specific point; instead, the border continues almost like a living organism. The border, to Raymond, "is a living, breathing entity, rather than a doorway. Real life flows almost undaunted by man-made divisions."

Defining the border, *Justin Taylor* says, "It is a unique place that is greatly misunderstood by people living elsewhere in the United States. I heard the story of Donald Trump visiting Laredo during the presidential campaign. He was too scared to get out of his limousine! He had to be escorted from the airport to the customs at Laredo International Bridge 1." The power position of the president magnified the misconceptions. Crimes always took place on the border, but the new iconology of the border being out of control was largely staged by Trump himself. *Ben Tristan* also defines the border as merely a line between two countries. Growing up in the wake of the McCarthyite Red Scare of the 1950s, holding the line against a foreign enemy was ingrained in his training. But it is difficult to look at Mexico from Laredo and think of it as a foreign country. Borders are artificial but real, according to attorney *Ishmael Reyes*, who bemoans, "This particular border divides, as do other borders, between school districts or cities, which has legal, political, and economic significance. Kids who regularly come to Laredo to go to school are detained at the bridge and rounded up. This has happened in Laredo since the 1980s and 1990s. Do we police the borders of other school districts the way we police the bridge?"

The border signifies regulation as opposed to collaboration in the present era. *Jake Ruiz*, a retired law enforcement officer, remembers the ease of communication with his counterparts in Nuevo Laredo. Often the Nuevo Laredo police sought help from the Laredo police to apprehend bank robbers. As he remembers, "I would be deputized, carrying on exactly the same duty in Nuevo Laredo as in Laredo, and return after finishing the job." When this relationship changed with the narco wars, it diminished the common weekend practices of clubbing and shopping in Nuevo Laredo as well. Sylvia Longmire describes the "telephone effect," where unsubstantiated stories of crimes become widespread but are later proven to be untrue. The murder and decapitation of an oil field worker by the Mexican criminal syndicate Los Zetas created panic in Laredo, but the story turned out to be false.[60]

"The border is defined by governments and not necessarily by the people who live there," observes *Giselle Lamar*. She recollects her college days when she took an honors class in political science. One of the projects involved the strategy board game Risk, in which the students had to represent different countries and write out the reasons behind their moves for conflict, diplomacy, and conquest. Her classmates wanted to take over the world, but she just wanted to stay in her own country. She was the least enthusiastic yet ended up winning the game as her more gung ho friends ended up destroying each other. She did not attack like the others and left her army stationary. The three other players attacked each other, their countries were taken over, and she won by default. The more they tried to win, the more they were susceptible to losing. She feels that "America, which is so powerful, is playing a similar game and winning the battles while losing the war."

The discourse over the border wall is a reflection of the anxiety, and the proposed wall is an inevitable manifestation of the fortification of the border. Failing to stabilize the border is threatening because it means the lapse of control. Similarity or familiarity between the different ends of the border is also threatening because this challenges the very justification of the border.[61] Throughout history, the connections between Laredo and Nuevo Laredo were fluid and natural, like the Rio Grande. When Laredo became an epicenter of globalized trade routes in the neoliberal economic era, which prioritizes profits over regional or even national interests, the need for the border as a tangible structure emerged to counter the notion of a loose border. The violence in Nuevo Laredo further justifies the presence and intrusion of law enforcement on the border and in fact all over the city. Even as the border opens up more and more for trade, the need for control and symbols of control becomes almost obligatory.

CHAPTER 3

||||||||||||||||||||||||||||||||

The Bazaar on the Border

How Did It Evolve?

> It [the border] is a golden calf for a lot of people. The reason why we do exist and are somewhat prosperous as much as we have poverty is because of our trade.
>
> *FELIX RIVERA*, LAREDO RESIDENT

> This town always looks to the south, never to the north.
>
> *TRAVIS MACE*, LAREDO RESIDENT

The story of Laredo as a marketplace can be told by means of three interlinked threads: its transition from a trade route to a flourishing community, its shifts back and forth between corridor and destination, and its local affluence and self-sufficiency morphing into a global trade network. The way Laredo evolved from a minor node of exchange into a full-fledged city and then a major thoroughfare after NAFTA is etched in the memory of its people. The story of downtown is about prosperity when the community was smaller and local merchants were the arbiters of their own economic fate rather than being subject to larger global forces. The identity of the city is tied to these transitions: how the local powerhouses dissolved into the amorphous international network and how after establishing itself as a vibrant community, becoming one of the ten major cities in the state, Laredo again became relegated to a trade corridor, funneling billions of dollars' worth of merchandise through its well-developed transportation grid. The policies and priorities for Laredo are usually focused on the smooth operation of transportation channels, often at the cost of other aspects of governance.

The marketplace in Laredo began with a history of sprouting into a smuggling racket during the Civil War. The small border town eventually advanced to a thriving marketplace in the 1920s. Local myth compares the prosperity of the historical downtown in the 1950s with that of New York. The downtown boom faded when Mexican shoppers withered away after the 1982 peso devaluation. The 1990s ushered in a period of spatial reorientation, especially for downtown, as the border city progressed into a major inland port for global commerce. NAFTA revived the significance of the declining downtown with expansive international bridges, turning the relentless traffic on the bridges into a prime source of revenue. Globalization decenters capital and local economic processes by new alignments that follow profits.[1] Instead of being a center for trade, Laredo transitioned into a passage for trade. This shift in trade and finance was grounded in the limited utility of the downtown. The spatial terrain of the city center did not augment the trade network, but it was valuable for its location and thoroughfares. Trade has always been the crux for Laredo, but residents are aware of and disenchanted by the trifling proportion of trade revenue that actually settles in the local economy.

Trade Route/Community

The most important and stable resource for Laredo has always been its location. This dusty outpost of Spanish colonizers was located along one of the

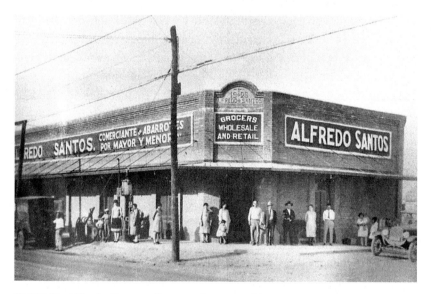

FIGURE 14 Alfredo Santos Grocery Store. Webb County Heritage Foundation.

oldest commercial roads on the North American continent. The historic trail known as El Camino Real de los Tejas linked Laredo to Louisiana. Throughout the periods of Spanish colonization and Mexican independence, trade routes with the French and the British passed through Laredo, although trade with the French in Louisiana was prohibited for a while. Laredo was connected to the presidios in San Antonio and Goliad, opening up trade opportunities all along the Nueces Strip. Ironically, major roads within the city were not even paved until the 1970s. Regardless of the city's infrastructure (or lack thereof), the advantage of proximity to the river as well as access to road networks shaped its commercial outlook. With limited agricultural products and the absence of industries, it was these external elements, rather than any internal economic feats, that shaped Laredo as a trade outpost. The major hindrance to the flow of trade was not legal barriers but repeated attacks by Indian tribes.[2] Much of this confrontation between Native Americans and local Mexicans continued until the mid-nineteenth century. As late as 1850, the federal government provided security against such assaults to free trade in the region.[3] More trade posts opened in Laredo after the Spanish Free Trade Act of 1865, originally intended to remove protections in the Caribbean Sea, was expanded to the city.[4]

The first trade treaty involving Laredo was authorized in 1831 when Laredo was still part of Mexico. A "Treaty of Amity, Commerce, and Navigation" was signed between the United States and Mexico, probably the first binational accord between the two countries. It focused on free trade, tariffs, market access, competitiveness, and mutual respect, even advancing the most-favored-nation concept.[5] For a brief period of ten months in 1840, Laredo was the capital of the Republic of the Rio Grande, which served as a buffer between Texas and Mexico.[6] When the Republic of Texas joined the Union in 1845, Laredo was not part of Texas. Laredo was seized by the Texas Rangers in 1846 during the Mexican-American War, and only after the Treaty of Guadalupe Hidalgo in 1848 did Laredo become part of Texas and the United States.

The first defining moment in Laredo's history, which elevated it as a trade route, was the Civil War. Laredo functioned as a major commercial center during the key turning points of the Civil War and later during the Mexican Revolution. During the Civil War, cotton from Texas passed through Laredo to Mexico, and supplies for the Confederate army came through Laredo.[7] The period of the Civil War was referred to as "Cotton Times"[8] in the Rio

Grande Valley, where vast quantities of cotton were smuggled to Mexico and the money was used to finance the war. A number of cities and ports in South Texas, including Laredo, evolved as hubs of smuggling, where it was difficult for the Union army to set embargos. In 1864 five thousand bales of cotton were hoarded in San Agustín Cathedral to safeguard them from the Union army. Compared to the other war-ravaged Confederate states, the practice of smuggling ushered in an era of prosperity along the southern border. Under the Anaconda Plan, President Lincoln employed blockading squadrons along the Confederate coastline to seize contraband goods from blockade runners. While the blockades were successful in the ports of New Orleans and Savannah, the distant southern border was never controlled by the Union army. Although Mexico officially remained neutral, unofficially it was the major trading partner of the Confederate states. Border towns like Brownsville, Matamoros, Rio Grande City, and Laredo emerged as important locations from which cotton was transported to the small coastal town called Bagdad (or the Port of Matamoros) in Mexican territory.[9]

The reasons why Laredo came into prominence during the Civil War are tied to geography and economy rather than political ideology or racial complexity. *Richard Andrew*, a native of Laredo, explains that South Texas did not organically lend itself to be part of the Confederacy because slavery was not a driving force of the economy in the region. People from Laredo fought in the Civil War on behalf of both the Union and the Confederacy. He elaborates:

> Santos Benavides, the highest-ranking Tejano soldier fighting for the Confederacy in the Civil War, is hailed for his military career, but he was in fact a merchant who saw the opportunity to make a profit by smuggling cotton to Mexico. Because of the Union blockade against the export of cotton, Laredo served as the locale for a smuggling ring organized by Confederate soldiers. The responsibility of Colonel Benavides was to make the Rio Grande Valley a safe passage for trade with Mexico. Confederate troops would send the cotton to Laredo, and then local soldiers would take control of the cotton and deliver it to Mexican ports. In the heart of downtown there are still buildings where cotton used to be stockpiled.

One of these historical houses belonged to John Zirvas Lyendecker, the quartermaster of the Confederate troops, who was married to Benavides's sister.

The very reason he was chosen to be quartermaster is that he was a merchant who kept track of the merchandise.

The trade policies and practices of the two countries on the banks of the Rio Grande easily lent themselves to progression as a smuggling hotbed. In 1858 Ramón Guerra, the interim governor of Tamaulipas, established a Zona Libre (a free zone where goods could be sold without duties or tariffs) along Mexico's northern frontier. American businesses could also take advantage of the special trade privileges within a narrow territory that started at the mouth of the Rio Grande and ended in Nuevo Laredo. United States customs and tariff laws had loopholes that were easy to take advantage of. The collection district at Point Isabel, established in 1849, granted duty refunds on all foreign imports that would be exported to Mexico in original packages within a year and also allowed two-year storage in government-owned or approved storehouses, either to be exported duty-free to Mexico or sold anywhere in the United States after paying duties. Selecting Laredo as a port of entry came to signify duty-free goods, easy storage, and friendly customs inspectors who would falsely certify merchandise.[10]

Zona Libre (1858–1905) existed before the Civil War and continued afterward to fuel economic activity across the Tamaulipas-Texas border. The illegal market reignited the stagnant economy of Tamaulipas by connecting it through shopping and smuggling with cities to the north of the Rio Grande. Easy navigation, the protection provided by the covering of thick chaparral, and the general lack of oversight led to flourishing contraband trade and attracted residents to Texas border towns.[11] Economic activity started to shift from Texas to Tamaulipas, negatively affecting American manufactured goods. Zona Libre remained uninterrupted through the Civil War as well as the French blockade of Mexico. It was merchants on the Texas side who launched a campaign against Zona Libre, and after decades of political agitation, disgruntlement, and blaming the Mexican policy for destroying Texas's economy, they succeeded in abolishing it in 1905.[12] It is notable that some signposts of Zona Libre are still visible in downtown Laredo. The historical significance of the term may have been smothered with the passage of time, but the idea of the border being a free zone remains alive in the imagination of border residents.

Commercial relations between Laredo and Mexico flourished after the Civil War. Merchants on both sides often used to be at odds with each other over trade conditions, claiming that the rules favored the competition. The Civil War ended such hostilities and established illicit trafficking as a norm for border transactions. Profits from cross-border trading, both legal and illegal, kept the two cities prosperous and the people content.[13] In an interesting twist of history, in post–Civil War Laredo the people who played major political roles were those who did not fight in the war. Mayor Jarvis, who laid out the plans for Laredo, was an American who was in Mexico with his Mexican wife during the Civil War and was selected for his position because he was the only elite American who did not fight for the Confederacy.

The trade route on the Rio Grande also went through massive transformations with time. In the late nineteenth century, along with canoes and small boats Laredo and Nuevo Laredo were connected by wooden passenger ferry.[14] Laredo had the right to lease the ferry to a private company, and legal battles ensued over the leasing operation. These disputes and the resulting delays in trade led to the demand to build a bridge on the Rio Grande. The bridge was eventually built in 1889, with walkways and steel tracks for an electric trolley system, the first of its kind on the U.S.-Mexico border.[15] The bridge was destroyed time and again by floods (1903, 1932, and 1954) and war (the Mexican Revolution) and had to be rebuilt over and over.[16]

The significance of Laredo magnified once the railroad joined Laredo to other cities. In 1874 efforts began to link Laredo with major cities by means of the railroad. By 1881 Laredo was connected to Corpus Christi in the east by the Texas Mexican Railway and to San Antonio in the north by the International–Great Northern Railroad. Nuevo Laredo was linked with Mexico City via railroad by 1887.[17] The outcome of these new developments was that Laredo was not only connected with U.S. cities but also with Mexico City through an 842-mile narrow-gauge railroad to facilitate imports and exports with interior parts of Mexico.[18] Instead of depending on cumbersome manual labor involving mules,[19] the trains easily transferred heavy loads of merchandise to cities north and south, making trade more dynamic for Laredo's economy. It was the railroad that spurred marketplaces in the two Laredos, along with construction of a new city hall, an opera house, public schools, churches, saloons, and banks.[20] Laredo's sheep farming provided wool as a valuable commodity for exchange with the United States in the 1820s.[21] Merchandise that left in steamers from Corpus Christi to New York originally came through Laredo from Mexico and included gold, precious ores, animal hides, skins, and wool.[22]

During the Mexican Revolution, covert commercial activity persisted, often in the form of gold and silver from Mexico when hyperinflation devalued its currency.[23] As John Adams observes, "The dynamic expansion of the Laredo economy, backed by railroads, ranching, mining, and onions, during the first decade of the century transpired concurrently with economic and political unrest that emerged in Mexico."[24] Laredo became even more prosperous after oil and gas were discovered in the early twentieth century. The U.S. Postal Service started door-to-door mail in Laredo in 1894.[25] The Laredo Chamber of Commerce was established in 1915. Before that the pivotal organization in charge of Laredo's economy was the Laredo Board of Trade, which acted to promote the business interests of both Laredo and Nuevo Laredo and foster commercial relations with San Antonio and Corpus Christi.[26] This is an important moment to locate transnational efforts at interdependence, which have evaporated in the neoliberal mode of international business. Laredo's status was further elevated with increased revenue and formal networks, such as the establishment of the Laredo Rotary Club in 1920.[27]

Although in the late nineteenth and early twentieth centuries Laredo explored its manufacturing sector, industrial investment in Laredo has always lagged behind trade and energy. There are exceptions, such as commercial brick production, where Laredo emerged as the largest manufacturer on the Rio Grande by 1900.[28] The discovery of oil in the 1920s also opened up a new set of industries, but Laredo has always focused more on economic exchange than local production structures. Kathleen Da Camara records that in 1942 a key business in Laredo was customs brokerage, with annual income from the port exceeding eighty million dollars.[29] Mostly agricultural goods were being transported through Laredo, which was famous for onions and other farm products such as winter vegetables and citrus fruits. Da Camara specifically mentions tomatoes, watermelons, broccoli, oranges, and grapefruit.[30] Local entrepreneur *Barry Rivers* notes that Laredo had orange groves and produced ample quantities of onions, zucchinis, and watermelons that were exported to nearby regions before the discovery of oil and gas. Ranches were always pivotal to the economy as sources of both agriculture and oil. Da Camara describes how oil was discovered when shallow wells were dug for irrigation. Low-cost labor and agricultural goods provided the basis for extensive truck farming.[31] Exports and imports on the U.S.-Mexico border were formally recognized in 1939, when the headquarters of the Twenty-Third Customs Collection District was established in Laredo.[32]

The expansion and contraction of Laredo's marketplace has historically followed the economy of Nuevo Laredo and the fate of its Mexican consumers. The central business districts (CBDs) of the two conjoined cities were designed to be focused on Spanish plazas, but these plazas became settings for divergent activities. Different land-use patterns, economic behaviors, and cultural meanings of downtown made the two cities interdependent yet complementary in the services they offered to the people.[33] Generous financial underpinning on the American side made Laredo a pivot for trade, while Nuevo Laredo advanced as the nucleus of recreational activities. In the 1920s there was unprecedented expansion of the customs brokerage and freight forwarding businesses, which elevated Laredo's stature as a border port. The downtown commercial district continued expanding to reflect the overall growth of the economy and population.[34] Even during periods of economic downturn, Laredo functioned as a vibrant trade locale as long as production and manufacturing from Mexico continued flowing.[35]

Historically, land use in Laredo and Nuevo Laredo was complementary. People lived in Laredo but owned ranches across the river. When Laredo became part of the United States, legal protections, economic opportunities, and superior infrastructure enhanced Laredo's commercial profile. Lagging behind in financial organization, Nuevo Laredo became more of a cultural terminus. People flocked to Nuevo Laredo to watch bullfights. Even during the heyday of downtown business in Laredo, Nuevo Laredo was the preferred destination for a colorful evening or a quiet weekend with the family on the ranches. Laredo was also a tourist town when *Samantha Taft* was growing up in the 1970s. Even with all the freight passing through, Laredo retained an eclectic character that attracted out-of-towners. People who wanted to taste the flavor of Nuevo Laredo would spend the night in Laredo even when it was a sleepy little town with just five or six motels. Both shoppers and tourists abounded in Laredo. Echoing other residents, Taft remembers, "I heard that more money was made per square foot in downtown Laredo than in New York City."

The reliance of border communities on each other's possibilities is not unusual but is instead very common throughout the border corridor. As James Giermanski notes, "Retail and wholesale trade along the border has become so reliant on the Mexican buyer that any reduction in the buying pattern of Mexican consumers along the Texas border would be critical for that already depressed area."[36] In assessing the impact of NAFTA, a late-1990s study described the border region as the fourth player in the trade treaty: "An estimated 50 percent of all sales at two El Paso malls, Cielo Vista and the Bas-

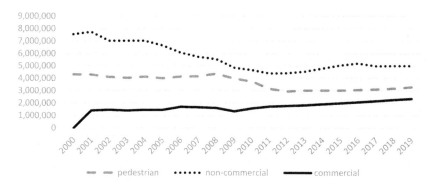

FIGURE 15 Traffic from Nuevo Laredo to Laredo. Compiled from statistics from City of Laredo website.

sett Center, are to Mexican cross-border shoppers; the city's top Kmart and the large Sam's Club depend for over half their sales on Mexican customers; and . . . retail store dependencies in downtown El Paso reach 90 percent or more. As was demonstrated in 1995, when the Mexican economy sneezes, El Paso catches pneumonia."[37] Although Mexican shoppers remain import-ant to retail outlets on the border, the proportion of proceeds has become much smaller in relation to the monetary value of the merchandise crossing the international border. Then again, however small the ratio, the profit to small businesses remains inside and benefits the local economy.

Downtowns or CBDs in nearly all major American cities experienced decline from the 1970s onward once retail patterns became multicentered; the urban revival in a number of cities in the 1980s and 1990s sought to establish the city center as more of a cultural than business axis in order to attract residents as well as tourists. Such examples can be found all over America: Cleveland experimented with the Rock and Roll Hall of Fame in the 1980s,[38] while Houston developed green spaces in the heart of downtown in the 1990s to draw residents back to the core.[39] Ian Burton uses the exam-ple of the Lower Rio Grande Valley to depict another model, where people buy their most desired items in neither downtown nor scattered centers but instead leave the city to venture to a close but bigger city for high-value shopping.[40] This model fits Laredo to some extent, as people travel to San Antonio quite regularly to acquire their peak consumption goods. It is im-portant to note that this trend has been present historically and continues today for different purposes.

When Laredo advanced as a city, it followed the classic example of central place theory where everything evolves around downtown. At one point in history, downtown was the only destination for high-quality consumer goods, whereas now it only attracts consumers who want cheap substitutes for brand-name or imported products. The urban landscape in Laredo has been reshaped by the hollowing out of downtown and the shift of the cultural and social focus to the northern environs. The decline of downtown has not occurred because of residential flight out of the core or the financial decline of the CBD. Moreover, tolls from the four international bridges remain the most important source of the city's revenue. Even though businesses are flourishing in other parts of town, it is difficult to imagine Laredo as a dispersed city where different urban concentrations, physically separated but functionally interrelated, replace a single CBD.[41] The transition of downtown is more a manifestation of national and international trends as opposed to local factors.

James Curtis has compared the CBDs of Laredo and Nuevo Laredo and analyzed the twin cities as a dynamic transborder consumer market. He found that in 1993, "Laredo had almost three times as many financial institutions as did Nuevo Laredo (fourteen to five), but Nuevo Laredo had more than twice as many bakeries and grocery stores (fifteen to six)."[42] He argues that Nuevo Laredo's downtown reflects the interspersed commercial and residential ways of life that are at its social heart. In contrast, Laredo focuses on the financial aspects of downtown, with more banks than entertainment venues.[43] Laredo and Nuevo Laredo might have been based on the same structural design, but one focused on the practical aspects of those structures to lure business and investment while the other utilized the same structures as cultural and social spaces.

Interdependence between the sister cities was rooted not only in overlapping ethnic and cultural characteristics and strong family ties but also in the aforementioned land-use pattern where people did business in Laredo and entertained in Nuevo Laredo regardless of which city they actually lived in. This symbiotic bond was scarred by NAFTA, which unshackled Laredo's economy from Nuevo Laredo's by relocating the nucleus of revenue to wholesale transportation from mere exchange of products and services.[44] The benefits of the international trade route have been accompanied by the potential for massive profits from illegal drug trafficking, so that by the early 2000s the drug cartels usurped power in Nuevo Laredo with their dominance in the unstable Mexican political system. The lack of safety and the void in cultural offerings have stalled the common practice of going across for the first time in more than two hundred and fifty years. Many of Laredo's stores, especially at the outlet mall, remain dependent on Mexican customers for their survival. But the current situation is a new and lesser functional relation that has replaced the age-old synergy between the two cities.

Laredo has always been a transportation town, stresses *Bianca Frey*, who has served as an elected representative in the city government and is acutely aware of the significance of Laredo's location in the border corridor. The transportation industry—one of the strongest industries in Mexico—is concentrated in Nuevo Laredo. People with dual citizenship took advantage of these resources and built local businesses from warehouses to end-to-end supply chains. This sector saved Laredo's economy when the air force base closed down in 1973. Frey concedes, "The flow of money from Mexican towns was always directed to Laredo, and banks seldom bothered to check the legality of the sources of money." The economies of the two cities were so integrated that peso devaluation brought about economic collapse in Laredo, the impact reverberating on the health of businesses more than the contemporaneous swing in federal interest rates.

The latest recovery in Laredo was spurred by the onset of NAFTA in the 1990s, which elevated Laredo to an international commercial base and the second-fastest-growing city in the country in the 2000s. Within six months of the treaty's passage in 1994, trade with Mexico grew by 20 percent na-

FIGURE 16 Laredo Airforce Base. Webb County Heritage Foundation.

tionwide. The twin cities of Laredo–Nuevo Laredo accounted for 60 percent of rail traffic as the number of freight cars tripled from fifty thousand to one hundred and fifty thousand. Intraindustry trade includes electrical and telecommunications machinery and equipment, office furniture, and auto parts.[45] Nuevo Laredo has the most extensive trucking industry in Mexico, and much of the transportation business still maintains dual headquarters and staffs on both sides of the border. Before the advent of NAFTA, Laredo was gradually growing as a city. But the city that had developed was interdependent with Nuevo Laredo, both functionally and culturally. NAFTA severed this traditional alliance by shifting the revenue source from the immediate transactions of buying and selling to the more profitable pursuit of imports and exports.

Destination/Corridor

The city of Laredo would never have become the largest inland port without NAFTA. Having become elevated as a major transportation city, its internal characteristics, especially those related to local businesses, changed drastically. Laredo's financial future is no longer tied to local economic success but international transport mechanisms. It takes only a week for any merchandise from Mexico to reach Canada, with Laredo claiming the credit for providing smooth passage. Instead of local interests being a focal point, Laredo is again important for being a corridor in the international web of shipping and hauling.

Some local business owners complain about the lack of facilities and support for trade within the city. *Max Green*, a handyman, had a hard time starting a business in Laredo, as he had to compete with cheaper labor rates from Mexico. He points to another impediment: "You have to be connected to the import-export sector, be a driver or work in a warehouse, if you want to prosper." The number of shoppers from Mexico fluctuates as the rate of the peso goes up or down. Moreover, the customer base in Laredo is always shifting. Green explains, "The exploration of natural gas by Eagle Ford Shell Company also produced migrants from other cities. They came when the oil price was high and left when it went down. A bunch of oil field workers would rent an apartment for $1,500 a month and leave within a few months."

Older residents have a different recollection about the ease of starting a business in Laredo. *Mimi Rose*, a schoolteacher, opened a flower shop without any knowledge of business but was able to acquire a sizeable loan because one of the employees at the bank, whom she did not know previously, believed in her project. Rose loved to arrange flowers for friends and family when they had parties. Her husband joked that she should try to make a living out of her hobby. This sparked her interest because she had friends who were florists. She decided to go to San Antonio to find out about the business aspects of a flower shop. There she looked up the phone number of a wholesale flower shop and called from a public telephone booth. The person on the other end was expecting orders, but instead Rose asked for ideas and advice. He was surprised to hear that she had neither money nor business experience but was impressed by her courage and promised to help her when she opened her shop. When Rose and her husband went to meet him, he turned out to be a large African American man who asked, "Are you the one who wants to open a flower shop but knows nothing about it?" He sent her to another supplier with the warning, "Have you seen any florist who is rich?" But Rose was adamant about trying her luck and exploring her passion:

> I needed to buy a box of accessories that cost four hundred dollars to start my business, which was a lot of money at the time. I headed to the Union National Bank where I did not know anyone. I approached an officer and he would not give me any money without a cosigner. The only person I could ask to be a cosigner was my uncle, and he was at a funeral. I went to another bank, and the officer heard my story. He agreed to lend me the money without any cosigner. I went to cemeteries at night and unwrapped flower arrangements to learn how they were done and wrapped them up again. I did not even know basic wiring, so I took some formal classes as well.

She started getting supplies from San Antonio on the trucks, as the little shop in her home took off by word of mouth, courtesy of kind customers who spread the news better than any advertisement. Despite being located in a quiet part of town, her business started flourishing.

For her first wedding decoration, her client convinced her that she could deliver what he desired, arranging to get the flowers from the Mexican side. As Rose's customers developed confidence in her, she started getting more and more orders for weddings, both within the city and from Nuevo Laredo. Providing service to Nuevo Laredo was legal and simple. One only had to get a permission form from Mexico City, which the client would arrange for. There was an instance when her client failed to get the permit and she was accosted by the Mexican police. On the day of the reception, she was charged with a fine of six hundred dollars. In the end, her rich client paid the fee as it was his mistake and the fine would have been more than the value of her business at the time. While Rose never feared any competition from her peers, namely other florists, she has found it hard to keep up with a large grocery chain like H-E-B, which also sells flowers and is more convenient for customers. She complains that now everybody sells everything and there are no protections for any line of work.

The people of Laredo remember the 1950s and 1960s as a golden era for downtown businesses. *Richard Andrew* recollects that in the 1950s Mexico entered a protective phase in order to produce light machinery and consumer goods such as washing machines, electronic equipment, and automotive parts. These policies drove a lot of trade to Laredo, as Mexicans preferred buying cheaper products available on the other side of the border. He recounts,

> Well-paid civil servants and well-off people in general cherished designer clothes, which were no longer available in Mexico. They would spend huge amounts of money to buy fashionable clothes, but instead of taking the risk of carrying the commodities, they paid others to sneak them across the border. Small gangs of smugglers grew and thrived in Laredo. They would smuggle clothing or automotive equipment to Mexico City worth as much as twenty thousand dollars, paying off customs in Mexico.

As a result, Laredo's commercial volume revived in downtown, but the devaluation of the peso in 1982 could not sustain downtown businesses in the long run.

Residents remember past opulence with more affection than the present economic upsurge. The prosperity of the 1950s and 1960s was much more tangible in the flourishing downtown businesses and the social interactions that occurred both within the growing city and as part of urbane interchange with Nuevo Laredo. The affluence that has come in the twenty-first century may have ushered in more dollars but has left less of a mark on the social landscape. Instead of new spaces of cultural dynamism, the city is now checkered with truck-and-trailer stops and encircled by warehouses along Mines Road.

The economic destiny of Laredo has mostly been shaped by forces outside its local confines. *Travis Mace* arrived in Laredo when the air force base was closing down and the city was facing a serious threat to its survival. That was when downtown merchants initiated a revival and rescued the economy. He started working in a downtown shop and remembers, "It was an incredible time. Back then, business went on a six-year cycle with the rise and fall of the Mexican president. The president would have a tendency to grab all the power and money he could and then have to leave. The incoming president would blame the woes on the outgoing one and start the cycle all over again." He stepped into a tremendous boom but also recalls downtown's bust: "We were a little store downtown. We had eleven employees, but within two years, we had one employee only part-time. Business had plummeted to less than 10 percent. By 1983, 50 percent of all the businesses in Laredo had closed. It had to do mostly with the devaluation of the peso."

At the end of the twentieth century, NAFTA spurred industrial nodes all along the border, such as in El Paso, but the share of manufacturing plants in Laredo has remained negligible. Laredo has always been a place of transit, whether for agricultural products or processed goods. Even the number of maquiladoras in Nuevo Laredo is much smaller than in Ciudad Juárez or Tijuana.[46] When we look at maquiladora manufacturing along the U.S.-Mexico border, we find a wide range, from low-tech assembly plants to high-tech sectors such as electronics and auto parts. These high-paying industrial clusters did not form in Nuevo Laredo as they did in other border towns, such as Tijuana (locally called "TVjuana" for its proliferation of television manufacturing plants), where they are supported by supplementary services in San Diego.[47] Mike Davis claims that quintessential maquiladora industries such as garments and electronics in Ciudad Juárez and Tijuana have attracted large amounts of Asian capital and reshaped the economies of El Paso and San Diego.[48] The absence of capital investment, both foreign and domestic, in either Laredo or Nuevo Laredo might well be the explanation for the lack of industry.

The impact of NAFTA on Nuevo Laredo has also been limited to trade and transportation. Instead of creating more jobs in Nuevo Laredo to expand its economy, NAFTA has created a binary safe/unsafe zone that has pushed businesses and people from Nuevo Laredo to Laredo. Historically, economic or political upheaval in Mexico pushes migrants to the U.S.-Mexico border. Border cities confronted one of the most significant immigration upswings because of NAFTA in the 1990s. Under the treaty, the Mexican market was flooded with cheap imported corn from the United States. Small farmers in Mexico were driven to the border in search of work because they could not compete with imported corn. After NAFTA, 2.7 million corn producers in Mexico were economically devastated and displaced.[49]

NAFTA was not an altogether new policy but instead only formalized already existing ties between border communities.[50] It is interesting that neither migrant labor nor drugs were addressed as issues in the tripartite agreement. While NAFTA removed obstacles to trade and allowed Mexican consumers to easily cross over to shop, because of uneven access and investment risk barriers Mexican businesses felt inhibited to compete with U.S. counterparts.[51] According to Peter Andreas, "While trade liberalization and economic integration help Mexico's traffickers penetrate the U.S. market, the privatization of state-owned enterprises and the deregulation of the Mexican banking system facilitate the laundering of their drug profits."[52] Lawrence Herzog notes that Mexican cities close to the border tend to have more per capita income than average Mexican cities while American border cities demonstrate almost half the average wage levels compared to other American cities.[53]

Andreas describes how the collapse of Mexican agriculture fueled illegal border crossings and how these led to the structures and practices of the security industrial complex that continues hiring more Border Patrol agents and building more infrastructure to monitor border crossings. In a mere six years after the passage of NAFTA, the increase in Border Patrol agents and support staff jumped by 65 percent and 89 percent respectively.[54] Andreas concludes that the border is closed and the market is open, as two key transactions on the border, namely illicit drugs and migrant labor, remain under strict scrutiny, while only a small percentage of trucks is examined so as not to inhibit commerce.[55] After the rise of the drug lords in the Mexican economy, much of the investment for small businesses like restaurants and gas stations has been displaced from cities like Monterrey to safer and more business-friendly Laredo. The most visible users of Laredo's public transportation are women who daily cross the river and work as maids or caregivers to the people of Laredo.

If NAFTA is an example of how globalization influences federal policies,[56] the United States-Mexico-Canada Agreement (USMCA), the more recent trade deal orchestrated by the Trump administration, exemplifies the crossroads where nationalism, populism, and globalization collide. USMCA is not fundamentally different from NAFTA even if it has been publicized as a policy that favors American interests. The changes in the treaty have had little structural impact on trade, but overall the Trump administration exhibited substantial departure in the areas of immigration and asylum. Most asylum seekers cross the southern border, so the impact of the policy changes—such as the chaos of the inhuman practice of separating children from parents and keeping them in cages—is being disproportionately borne by border communities.[57]

Social and cultural ties between the two cities have always been strong because Laredo's residents are overwhelmingly Hispanic with frequent family relationships on the other side of the river. In the pre-NAFTA era, it was common for family members to live on both sides of the border to manage businesses that spanned the sister cities. NAFTA defused this practice to some extent, but with the eruption of the drug wars and accompanying violence, people—or at least the elites—from Nuevo Laredo started moving to Laredo for safety reasons. Navarro and Vivas note that at the peak of the violence, every month about fifteen hundred families moved to Laredo from Nuevo Laredo.[58] There has also been a steady drain of small businesses, such as restaurants and shops, in the same direction. Unlike the previous era, when business was fluid and migration often temporary, drugs and violence have produced a permanent one-way movement toward Laredo.

It is also important to note that despite the economic development induced by NAFTA, border regions host many more poor residents per capita than the national or Texas average. One-third of Webb County residents live below the poverty line. James Peach and Richard Adkisson argue that regional income levels and wage rates have always remained low in the border cities, causing the border regions to remain "economically depressed."[59] Historically, Laredo suffered from considerable poverty even when it went through several cycles of economic recovery. A study on El Paso reveals economic segmentation disfavoring women,[60] and Laredo is probably no exception to the exploitative structure. The border economy is flush with low-cost unskilled labor available for menial jobs under both legal and illegal arrangements.

Laredo's economy might have been shaped by U.S. policies, but it has always demonstrated a closer connection with the Mexican rather than the American economy. As mentioned earlier, the collapse of Laredo's downtown in the 1980s has been linked to the peso devaluation in Mexico, while the second peso devaluation of the 1990s was prompted by NAFTA. Political and economic uncertainties in the two countries have functioned as persistent historical limits to steady growth, keeping the border economies fragile and susceptible to such changes. James Giermanski argues that economic development on the South Texas border has not occurred in an open and competitive market but has been driven by artificial barriers between the United States and Mexico.[61] He further stresses that despite the impediments put in place by the two countries, the actual economy of the border regions on both sides remains intertwined, and U.S. federal laws cannot protect the border towns from the impact of the ups and downs of the Mexican economy.[62]

As a partner with access to less-specialized labor, Nuevo Laredo lured affluent tourists to bars and restaurants, offering food, music, and a lively vibe that was absent in its more efficient and utilitarian counterpart until the late 1990s. James Curtis notes that even with low per capita income Laredo emerged as one of the cities with the highest retail sales, with much of the spending originating from Mexican consumers regularly crossing the bridge in search of better goods and services.[63] Although devaluations and adverse political rhetoric influence the ebb and flow of such customers, Laredo's economy would significantly dry up without the steady stream of border crossers. The largest cluster of bars and cabarets in which prostitution was allowed fell outside the urban core on the margins of Nuevo Laredo in a designated Zona de Tolerancia, known as Boy's Town in local vernacular.[64] *Grace Terry* notes how catering to oil-field workers and truck drivers requires raunchier entertainment options than currently available in Laredo. Perhaps this explains why the vice districts in Laredo never acquired the notoriety usually associated with border towns.

Most of the shops in downtown tried to lure a high volume of customers with cheaper merchandise rather than the high-quality goods for which they were once famous. *Charles Vega*, a native of Laredo who has spent all his life in the city and served in local government, blames the availability of merchandise on the internet for the collapse of downtown stores. He notes, "A number of shop owners even turned down money available through the city to renovate their facilities. They were afraid of losing customers who would equate the renovated stores with more expensive goods." Vega reminisces that at one time Laredo sold the most Joe brand shirts by Arrow in the entire country. People from Mexico used to buy luggage in Laredo and fill it with American goods. Because of the availability of everything imaginable online, even the need for smuggling has diminished. Vega feels that Laredo's retail stores have failed to adapt to changing times.

The city's ever-expanding trade perimeter now encompasses Canada as well as Mexico. *Samantha Taft*, a longtime native resident, inherited her father's motel in the bustling part of town, along San Bernardo Avenue, and would hear cars screeching and trucks and eighteen-wheelers thundering along until the bridges were expanded in the 1990s. At the time investors eagerly wanted to cash in on Laredo's homegrown potential. Laredo's economy was historically turbulent until oil was discovered on ranches adjacent to Laredo. To a degree the local millionaires stabilized the economy from the effects of the fluctuations of the peso. Taft feels it is bad enough that Laredo is losing shoppers from Mexico but also finds itself in the political crosshairs with a negative image that reduces the number of American visitors as well. Even people from Corpus Christi, which has more crime, hesitate to visit Laredo. The dictates come down from Washington, and local businesses are unable to fend off the detrimental representations pervasive on national television. Local efforts to revive downtown have collided with the national policy of proclaiming the border as a national emergency and building a wall that would literally pierce downtown.

The shift in the image of downtown also contains the story of the transition of this city. In the early to mid-2000s, Laredo wanted to change its image to a "destination city" and began exploring river development plans to attract tourists. At the same time, there was a concerted effort to reclaim the city's logo of the "gateway city" and nudge it toward a stable and desirable symbolism. One plan was based on a dual downtown that would include Nuevo Laredo. Another ambitious plan called River Vega marked off a huge slice of downtown from Tres Laredos Park to the small shops on Santa Ursula Avenue for renovation. The idea was to get people from the Rio Grande Valley and South Texas as well as Nuevo Laredo to downtown Laredo in larger numbers. The present outlet mall is a limited manifestation of that desire. *Rachel Lawrence*, a longtime resident of south Laredo, observes, "Although it is called an outlet mall, it is not cheap but targets Mexican shoppers by offering brand-name merchandise not readily available across the border. It offers very little local flavor and instead is crammed with major labels. Rather than developing the riverfront with a larger vision, the outlet mall is an aesthetically pleasing complex with limited commercial aspirations." It was tough to get the various components of the broader plan in sync, and the long delay swung the plan back to conventional space/money/square footage calculations that departed from a holistic vision for downtown. Barely a decade passed when the discussion switched to the border wall, meaning how to exclude people from coming to Laredo. This paradoxical turn in border discourse is rooted not in local determinants but intrusive national politics. As a gateway city, Laredo had customarily swung its gate both ways as it welcomed people and businesses from north and south. But when it is redefined as an international corridor, what comes into being are tangible control mechanisms rather than implicit and explicit interdependencies.

Local Control/Global Port

The conversion of Laredo from a city to a trade corridor preceded NAFTA. This success in the 1970s brought external investors who were different from previous generations in that they did not stay back and become part of the social fabric. Rather, they financed chain stores that competed with local businesses and shifted money away from the community. This is not a story unique to Laredo, but the unfolding of the process of how a new mall with national-brand stores choked downtown businesses is worth evaluating. Urban revival in American cities has often been built around consumption, especially retail and restaurants, often in the form of shopping malls.[65]

Downtown Laredo was the vital center of civic life because of thriving businesses and movie theaters interspersed with the peaceful bliss of residential neighborhoods, all of it minutes away from a hassle-free passage to the fascinating nightlife of Nuevo Laredo. Local residents remember the homegrown entrepreneurs who owned Alexander Department Store. National-brand stores like Woolworth's did business in harmony with locally owned stores. Lunch at Woolworth's counter after Sunday church was a common practice among the ladies. The KGNS TV station stood at the corner of Convent and Houston with a popular restaurant on the first floor. Richter's Department Store, with its lush wooden floors, was a focus of pride. Precio Fijo (One Price) was a famous department store on Zaragoza Street and a popular destination for locals. Guarantee Shoe Store was located across the street, one of many shoe stores that reveled in local pride and excelled in their craft. In the 1930s Guadalupe San Miguel owned La Esmerelda and even owned branches of the

FIGURE 17 One Price Department Store. Laredo Public Library Foundation.

restaurant in other cities. At the northeast corner of Iturbide and Convent, across the street from La Perla, was fashionable Tres Hermanas (with another branch in Del Rio) selling clothing from intimate apparel to formal wear.

It was not only downtown that boasted of proud native-owned businesses. Small bakeries, tortilla factories, and stores like Alfredo Meat Market, Casso Guerra Groceries, Western Auto, Garza Bargain Center, and El Mejor Pan Bakery existed in every barrio. Neighborhoods all over the city had small stores and locally owned factories. Local residents still remember the taste of the cupcakes and coffee cakes with pecan and coconut from Borchers Family Bakery in downtown. El Aguila Bakery across from the old H-E-B in downtown served the most delicious pan dulce. The little taco stand next to the bakery had the best *tacos al vapor. Elena Cruz*'s grandfather had a butcher shop in the downtown area. She remembers getting candy anytime she walked into the shop. The clamor of downtown shopping, the rustle of her prom dress, the fragrance from La Fruteria on Zaragoza Street, and the taste of Pixy Stix candy linger in her memories of downtown. *Bianca Frey* remembers a tortilla factory at one corner and a bakery at another corner of her street along with a candy store about a block away on Clark Street. One of her neighbors was the owner of a downtown shoe store. In her neighborhood with just two paved streets, there were tennis courts and a Girl Scouts House. People remember buying school supplies from Perry's and art supplies from Carousel, or frequenting ordinary discount stores or Western Auto. All of these stores went out of business when Walmart came to town, replicating the prevalent trend in urban America.

Downtown flourished well into the 1960s and for much of the 1970s as the fulcrum of social and cultural activities. Many older interviewees were born and raised there, and all have memories of walking around there as part of daily life. One interviewee, *Bianca Frey*, recounts that her father had a business in downtown, loaning money and getting it back in installments with interest. In a town of seventy-five thousand people, the largest loan he made was around a hundred dollars, but the enterprise was enough to comfortably raise six children and save money to buy land for retirement. Her father was the only brother who stayed behind in Laredo to take care of aging parents, yet he ended up being far more successful than his brothers who left for California. The major change in their lives occurred when they moved a few miles into the interior and had to take a bus to downtown. Although taking the bus to go to school or downtown was quite safe, they felt as if they had been cut off from social intercourse, much to the chagrin of Frey's mother. Easy access to downtown, whether on foot or by bus, was a prerequisite for social life, which was entirely based in downtown.

Laredo's location has always enticed diverse groups of people not only to do business but also to make their homes there. *Richard Andrew*, with his keen knowledge of local history, describes Jewish refugees finding their way to Laredo during the Second World War. He explains,

> Along with Jews came Palestinians who had also become refugees in their homeland. Like Spanish immigrants from old Mexico, merchants from the Middle East, both Jews and Arabs, set up commercial seats in Laredo. Often the mercantile class came from Northern Mexico and could be Latino or Jewish or Arab. This mercantile class actually triggered Laredo's commercial boom.

Laredo also attracted Chinese and Indian businessmen who opened shops in downtown. Electronic goods stores used to have Chinese owners, and gold and jewelry shops were dominated by Indians. Immigrants from distant lands tended to be entrepreneurs, while workers—especially on the farm—were overwhelmingly Mexican. As Andrew sums up, "If one draws a straight line to connect New York City with Mexico City, it goes through Laredo."

Along with important individual stores located in the well-worn buildings of downtown, there was River Drive Mall, built in 1970. The first indoor mall overlooking the Rio Grande at the edge of downtown quickly became the magnet for shopping. It was an enclosed structure with sixty-eight stores, flaunting flagship emporiums and signaling to residents that the days of traveling to San Antonio to obtain classy merchandise were over. Many Laredoans cherish fond memories of River Drive Mall and the pleasure derived from exposure to quality products without having to leave the city. Prestigious stores like J.C. Penney, Frost Bros., Weiner's, and Orange Julius replaced the need to go to Ingram Park Mall in San Antonio.

With the mall still at its peak, within seven years Mall del Norte[66] was established in the emerging northern part of town. The new mall was built along the I-35 corridor, the location of the new focal point of commerce. *Felipe Calderon* believes that what made Mall del Norte special was St. John Neumann Catholic Church inside it. It might have been the only mall to have housed a church within its edifice. The church remained inside for over twenty years until it moved to a bigger location at Hillside and Springfield. Its archaic exterior felt almost classical, and its interior was distinctive as well, with an upstairs balcony where one could sit and enjoy Mass. Sunday started with church for the Catholic community, so with the church inside the structure, the mall competed well with downtown businesses.

Mall del Norte and the burgeoning strip malls along I-35 swelled to contain more than half the city's retail volume according to the 1987 U.S. Bureau of the Census, while River Drive Mall and surrounding downtown stores shriveled into cheap substitutes for poorer customers. As James Curtis observes, "Retail and service outlets in Laredo, though dispersed in typical United States fashion, are most dense along the 1–35 corridor, where stores of large discount chains such as Walmart and H-E-B are located, as well as the enclosed Mall del Norte."[67] By the time Mall del Norte was built, a considerable portion of residents had left their downtown abodes and settled in the northern parts of the city. Having a mall in close proximity slashed their need to visit the downtown area.

Mall del Norte started out as the ninth-largest mall in Texas, with 2.4 million square feet of rentable space and many more nationwide stores than

River Drive Mall. In the hot Laredo summer, the mall functions not only as a shopping complex but also as a place to stroll for older inhabitants and for activities for children, which are considered valuable by family-oriented residents. *Elena Cruz* remembers that despite the various new stores in the mall, people kept going downtown for some items like prom dresses and jewelry. If Mall del Norte offered more options, downtown offered cheaper prices. Nevertheless, Mall del Norte became the indispensable shopping center after the fall of downtown, and it was subsequently remodeled and expanded in the 1990s. River Drive Mall could not withstand the new competition in town, and by the mid-1980s had lost its allure. It was finally abandoned in 2003 because of high vacancy and demolished in 2014. Curtis finds that the location of River Drive Mall at the border was always disconnected from the rest of downtown. In his words, "Situated on the southwestern margins of downtown, the mall appeared to have little physical or even functional relationship with the rest of the commercial core."[68]

The Outlet Shoppes at Laredo is the latest entity to have replaced River Drive Mall, with the expectation that it will revive downtown. River Drive Mall was enclosed in an office-like complex, while The Outlet Shoppes, although built on the same land, has a more open architecture, with a footbridge linking it to the pedestrian bridge to Nuevo Laredo. Reversing the strict commercial model of River Drive Mall, this private mall is actively seeking to connect with grassroots organizations. When world-famous cellist Yo-Yo Ma came to Laredo and held a concert on the border—in Tres Laredos Park across from The Outlet Shoppes—the mall not only opened its parking to spectators but also lent its stage and audio equipment for the concert. Its watchword seems to be to include the populace as much as possible, and more and more public events in south-side neighborhoods are now moving to its facilities. The mall has already resuscitated the popular event of Santa's arrival and the lighting of the Christmas tree, events that had faded along with the prosperity of the 1980s. About five hundred people recently showed up for the lighting of the tree, which used to take place at San Agustín Cathedral in the fondly remembered days. In short, the mall is trying to fuse modern commerce with continuing nostalgia for a soaring downtown.

Although the new mall attracts plenty of customers, particularly from beyond the southern border, it has yet to meet the revenue targets that had been much ballyhooed. *Elena Cruz*, a young professional working at The Outlet Shoppes, claims, "We are bringing more visitors to Laredo and trying to help make it a destination place. We are seeing people not only from across international borders, but also people from Dallas, from up north in Texas, and from California." The significance of Mexican buyers for the mall cannot be overemphasized. Roughly 70 percent of patrons are from Mexico. Sales go up during Mexican holidays but not necessarily American holidays. There is special emphasis on enticing Mexican customers and assuring them of privileged treatment. As Cruz explains, "We treat them like royalty because we are here because of them, and the relationship with neighbors is very important for a border town because we feed off each other."

Neither The Outlet Shoppes nor any other stores in downtown consider the stores in Nuevo Laredo to be their competitors. What scares them is competition from increased investment in retail and other businesses in the northern part of the city, which has succeeded in attracting national stores. In October 2000, Home Depot opened its largest U.S. store (a hundred and fifty-thousand-square-foot facility), and Lowe's Home Improvement also has a similarly large store in Laredo. The Walmart along I-35 brags about earning the most profits per square foot in the nation.

In terms of physical landscape, the CBDs of the two cities are based on an identical design centered on Spanish plazas, which are meant to serve as the nuclei of commerce and culture. Laredo started out with a vision for a plethora of plazas, but the five that remain are underutilized as public spaces. On the whole, local flavor seems neglected and underrated today. Only a few miles from downtown, on San Bernardo Avenue (which linked downtown to other parts of the city before the construction of I-35), there are stores that sell Mexican artifacts. Generally family owned and operating for generations, they are scattered along the tourist strip and offer cheap merchandise to out-of-towners. The most striking image of these stores is the "For Sale" signs almost always accompanying the artwork, acquired as souvenirs and probably costing a lot less than at the organized El Mercado in San Antonio.[69]

Despite the significant attempts to revive the downtown, it remains a food desert. The only real grocery store there, H-E-B, closed in the 1970s. In a city of over three hundred thousand people, H-E-B continues to dominate the food market, thriving amid limited competition from Walmart and Sam's Club. Older residents remember the presence of Kroger and numerous smaller groceries all over the city. While new bars and stores have emerged in downtown, the residents of downtown and neighborhoods in the south rely on the smaller H-E-B near them, while the bigger H-E-Bs with more food choices open on the north side. H-E-B has expanded its locations around the city yet closed its doors where the poorest people live. *Ria Sandoval* laments that most of the new businesses, with their cultural diversity, have shifted to the north, leaving the city center hollow. She would love to see the downtown of her childhood spring back to life. The residential part of downtown remains underappreciated, as most of the inhabitants are the working poor, in close proximity to the few existing elite historic neighborhoods. Amid the bars and fast-food outlets, both chains and family owned, a lone *frutería* and a discount food store (mainly offering nonperishable items) have cropped up in recent years.

Bianca Frey, who has worked in both the private and public sectors, believes that the solution to Laredo's fluctuating economy lies in manufacturing plants creating stable employment and nurturing growth from within. She muses, "If even one person takes an opportunity to bring a manufacturing plant with high-skilled workers here, they'll find that this is the place to be and we can do this." *Barry Rivers*, a younger resident who left the city for college but returned after a family emergency, agrees. He has discovered business opportunities in the otherwise blank slate of the city, where there had been little interest other than in trade and transportation. Settling down as an entrepreneur in his hometown, a place that offered scant promise only a few years ago, he argues, "The pro for Laredo is that it's a great place to start something because you're going to have the tight community that's going to be of assistance to help you get going and at least build a model for yourself. And then from there you can figure out what you want to do, but it's a good place to get started and especially now that there's room to experiment a bit."

One of the rare local industries in Laredo is La India Herbs and Spices Packing Company, which has been in business for nearly a hundred years. It was established in 1924 by Don Antonio as a small grocery store that sold Mexican chocolate. Antonio Rodriguez was from Lambatos, Mexico, and used to go back home to get medicinal herbs for soldiers during the Mexican Revolution. He became blind but compensated with a heightened sense of smell and taste. According to his granddaughter, who now runs the business, he could tell everyone not only by their voice but even their footsteps. He had the intuition to include medicinal herbs in his blends because he was aware of their impact on gastric acids. His spice blends derived from his unique knowledge of herbs and their nutritional and healing characteristics. For example, chili has a natural acid neutralizer. The formulas for chimichurri, chorizo, menudo, and chocolate blends still follow his original recipes. Their house had the small shop in the front, which is now an eclectic restaurant, with the packing factory in the back. Some of their products are still hand packed, and aside from the local market, they deliver spices to Houston, Dallas, Austin, Fort Worth, the Rio Grande Valley, and even Oklahoma. When the local H-E-B decided to drop their products, residents protested and convinced the supermarket to carry the popular spices. With twenty employees at the factory and a few more at the restaurant's kitchen, La India is one of the few industries to have survived both the downturn and the prosperity and held its own despite competition.

The 1.5 million square feet of warehouse space that contains its commercial freight testifies to the significance of trade for Laredo. The city is heavily dependent on the Mexican shopper, but *Paul Sergio*, who works in city government, believes that Laredo exhibits a marked disadvantage compared to McAllen and other cities in the Valley. He complains,

> McAllen gets to keep a higher share of the state sales tax. The sales tax throughout Texas is eight and a quarter percent, and communities can vote to increase it by one percent. The state takes six pennies, the city gets one penny for transit and a quarter penny for the sports venue tax, and the county gets half a penny, so that makes up almost two pennies that have to be shared locally. The city of McAllen gets the two pennies outright without having to share it with the county.

NAFTA and subsequent national trade policies have created a surge in revenue growth for Laredo, but the profit is dispersed among distant investors rather than local entrepreneurs. Until the 1950s and 1960s, most downtown businesses were established and run by local owners. The profits they generated flowed back to the local economy. People become misty eyed when they remember the Alfredo Santos grocery store, where local snacks were available, at the same time as there were large retail stores, where shoppers could socialize. Although a far greater amount of money and merchandise passes through Laredo now, only a negligible portion of the money is retained for the city.

FIGURE 18 Downtown Hidalgo Street. Webb County Heritage Foundation.

The Global Port in the Local Community

David Byrne explicates how globalization has added a new dimension to urban theory. He selects certain cities because their location maximizes profits
to transnational capitalist interests and because they are transformed following neoliberal economic arrangements.[70] Laredo since the mid-1990s, ever
since NAFTA, fits the model very well in terms of the impact of globalization
and new networks of transnational trade. The transportation sector in Laredo
multiplied, and key institutions such as the first four-year university, Texas
A&M International University (TAMIU), came into existence in 1995.[71] The
emphasis on transborder security resulted in escalated Border Patrol presence and federal funding allocated to national security. Laredo temporarily
surpassed Los Angeles in 2019 to become the largest inland port in the country.[72] According to the Port of Laredo Annual Report of 2017, merchandise
worth $177 billion was imported while goods worth $126 billion were exported.[73] Even if we remember that for Laredo the significance of its location
predates globalization, the magnitude of the transformation is indisputable.

In terms of the sheer size of economic activity, it is difficult to deny Laredo
the status of a global hub. Michael Smith distinguishes between the global

and the transnational, the former representing a restructuring of economic networks to take advantage of locality in the post-Fordist global capital market and the latter constituting more of a social and cultural connection built on kinship and migration networks that can amplify in a crisis situation.[74] We need to remember the historical evolution of the city of Laredo to understand both its global and transnational elements. Smith defines transnational urbanism as "a marker of the crisscrossing transnational circuits of communication and cross-cutting local, translocal, and transnational social practices that 'come together' in particular places at particular times and enter into the contested politics of place-making."[75] Laredo started out as a transnational hub of commerce but has evolved into an important node in the global market where transactions of auto parts and machinery serve the dual markets of the United States and Mexico.

Saskia Sassen focuses on the impact of corporate globalization on restructuring local politics through innovative economic networks and institution building. She notes how small local entities prioritize technical connectivity and form new economic ventures that trigger new sets of political actors and activities. These transnational places open up to fresh immigrants and diasporas and challenge existing civil society.[76] Although global trade has resulted in rapid growth and brought many newcomers, a large portion of the people who came and settled in Laredo are affiliated with institutions— the Border Patrol, TAMIU, Laredo Independent School District (LISD) and United Independent School District (UISD), Laredo Medical Center— and hence did not disturb the existing power structure in any fundamental way. The categories of "immigrant" or "diaspora" or even "outsider" have remained inconsequential given Laredo's demographic profile and history of ethnic harmony. Nevertheless, urban politics in Laredo underwent unaccustomed challenges toward more accountability and transparency from existing civil society.

Given the copious amount of federal dollars associated with border security, the Border Patrol has emerged as a major power broker as its interactions with the city council have acquired overt political features. As an example, during the Trump administration, when contracts for building the border wall were granted by the federal government, the Border Patrol needed the city's approval to examine the construction locations for "right of way." The city council (under pressure from citizen groups) denied the permit for almost two years, essentially stalling the construction until the

2020 election. This is precisely what sets a border city like Laredo apart from other participants in the global economy. Local stakeholders in Laredo are motivated by profits accruing from federal funds but are also acutely aware of national policies that undermine local economic priorities. The contradictions between local and national financial interests may not mirror partisan ideologies and thus may elude political analysis.

The processes involving formal cross-border or transnational institutions have come into vogue after globalization, but for Laredo strong informal networks of institutions—business, family, and cultural—existed with Nuevo Laredo before the neoliberal wave of globalization. In fact, security issues associated with globalization weakened preexisting economic and social patterns of interdependence. As the trade zone stretched into the mainland, the border became integrated with the national economy. Borders have acquired a security/economy nexus in the aftermath of geopolitical reorientation.[77] Similar to other border areas, for Laredo it is the economy that multiplies interdependence while security restricts customary linkages with Nuevo Laredo. Ultimately, it is local people who face the scrutiny of enhanced security and the recasting of the economy toward global commerce. The internationalization of the border in the national economy has intensified a hierarchy of authority, privileging the federal government over local or regional power structures.

Commerce has remained the heart of Laredo, so much so that the metaphor of the market has often been used to analyze the city itself. Vincenzo Ruggiero and Nigel South apply the concept of the bazaar—the Oriental marketplace driven by informal rules and transactions and apparent chaos—to decipher the drugs network that often parallels the structural network of cities.[78] Boundaries between legality and illegality are ambiguous, constantly shifting, and being renegotiated in the chaotic bazaar, which might be an apt way to conceptualize the commerce and marketplace of Laredo. Ruggiero and South employ the interesting concept of barricades, factors imposing limitations on the bazaar.[79] For Laredo, historically the barricades have been federal regulations. Time and again, trade and immigration laws have served to expand or restrict the marketplace of Laredo, thereby literally altering its physical space with new groups of entrants, such as merchants or Border Patrol officials. If federal laws have functioned as the external barricade to the marketplace of Laredo, then the internal barricade has been the competition between downtown and respectable neighborhoods in the north of the city (although the definition of north keeps shifting as the city expands) in addition to the city government's attention to and investment (or lack thereof) in the downtown area. Although trade is the lifeblood of Laredo, the actual income for the city comes from transportation rather than interaction between buyers and sellers.

Instead of constituting an in-between space, Laredo is better seen as having a dual identity. It proudly proclaims its position as the largest inland port while recognizing that it serves as a major corridor for drugs and counterfeit goods. Both types of trade bring profits. Trade through prohibited routes gets all the attention and is monitored, but the same trade through lawful routes often escapes strict vigilance. Drugs enter the United States through the legal channel of the bridge and rarely through the risky route of backpacks loaded on human carriers traversing the river. The little bundles of marijuana that come through the river are negligible in quantity and monetary value compared to the harder drugs that add up to tons. Everyone is aware that most of the smuggled goods actually pass through the bridges, which process fourteen thousand trucks a day. If each of these trucks were inspected, the checkpoints would experience colossal jams.[80] Miniscule numbers of tractor trailers are checked for drugs, since disruption of trade is not realistic. By shifting attention to trade routes rather than trade, business continues seamlessly in Laredo.

Conclusion

Borders tend to be paradoxes, as they simultaneously open up economic spaces (markets) yet control the participants (workers). Like its much earlier predecessor the Zona Libre, NAFTA redefined the border to allow more economic activity, yet at the same time control over the border often occurs beyond it, within what we typically consider sovereign territory. In Laredo, citizenship—which confers certain inalienable rights—has been separated from consumer rights. An implicit devil's bargain has been struck by protecting consumer rights, because they are seen as more important to the economy, but only within the parameters of the city. Mexican shoppers rarely face hindrances in visiting Laredo, but the scrutiny alters at the checkpoints, where they are regarded with suspicion as opposed to legitimate participants in the local economy. American citizens are not free from such inspection

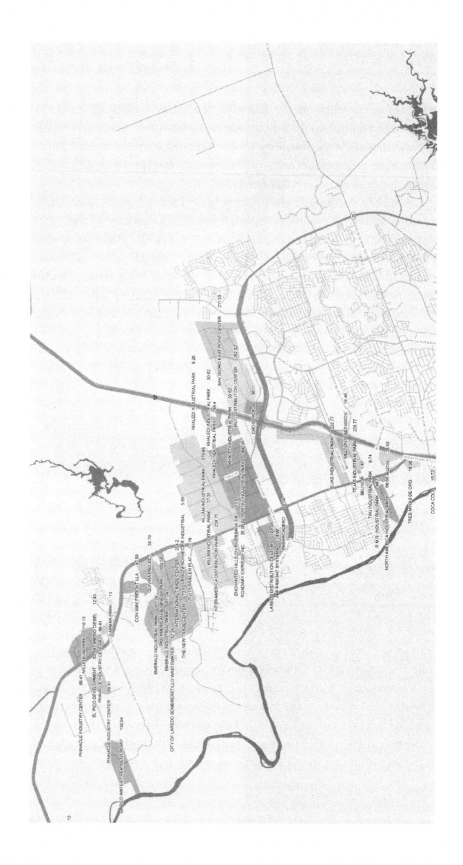

PINNACLE INDUSTRY CENTER

EL PICO DEVELOPMENT 6541 LAREDO DIESEL 88.41

PINNACLE INDUSTRY CENTER 55941

CITY OF LAREDO SOMBERETILLO WASTEWATER

PINNACLE INDUSTRY CENTER 116.13 MILLENIUM PARK

PINNACLE INDUSTRY CENTER 130.94

GARMAR PARK 13

BEBCO WATER TREATMENT PLANT

CON-WAY FREIGHT ILLA 47.59

OLIVIRA PROJECT 38.79

EMERALD INDUSTRIAL PARK 61.24
PAN AMERICAN BUSINESS PARK 183.04
EMERALD INDUSTRIAL PARK 61.24

THE NEW TRADECENTER 62.24 INTERNATIONAL TRADE CENTER
7.19 LA BOTA SCHREIDER INDUSTRIAL
UTILITY/TRAILER PLAT. 10.78

INTERAMERICA DISTRIBUTION PARK

KILLAM INDUSTRIAL PARK 29.2

5.05

KILLAM INDUSTRIAL PARK 570.68

KILLAM INDUSTRIAL PARK 37.31

KILLAM INDUSTRIAL PARK 254.75

ENCHANTED HILLS ON RIVERBANK DR 13.37
ROADWAY EXPRESS INC 25.00 EL-PORTAL INDUSTRIAL PARK 499.91

LAREDO DISTRIBUTION CENTER 1.03.04
ABF-FREIGHT SYSTEMS 24.99
EMBARCADERO 35.04

KHALED INDUSTRIAL PARK 9.26

KHALED INDUSTRIAL PARK 30.62

KHALED INDUSTRIAL PARK 136.4

KHALED INDUSTRIAL PARK 30.62
MICO DISTRIBUTION CENTER 252.32

SAN ISIDRO EAST POINT CENTER 211.53

CROSSROADS 36.11

TEXAS INDUSTRIAL PARK 228.77

MELTON SUBDIVISION 19.46

TEXAS INDUSTRIAL PARK 226.77

BEL NEA 1.47

R M R TWO INDUSTRIAL PARK 6.74

NORTH AMERICA INDUSTRIAL PARK 66.68 KAIZON 75.53

TRES MINAS DE ORO 18.38

COCA COLA 1572

13

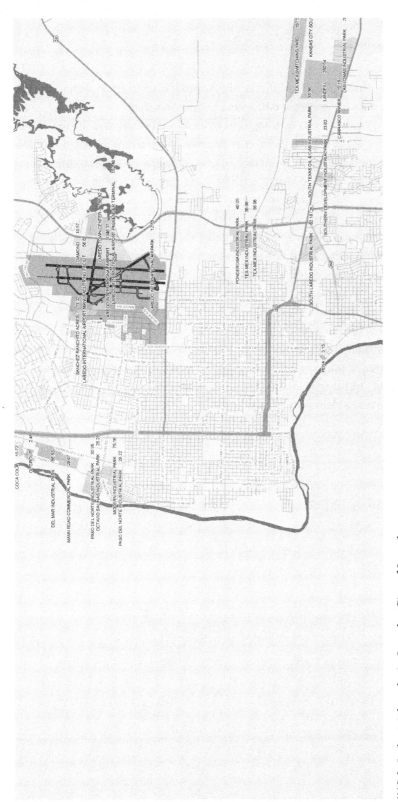

MAP 3 Industrial parks in Laredo. City of Laredo.

tinged with distrust. By asking to validate proof of citizenship at checkpoints, the privilege of American citizenship is compromised.

Laredo's identity has strong roots in localized culture and the way of life defining the border. As the border lifestyle of coexisting in harmony with Nuevo Laredo has been upended by global trade, the underlying ethnic identity is becoming more visible, with political demands accentuating citizenship rights. Globalization is expected to weaken the power of nation-states by prioritizing the neoliberal economic rationale, but in Laredo clashes between the national government and civil society to define the border continue in full swing. Laredo has emerged as one of the key strategic sites to confront pressing issues of transnational identity. It has always been a city of commerce and has welcomed entrepreneurs, but what has changed is the relationship between the entrepreneurs and the city. With the shift in power from local to global moguls, business enterprises have grown in volume but become spatially contained within the transportation corridor. The city's outer layer is being shaped by national and international interests, but within the inner layer there remains a vibrant community wrapped in nostalgia and ready to make claims on its own terms.

CHAPTER 4

Public Spaces and Community Engagement

Claiming Laredo

> In response to the overwhelming community desire to retain the natural habitat and biodiversity that make Laredo and the wider region adjacent to the Rio Grande distinct, efforts to protect and restore natural features as the city grows will be central to realizing this vision. Natural areas serve multiple functions, acting as both infrastructure and open space.
>
> VIVA LAREDO, 6.13

> We are beginning to understand how to have a conversation about who we are. The border wall coalition is part of learning how to have a conversation about our city.
>
> *CHARLES FOX*, LAREDO RESIDENT

Laredo has a rich history of civic engagement despite its elite-dominated social fabric. As long as Laredo remained a small town, its activism remained focused around local issues and largely forgotten. The recent national spotlight on Laredo has reshaped local assertions about the future direction of the social order. The transformation of public spaces in Laredo reflects the contradictions between local and national priorities. The comprehensive plan for city development, Viva Laredo, was assembled through a long public participation process. After years of neglect, some of the downtown plazas are being reclaimed and utilized as lively spaces where clashing meanings of fellowship and belonging are being enacted. The city has refocused its attention to develop new green spaces and maintain existing ones with much greater vigor and investment. Local voices now congregate around the new spaces to challenge national and state policies. The story of the civic square in Laredo is woven with three interconnected strands: the expansion of actual public spaces, the institutional planning process, and community engagement, which is often forgotten and remains hidden from the public eye.

A vibrant saga of activism runs through Laredo's history, stories that are often retained in collective memory rather than explicit documentation. This chapter attempts to narrate the changing shape of the civic square in Laredo and analyze the underlying reasons for the transformation. Azteca Economic Development and Preservation Corporation (AEDPC) successfully thwarted a gentrification attempt that would have turned a working-class neighborhood into a commercial zone. The Holding Institute educated Jovita Idár, one of the most famous civil rights defendants for Mexican Americans, and has recently reasserted its presence in the public welfare dimension. Rio Grande International Study Center (RGISC) stands out as the lone environmental nonprofit organization seeking to preserve the precious river. Laredo Main Street is an ongoing partnership between the city and private businesses to coordinate downtown revitalization. The #NoBorderWall Coalition was formed to challenge the Trump administration's border wall project and has more recently opposed Governor Abbott's comparable initiative. The first contracts for the border wall that were canceled by the Biden administration in July 2021 were those in the Laredo Sector.

The premise behind most global or transnational cities is their operation as sites of production. Saskia Sassen describes how transnational economic and political processes open up new places and new claims to the city.[1] As Laredo's economy has always depended on transportation rather than any particular industries, the most visible new spaces in town are the warehouses that support the burgeoning trucking traffic. At the same time, the city has responded seriously to local pleas for more green spaces and quality-of-life indicators, which have reenergized public involvement on a new level. Laredo is not immune from the nationwide trend in which private capital dominates investments in entertainment and codifies a different norm of participation than traditional public spaces. But it should be recognized that at a time when most of the reshaping of public spaces has been accompanied by surveillance technology that implicitly aims to keep out the poor, a large number of new public spaces in Laredo have been formed by the city in response to calls made by residents. Different groups—youth, young professionals, progressives, activists making political claims, slam poets—are asserting their right to these revitalized spaces.

FIGURE 19 Bruni Plaza. Webb County Heritage Foundation.

The City of Plazas

The history of public spaces in Laredo begins with magnificent plazas, which remained underutilized as civic places despite their rich cultural history. As discussed in chapter 1, the city was established in 1755, making it one of the oldest cities west of the Mississippi. *Felix Rivera* regards Laredo as one of the most unique urban centers in the country, with its seven original plazas based on the Law of the Indies.[2] The five existing plazas are El Mercado Plaza, San Agustín Plaza, Jarvis Plaza, St. Peter's Plaza, and Bruni Plaza. Tex Mex Plaza was razed in 1966 to accommodate the offices of Tex Mex Railway, and Plaza de la Noria (School Plaza) was bulldozed and later resuscitated as part of the greenbelt along I-35.[3] Along with the plazas, the vernacular architecture of buildings bears the mark of many different structural designs seamlessly coexisting. The credit for Laredo's urban design goes to Mayor Samuel Jarvis, who took the helm after the Civil War. An engineer by profession, he expanded the initial grid of the city beyond the original settlement and established the well-thought-out city structure. *Alex Mead* recollects,

"When I was in architecture school, we were entering GIS [Geographic Information System] data and street grids. My classmates were showing street grids from Cleveland and Brooklyn. When I put mine in everybody fell quiet and my professor asked, 'Where are you from?' I answered, 'Laredo, Texas, and we have one of the most beautiful and symmetrical road grids in all of America.'"

Downtown is truly unique, *Felix Rivera* elaborates, as it contains a fifteenth- or sixteenth-century approach to settlement, its urban design characteristics dating back to the 1560s in Spain. In the layout of the downtown street grid, streets running north–south were named after saints, while streets running east–west were named after generals. Although the city can boast of a range of vernacular architecture ranging from Spanish to Mexican to Creole,[4] Rivera laments that Mayor Jarvis was the first and last genuine urban designer Laredo had. Instead of following the Spanish grid-plan design,[5] the city haphazardly adopted the suburban model,[6] making the beautiful inner city lose connectivity with the rest of the city. The original city hall was built in 1880 in El Mercado Plaza and was surrounded by an outdoor market. The present city hall was constructed in downtown following a modern architectural format. Laredo Center for the Arts and Webb County Heritage Foundation now reside where the original city hall used to be, while the surrounding spacious courtyard still evokes the aura of a plaza. Jarvis Plaza and San Agustín Plaza are the two functioning plazas, but they remain underutilized. Bruni Plaza, once one of the most popular spots to congregate, was turned into a public library. After the library moved to the northern part of town, the beautiful building of Bruni Plaza has stayed empty and forlorn. St. Peter's Plaza in the elite part of downtown is comparatively well kept and used for afternoon strolls or recreation by residents. Mayor Jarvis had allocated 160 acres of green space (four blocks by four blocks) for a park in the center of the city as long ago as 1868, which remained empty for decades. In 1937, Martin High School was constructed on the land. A few other reserved spaces for either parks or plazas were turned into functional buildings such as a fire station or a baseball field.

The Spanish plazas have the traditional kiosk in the middle while the sidewalks are graced with benches and beautiful trees, creating additional spots for visitors to sit and chat. People still remember walking or jogging around Jarvis Plaza while an orchestra would be playing in the kiosk following the old Mexican tradition. According to history professor *Justin Taylor*, everything from concerts to public hangings took place in Jarvis Plaza. The hangings occurred mainly during the Civil War, and the last one was in 1912. Most residents have more pleasant memories associated with the plaza. According to one respondent, *Sylvia Bruni*, in the earlier part of twentieth century, Thursday and Sunday concerts or *serenatas* used to take place at the plaza, and young girls and their suitors had the social sanction to meet and flirt. Young men and women strolled in opposite directions, and occasionally a young man would offer a flower to the girl he admired, and she might reciprocate by wearing the flower in her hair.

The custom of offering flowers to the Virgin Mary on Sunday evenings in the month of May took place at the plazas. *Millie Allen* remembers procuring fresh flowers to present them to the Virgin Mary after a half-hour procession and then playing at the plaza outside the church as a young girl. The plazas served struggling artists or street vendors when they were being utilized as venues for congregation. San Agustín Plaza used to be the center for Easter parades and a number of Catholic ceremonies that have withered away. In the 1970s there were many political rallies at the plazas by small groups allied against the dominant patron system that ruled the municipality. Vendors selling tacos and other types of food used to be a permanent feature of the plazas before the city installed the permit system and started denying permits to small businesses in the 1980s. After downtown lost its allure, Jarvis Plaza became a refuge for homeless people and a waiting area for the adjacent Greyhound station. *Yvonne Sims* recalls participating in a Feed the Homeless initiative by TAMIU that took place on Jarvis Plaza in 2015.

Downtown Laredo was not only the cultural and economic magnet until the 1970s but also the location of the elite neighborhoods. The original core of the city was surrounded by commercial zones, while the outer layer consisted of residential neighborhoods expanding to the north of the city. Michael Yoder and R. La Perriére de Gutiérrez conclude that over time Laredo's urban geography became distinct from Spanish cities and now resembles the urban pattern found in other American cities. The inner-city zone surrounding the central business district (CBD) contains residential neighborhoods, but unlike the desirable neighborhoods in proximity to the plazas, they are mainly working class. Historically, barrios have accommodated a wide array of lifestyles, socioeconomic levels, and land uses, but El Azteca and Santo Niño, the two barrios near the CBD, have been converted into socially homogeneous working-class barrios.[7] The residential parts of downtown, which survived the economic collapse of the 1980s, thus remain very mixed with both historic districts and poor neighborhoods.

The formation of downtown neighborhoods is tied to the history and success of railroads in this region. The construction used local brick, an industry that flourished here, instead of lumber. Brick kilns were closed down when they started burning tires, which produced black smoke. The old buildings in downtown bear the mark of history in their architecture, ranging from adobe homes made of sandstone and covered with stucco to elaborate Spanish architectural prototypes. *Vera Gabriel* feels surrounded by history in her downtown home. Standing on her porch, she narrates:

> It was here that the gun battle in the downtown area occurred and Dr. Wilcox walked outside and ended up getting shot. This house was built in 1890. They were all military leaders and on the Confederate side in the Civil War. This is really an immigrant neighborhood and every house has the stamp of a different country because of the merchant class that lived in this area. You have French style bungalows and little green homes side by side. People recognize the African American experience here, how we had Buffalo Soldiers and a black tabernacle down the street. I wish people would appreciate more about this part of Laredo.

Downtown buildings have lived through continuous reincarnations. Hamilton Hotel has been converted into a nonprofit that rents apartments to the elderly. Plaza Hotel is now part of the BBVA bank system. The old county jail has been torn down, and the new jail has replaced the building that belonged to Texas Harvest. *Thomas Jeffrey* sadly notes that the city has done little to protect the historic buildings and beautiful plazas. Webb County Heritage Foundation is protecting historical resources by maintaining an archive that is a repository of both official and personal memoirs. It manages the Republic of the Rio Grande Museum along with two other landmark buildings. Historian *Justin Taylor* explains that the absence of gentrification has permitted the retention of beautiful houses in the downtown even if they have not been properly preserved. The downtown residential area has escaped gentrification because of spatial limitations and the lack of sharply escalating real estate values common to other metropolitan areas.

Neil Smith identifies gentrification as the new norm of inequality that reshapes both housing and the labor market.[8] The lack of gentrification in

Laredo has allowed the poor to live very close to the exclusive neighborhood of St. Peter's, but the city has been reluctant to improve the condition of the degraded housing stock in the adjacent barrios, which were detached by I-35 and remain spatially invisible. The new elite neighborhoods burgeoned on the north side as well as farther away on Mines Road, thirty minutes to an hour from the city center. Zoning or even city planning often carries a hidden agenda to preserve the interests of the powerful.[9] For Laredo, lack of zoning has made it possible for the underserved colonias to exist just outside the periphery of the city but close enough to provide an essential labor supply. Dearth of concerted planning and a gung ho, prodeveloper attitude have resulted in diverse new residential districts, ranging from upscale to working class, popping up wherever land is available. As part of the desire for affordable housing in Viva Laredo, the city has enticed developers to construct affordable housing in the mostly barren southern edge along Highway 83. Both United Independent School District (UISD) and Laredo College (LC) have opened new campuses in these neighborhoods. Now that the southern tip of the city is joined by the impressive Cuatro Vientos highway, residential districts and various urban amenities have emerged to absorb the middle and working-class populace.

While small merchants and vendors were kicked out of the plazas in Laredo in the 1980s, Nuevo Laredo sustains its plazas with crowds of passersby exercising or lounging, eating snacks from food sellers, and enjoying arts and crafts by local artists who set up tents surrounding the plazas. Only a few miles from Laredo, one can encounter mariachi bands or local artists drawing sketches. Birds prefer these plazas because there is enough for them to nibble on in contrast to the austere Laredo plazas. Christina Jiménez provides us the example of how street vendors in urban Mexico fought with the state and elite merchants to gain the right to be on the streets and sell their merchandise, and thereby to claim the public spaces. She highlights downtown plazas as the prominent crossroads of such conflicts.[10] The political climate, rural-to-urban migration patterns, economic pressures, and zoning laws are obviously different in the two countries, but how these differences define public spaces is visible in the downtown plazas of Laredo versus those in Nuevo Laredo. The current downtown revival effort, though associated with the language of cleaning up the image, has left alone the homeless people sleeping on the benches or the poor who squat idly in the plazas, often waiting for a Greyhound bus.

Laredo appears a passive place to *Vera Gabriel*, who grew up in Chicago. She asserts, "The community lacks a voice, with its top-down arrangement. I got involved in St. Peter's Historic Neighborhood Association[11] and pushed the city to take a number of actions such as issuing parking permits to accommodate downtown residents. It was very difficult to approach the city council. The city has designed master plans but does not implement them properly." The association started having different events each month—such as storytelling sessions, plant exchanges, and movie nights at the outdoor plazas—to form connections between neighbors. In contrast to the other plazas, St. Peter's Plaza remains a lively public space for residents who cherish the flocks of parakeets that have claimed this particular location for years.

Almost everyone agrees that Laredo historically has lacked green spaces, but its plazas, ranches, and easy access to Nuevo Laredo's public parks have made up for that deficiency. A lot of social activity took place at family ranches and Lake Casa Blanca State Park, which was developed in the 1950s as a county park, using the lake as a reservoir for the golf course. It eventually became a state park with one of the highest per capita usages on the weekend of any state park in Texas. *Giselle Lamar* remembers that going out to the ranches after church on Sunday was a common practice, as everyone had a relative who had a ranch. There would be potlucks with games such as three-legged races and sack races. Having barbecues at Lake Casa Blanca during Easter was also a tradition.

From the 1900s until well into the 1980s, the downtown along with Nuevo Laredo was a thriving cultural mecca. Laredo offered movies and music that complemented the vibrant nightlife in Nuevo Laredo. The colorful downtown contained the Royal, Tivoli, Azteca, and Plaza theaters. *Millie Allen* experienced her transformational moment when she saw the Beatles movie *A Hard Day's Night* along with a screaming audience packing Plaza Theater. As an avid moviegoer, *Ria Sandoval* used to diligently visit Plaza Theater three days a week—Friday, Saturday, and Sunday. As she remembers, "Often, I would be all alone in the entire theater as the downtown was already past its glory days. I felt like a VIP, having the complete theater to myself. I will never forget seeing *The Rocky Horror Picture Show* at Plaza Theater, its last hurrah before shutting down." There was a drive-in movie theater called Bordertown where, because it was beside a playground, one could watch a film straddling a swing or a merry-go-round. The downtown took pride in record stores, a bookstore, and various restaurants ranging from French cuisine to *panaderias* and small family-run restaurants. The continuation to more eateries, *mercados*, and bars with live music seemed seamless across the bridge. *Jill Webb* had heard stories about Nuevo Laredo's Cadillac Bar and its famous gin fizz from her grandmother. Fond memories of the tack room and the drink with an orange peel that was set on fire and how it curled were cherished and shared across generations in her family.

In the days before television, perambulating in downtown in the evenings when the weather cooled down was an important ritual. *Charles Fox* mentions walking around the track of Ryan Elementary School in the Heights, where evening promenades were common for families. Laredoans identify social intercourse with the organic congregations assembling around the plazas and the religious events where everyone participated with full vigor. Walking down the paved section of San Bernardo Avenue to the water fountains at Bruni Plaza, which shot out multicolored sprays with changing patterns, was a popular practice. Children played on the lawns and adults rested on the benches while peacocks strolled by well into the 1980s. In this friendly society, the streets were safe, and children's playgrounds did not require much adult supervision. Children climbing trees, riding bikes, going out to get ice cream, or running to the magazine store to get comic books were common sights in the neighborhood. The plazas functioned as bright public spaces where people hung around and did window shopping in the bustling stores around them. Since residents in the inner city now tend to be poor (except in the celebrated St. Peter's district), the nocturnal congregation is more feared than appreciated. Compared to the vast seashore in Corpus Christi or the huge city parks in Austin, almost all the avenues for entertainment became privately owned after the collapse of downtown.

Downtown lost its gravitas during the contraction of the economy and never regained its stature even when Laredo evolved into a major trade seat. The beautiful grid that underlies downtown was rudely sundered by I-35. Along with the freeway, the preference for suburban life flourished, and less dense residential housing evolved in the northern sector. The south end lies along the Rio Grande, where residential neighborhoods have lost their past glory and bustling marketplaces have been swallowed by a busy trade route for trucks. Interstate 35 recapitulates the story of spatial growth for Laredo: the original planning of the settlement gave in to conventional American suburban design as the interstate reached the newer and more affluent parts of the city. Most of the entertainment venues were constructed in these new neighborhoods, shifting resource allocation away from the inner city.

As the city grew in the early part of the twentieth century, a north–south divide that was both economic and cultural started to take shape. The most elite neighborhood evolved in the Heights area because of proximity to Mercy Hospital (originally founded in 1894, and now sitting abandoned for more than twenty years) and the doctors settling there. At the end of the twentieth century, sparked by trade and especially after NAFTA, most residential and commercial growth occurred in the north, away from the city center, displaying a more pronounced cultural as well as economic divide. The discrepancy between street names is a reflection of the north–south rift. As mentioned before, downtown street names commemorate saints (north–south) and generals (east–west), but streets in the north demonstrate a tendency to depart from local history, as they are often named after trees that may not grow in this part of Texas (dogwood) or fanciful history (King Arthur's Court/Camelot Drive). All the new institutions (except perhaps for TAMIU) that have been built try to escape from past lineages. The north is home to more restaurants and cafés, and the busier Mall del Norte is located here as well. Sames Auto Arena, although privately owned, is emerging as the new communal space on this side.

The withering away of downtown was not only the result of shifting economic flows but also a consequence of local government policies stripping investment from central city infrastructure. The fact that without the bridge and trade revenues collected from downtown, Laredo would be just another dust bowl was hardly a consideration in local planning and policies. *Charles Vega* remembers that the city had $21 million in reserve funds, and despite the economic downturn of 2007, was able to raise it to $42 million, which elevated the credit rating to AA. In spite of available resources, downtown was in a dilapidated state by then. It suffered by being divested of resources and unable to attract thriving businesses despite being a major trade junction. Except for preserving a few seminal buildings, there has been almost no attempt to capitalize on the cultural assets of downtown as with the Mercado in San Antonio, which is structured like a Mexican marketplace and attracts large numbers of tourists from around the country. Similar artifacts are available in Laredo but only in haphazardly situated shops on San Bernardo, where the cheaper cost of such merchandise is the main attraction rather than the celebration of Mexican heritage that takes place in San Antonio.

The city is warming up to the appealing features of public art, sculptures, and murals, all of which form connections, initiate new thinking about identity, and project a more appealing portrait of the city. In 2018 the Fine Arts and Culture Commission approved the Mural Arts Grants Program and called for artists to compete in beautifying Laredo and upholding its unique identity through their work.[12] Public art fosters tourism and is an effective tool to fight against the negative picture of the city. It is growing exponentially in Laredo. The city's Visit Laredo page now has a dedicated section that showcases the growing number of murals by local artists, almost entirely funded by the city.[13] At the Cultura Beer Garden in 2017, when local artist Poncho Santos installed an art piece that proclaimed "I love U Chingos," the site quickly emerged as a popular selfie spot, and the message was placed on merchandise such as T-shirts, mugs, and sandals, making it an iconic statement about Laredo.[14] The framing of public spaces with murals depicting Mexican ancestry and culture is another way of claiming the cityscape. Instead of urban graffiti denoting discontent, murals signify reclamation of a place as it undergoes changes that symbolize pride.

On the cultural front, Laredo Center for the Arts and Laredo Little Theater offer valuable venues for interaction. Laredo Center for the Arts—situated in archetypical San Agustín Plaza, the building that lodged the first city government—has gone through some fundamental changes. Although historically it was funded by rich benefactors, it has evolved into a more inclusive common space. The center was started by a couple of artists in 1983 after securing the building that had been the city hall and was vacant because the city hall had moved to its present location. The building had also housed the first library, a police station, and even a skating rink upstairs. The remodeled skating rink has become an exhibition space, with art classes for children held downstairs. There is a used bookstore on the premises, which for a number of years was the only bookstore in Laredo. Art and yoga classes are held in the mezzanine area. There are live shows hosting out-of-town artists and public events on a regular basis just as the classes for children are also offered routinely. *Ria Sandoval*, the young director and Laredo native, has turned the nonprofit into more of a communal space with yoga and dance classes and painting and photography exhibitions. She believes, "Spaces for arts and culture are integral to mental health on the border. The image of the city can change, and tourists get drawn in when people take pride in the city and get involved in creating the image." Along with the artistic flavors of the town, local music, dance, and food are incorporated in the events. Local mariachi bands, the Laredo String Quartet, and Mexican folk dancers grace the beautiful podium or the spacious courtyard during Cinco de Mayo or Día de los Muertos celebrations. Art can be assimilated in daily life in many different ways. Laredo Center for the Arts believes in this motto and is trying to introduce this critical element in people's lives from an early age. The center has become more of an event venue than a showcase for art, but this also makes it available to more intensive open-door engagement. An exhibit showcasing "the other border wall,"[15] which challenged the political narrative by presenting creative and communal sharing of border spaces, was well attended and appreciated.

Laredo Little Theater is over a hundred years old and has gone through several incarnations. *John Allen* reminisces about a couple of octogenarians (Hortense and Stanley Keilson) who revived the theater in the 1960s: "Stanley was trained as an actor in New York and landed in Laredo to teach at Laredo Junior College in the 1950s. He gravitated toward local artist Hortense, a music major from Julliard, and together they revived the existing small theater by moving it to the air force base. At the time Laredo was blessed to have other artistic talents, both homegrown, such as Bob Warren,[16] and newcomers to town." Allen claims that despite having a much smaller population than San Antonio, the theatrical community in Laredo is more robust as it is concentrated through the sole vehicle of Laredo Theater Guild International (LTGI). It has a live orchestra and an amazing set, and actors and artists from New York have performed here. The choreographer who arranged *Hamlet* for the stage in Laredo ended up choreographing Lin-Manuel Miranda's *Hamilton* in Puerto Rico. The international gala of *Man of La Mancha* was very successful as an event as well as a fundraiser. The theater is involved with LISD and tries to instill interest in art among students with plays by Shakespeare that they read in class. The average reading scores of senior students improved by 40 percent after watching the plays. Allen feels that a vibrant arts community is a must to attract major corporations to the city.

Laredo reveals an unsurprising trajectory of elevating elite preferences and neglecting needy regions. When downtown was booming, the adjacent neighborhoods to the south benefited from economic and cultural infrastructure, but when downtown business collapsed and the area became abandoned, poor communities in the vicinity were irreparably damaged. The spatial geography of Laredo was arranged in terms of economic functions, and as downtown became impoverished, the "south side" came to denote destitute neighborhoods. *Samantha Taft* grew up in a financially secure community, geographically located in the south but considered central because of its prospering businesses. All the hotels and motels in Laredo stood along San Bernardo Avenue, some with elaborate courtyards or open spaces or enormous lawns like Cactus Courts, nestled next to eateries like Sal's Pizza and other popular restaurants. Hotel Evelyn had two ponds with goldfish, and Taft used to ride her bike to feed them. The hotels would all be packed with tourists and scarcely an empty room was available on weekends. Traders stayed on in Laredo when they came here to conduct business and enjoyed the local flavors. People from all over South Texas, even from cities like Corpus Christi, came to the Jamboozie Festival. The same people from the Valley or Corpus Christi are wary of Laredo now, or more precisely, Nuevo Laredo's bad reputation. The speedy growth of freight trade, incited by NAFTA, has turned the commercial zone that once hosted people into a back alley for trucks, with a proliferation of stores like Auto Zone and cheap motels where truckers can get a few hours of rest before jumping back on the road.

Sociability remained conspicuous in south-side barrios, with small coffee shops presenting live music and poetry until the late 1990s, when fast-food chains finally gobbled up the cozy down-home spots. Coffee shops in the southern quarters, such as Espumas Pub & Café, that used to have live performances every week have closed down. This trend is not exclusive to Laredo and reflects the nationwide urban transformation, but what is notable is that new cafés that sprang up in the north, such as The Treehouse or Flip Flop Coffee Shop, have struggled to survive for the long haul. Meanwhile, older cafés such as Bolillos, Caffe Dolce, and Organic Man Coffee Trike, which relocated from downtown to the north, have been more successful in sustaining their presence. Food trucks are now visible both in downtown and in the up-and-coming Shiloh neighborhood adjacent to North Central Park. Even though new restaurants tend to select the north for their location, a few older establishments still exist to serve their loyal customer base in the south. Pan American Courts, a long-existing motel on San Bernardo, has added an arts complex and food trucks to cater to young people and has retained its landmark stature. Frontera Beer and Wine Garden now has a restaurant, two food trucks, and two art galleries on its premises. It hosts an open-air midtown market (El Tianguis) every second Saturday of the month. The courtyard has evolved into a space for political and cultural gatherings, as voter mobilization drives, election watch parties, and meetings of various activist organizations take place there. This space has filled a void as many other public venues have blocked access to local residents.

Over the years, private businesses have gradually usurped traditional public spaces. One of the most cherished locations for different groups to come together and celebrate was the downtown civic center. *Rosalie Wright* was disappointed when the civic center could not be preserved and was demolished to make space for the new LISD building. The civic center used to host community gatherings, including Thanksgiving and Christmas meals for people too poor to afford them, for which *Matilda Roy* used to volunteer each year. *Jack Hughes* remembers attending events where people would dance together when downtown was still joined with other neighborhoods through local avenues like San Bernardo before I-35 dislocated the barrios. The dismembering of localities through railroads or highways is an American ritual of urban planning affecting poor, especially minority, districts.[17] In the more integrated northern section, some of the events, such as the Thanksgiving dinner, have moved to Sames Auto Arena and are still hosted by H-E-B. Now that the venue has shifted to a private location, the composition of participants has changed. Similarly, the small food stores in downtown have also failed to survive even though they not only served their own-

FIGURE 20 Jarvis Plaza. Webb County Heritage Foundation.

ers' economic interests but also made the area vibrant by providing space and a reason for people to hang around.

Annals of Community Engagement

Laredo's residents are proud of their fraternal ties despite a hierarchical social structure and political domination that have captured and controlled most resources for upward mobility. Civic engagement in Laredo has flourished in small clubs, churches, and nonprofit organizations. The Boys and Girls Club, Junior Chamber of Commerce, Youth Council, and various church groups have provided opportunities to meet new people and cultivate team spirit among children. *Felipe Calderon* remembers the opportunity he had to volunteer for the Special Olympics as a middle school student. Much of the support came through religious initiatives such as the Sisters of Mercy or the Holding Institute, both fighting against poverty since the nineteenth century. True to the tenacious barrio-centered society, people have a history of mobilizing against adversities. Laredo has a rich history of activism but the success stories are rarely celebrated.

Before the existence of government services or various nonprofit agencies helping the homeless, the famished, or the abused, Mercy Hospital was the refuge for the downtrodden in underserved Laredo, where many people lack health insurance to this day. The Sisters of Mercy has been a part of the community since 1894. The first four sisters who came from Ireland in that year weren't even nurses but were invited by physicians and a bishop to initiate organized health care. They had $440 in their pockets, but in two weeks they opened a small hospital because they got along well with the people. The much-awaited Water Park has recently been named after the Sisters of Mercy, which *Cesar Villarreal* appreciates as an apt gesture for their long contribution to the people's welfare.

In contrast to other community organizations or nonprofits, Azteca Economic Development and Preservation Corporation (AEDPC) grew out of resistance to land use and urban policies. The nonprofit organization was founded to counter the city's takeover of a working-class neighborhood, El Azteca, to turn it into a commercial zone. In the late 1970s and early 1980s, the neighborhood was marked off for redevelopment by the Urban Development Action Grant program, essentially a form of gentrification. The grant came from the U.S. Department of Housing and Urban Development

(HUD) but would have been channeled through the City of Laredo's Community Development agency. *Rodrique Taylor*, who grew up in Al Azteca, was working in Philadelphia in the 1970s, but he was so disturbed about the impending fate of his neighborhood that he moved back to Laredo and started initiating public meetings. After failing to get any grants to protect the illustrious neighborhood, he formed a nonprofit that documented all the notable properties and submitted their nomination to the federal government. The organization went into full swing by the late 1980s with the aim of getting the neighborhood enrolled on the National Register of Historic Places (NRHP), which was accomplished in the early 1990s. Eminent domain provisions are now much stronger and more difficult to fight against. As commercial property earns more revenue, turning residential property into commercial property paves the way for easy expropriation by paying off private property owners fair market value, which is determined by the federal government.

Forming an association and getting designated as a National Historic Landmark District may have protected the Azteca neighborhood from demolition but not necessarily from urban decay. Although 133 properties were identified as historically significant, many have been lost through poor maintenance because property owners are under no obligation without formal assignment as a historic building by the city or some other political entity. As of now, there are fifty-six low-income housing units under the purview of AEDPC, enabling low-earning residents who qualify under the guidelines to rent these units. AEDPC maintains an office to develop affordable housing, and most recently it has ventured into supportive services in the form of business loans, income tax preparation, and financial coaching for residents. The organization serves about five hundred people a year and aims to make clients stable enough to either preserve their properties or move out of dilapidated housing. Though it lacks adequate funding, it has assistance from the city and the county as well as from the federal government's housing agencies. Besides providing services to the present occupants, it has kept the importance of the neighborhood uppermost in the minds of both nonresidents and the political leadership as it comes and goes at both the city and county levels.

The Holding Institute[18] has stood tall with past glories since the 1860s, established when Abraham Lincoln was president. Officially named in 1880 after an Episcopal missionary, Nannie Emory Holding, who was sent from

Kentucky, the institute was originally founded to provide academic resources to Mexican American children who were not allowed into regular public schools in Laredo. Jovita Idár, the famous scribe, educator, and social activist, graduated from here. Idár was a journalist and later the editor of *La Crónica*, a periodical established by her father that focused on the plight of Mexican Americans. She also served as the president of La Liga Femenil Mexicanista, the League of Mexican Women. She criticized President Woodrow Wilson for sending U.S. military forces to the border in 1914. The Texas Rangers attacked the newspaper *El Progreso*, which published her essay, whereupon she bravely confronted the Rangers, citing First Amendment protections. Although her life was spared, the press was destroyed in retaliation. Idár went on to continue her career of writing about Mexican American issues in *Evolución*, a new weekly journal she established. She eventually settled in San Antonio, but her struggles and fame are rooted in Laredo.[19]

The mission of the Holding Institute has always been to help the underserved. It is now a full community center with over twenty programs, offering everything from food, health care, housing, emergency shelter, hygiene counseling, and medication assistance to first-time mothers. *Mike Socorro* reports that his clients include the working poor, those who have multiple jobs, yet neither do they earn enough to buy groceries to last until their next paycheck nor do they qualify for help as they are not unemployed. With an annual operating budget of about $133,000, and donations from various faith-based institutions, the organization provides the invisible poor with basic needs. Laredo has a steady poverty rate that traps a third of its population in a cycle of immiseration with low-paid jobs. *Cecily D. Vega* taught GED classes at the institute and was impressed by the staff's dedication and motivation. The institute addresses immigration, welfare, and housing issues in conjunction with Bethany House, a coordinating agency providing food and shelter to the homeless. Deferred Action for Childhood Arrivals (DACA) workshops have been routinely conducted at the institute. A pilot project to prepare lists of handymen such as carpenters and make connections with anyone who needs such services is underway. The next goal is to build a community garden to deal with the food shortage blotting downtown's food desert. Also under construction is a hydroponic garden with raised beds and solar panels in the backyard, because food security is the first step to self-sufficiency. A communal laundromat (with only a washer) will be erected beside the garden, where people can socialize while they dry their clothes on the clotheslines. The sitting area will also have Wi-Fi availability, which is lacking in many homes.

A new group that aims to hold the city council accountable is Our Laredo,[20] formed in 2014. The transparency organization participates in city council meetings with pertinent questions demonstrating deep research. At the same time, it educates citizens about corruption, negligence, and abuse of power in order to build pressure. When the city proposed an additional fee for road maintenance, the organization galvanized residents and put a stop to it, posing tough questions about the existing funds for road maintenance. It also halted the city from building a jail costing $130 million. Founder *Van Vincent* claims that Our Laredo has been busy exposing a lot of crime and corruption. Getting licenses from the city is a problem, and fees keep increasing every which way they can. Water fees have gone up tremendously, even though immediately after the increases there have been consecutive citywide water boiling notices. These ongoing concerns are not new, but the growing number of people attending city council meetings and the heated debates that often take place on the council floor are a novelty.

Red Wing United[21] existed for three years and was made up of young people from Laredo who were willing to help out people (distributing food from their co-op garden, establishing a community fridge, giving out blankets and heaters by flashlight during winter storms) and raise pointed questions with the city government (why does Laredo undergo a water boil notice every couple of years?). *Alex Mead* is proud of the three-hundred-plus crowd at city hall who showed up for a protest against racial injustice in an effort to solidify connections with other minority communities. They raised awareness about past labor movements and critiqued the investments of the city in jails, weapons, and militarized police vehicles as opposed to poverty alleviation or even basic infrastructure. They also ran a community garden and stored the harvest in a community fridge for poverty-stricken people.

The Laredo Immigrant Alliance was set up to protect DACA recipients, arrange workshops for legal advice, and assist with filling out necessary forms. It even helped with the high costs of application. Lawyers from Austin came and held DACA clinics on a pro bono basis. DACA recipient *Sara Calderon* only had to cover the nominal amount of $195, a fraction of the excessive government fees. Coordinating with Laredo College (LC) and TAMIU, the alliance tried to raise awareness of the plight of Dreamers throughout the community. It established healing circles and deportation protection teams to provide assistance with active cases. This nonprofit, growing with volunteers and sympathizers, often responds to calls from similar out-of-state organizations.

The most politically charged group that has emerged is the #NoBorder-Wall Coalition,[22] formed to challenge the negative depiction of the border by the Trump administration. After the declaration of border areas as a national emergency, a bunch of local citizens organically coalesced in front of the Rio Grande, holding a sign, "Where is the national emergency?" From this public protest, a small team emerged that met regularly to discuss how to thwart the administration's border wall. It involved stakeholders who were in danger of losing their private property, those who were worried about the environmental impact on the river and its effect on local residents, and those who were horrified at the thought of a concrete wall bifurcating the historic downtown. *Charles Fox* explains how this coalition assembled some of the most progressive thinkers in Laredo. Starting from participating in city council meetings to bringing forth resolutions and holding public awareness campaigns through protests, the team joined Earthjustice along with private property owners to sue the Trump administration, even persuading the city to join the lawsuit. They arranged the first-ever local MLK rally in 2020, publicized as "I have a dream: No border wall." In mid-2020, they painted a huge mural in front of the federal courthouse labeled "Defund the Wall/Fund Our Future," which won a prestigious art award.[23] The alliance has created a space for people from very different realms to meet and articulate claims for their voices to be heard. Members of the coalition are now running for statewide public offices. After two years of dogged pursuit, which put this group at the heart of the border wall resistance, in July 2021 the Biden administration canceled the contracts for the border wall in the Laredo Sector, although Texas Governor Abbott has threatened to use funds from the Texas Department of Transportation to build the wall, at least partially.[24]

Downtown Revival in Viva Laredo

The comprehensive master plan of the city, Viva Laredo, was adopted in 2017 after two years of public participation. The process of coming up with the city plan was unique and dedicated to reflecting citizens' preferences. *Sophia Brown* was involved with the public outreach for Viva Laredo for almost a year, which involved bringing different blocs of people to the planning ta-

FIGURE 21 Jovita Idár. Webb County Heritage Foundation.

ble. Everything from transportation to zoning to poverty came under discussion, with widespread public concurrence. *Alex Mead* was also part of the Viva Laredo public outreach initiative, so he got to know the movers and shakers in the city firsthand. Extensive meetings were held at Hotel La Posada on the topics of arts and culture, economic development, and trade and logistics. A large number of the new green spaces and bike paths, derived from Viva Laredo, are in fact a result of public insistence. People unanimously agreed to restore and preserve the downtown. Christine Boyer believes that older city centers are repositories of collective memory,[25] and it is evident that the nostalgia Laredo's residents feel indeed hinges around their downtown.

Leonie Sandercock situates "story" at the center of the planning process as a way to include those who will be affected. Stories bring discrete groups together, help resolve conflicts, and generate meaningful participation between constituents and planners. In diverse populations, stories are often the most evocative expression of divergent experiences. Planners have a difficult task detecting the defining story of a locality amid neglected, nonverbal, and concealed narratives.[26] The planning process in Laredo has illuminated a central theme in Laredo's stories—its splendid downtown. There has been overwhelming agreement among participants about the city's next order of business: they want to revive their one and only city center. The collective memory of residents unwaveringly focuses on the downtown as the backdrop for social engagement and cultural identity. This kind of memory is often referred to as "place memory," and it connects identity with cultural landscapes.[27] The architectural vestiges of the plazas and brick roads contain memories of urban encounters and preserve lived experiences as part of the identity for Laredo's residents.

Viva Laredo was unanimously adopted by the city council on September 18, 2017, after a two-year-long inclusive process involving the entire population. The master plan went beyond urban design and attempted to enunciate the needs of the people in the built structures and the processes it would generate. The focus on quality of life is a reflection of the counterclaim expressed by the people. The planning team studied previous plans, city ordinances, and land development regulations as well as the physical, social, and economic characteristics of Laredo. A public charette including intensive, multiday, collaborative workshops was held from September 27 to October 6, 2016, along with press conferences, town hall meetings, and a New Urbanism Film Festival.[28] Boyer has criticized city planning as a mode of disciplinary control,[29] but Laredo's comprehensive planning process departs from the usual top-down model and highlights the needs of residents as they push the city to change its development priorities. Fourteen working groups made up of community members were established, each focusing on a different topic of concern for the city: urban planning, economic development, mobility and transportation, housing, greenspace, recreation and landscape, infrastructure, environment and natural resources, education, health and wellness, international border relations, logistics and international trade, technology and communications, and philanthropy and think tanks. The groups discussed how they wanted to see Laredo evolve over time. The common themes that emerged from the groups were to create attractive and walkable destinations, to make the downtown economically self-sufficient, to plan new and improved public spaces, and to do it all while maintaining a prosperous but still affordable city.[30]

The level of grassroots involvement and citizen collaboration was novel for Laredo, claims *Karla Garcia*, one of the participants. The exercise served as a platform not only for people to come together but also to vocalize their wishes with a growing sense of ownership toward the city. People with decision-making power actually listened and served as conduits rather than taking the lead on the planning process. The comprehensive city plan was presented to the public, and an overwhelming majority (92 percent) of participants supported the plan. Viva Laredo is available online and is written in accessible language that is uncommon in the realm of planning documents, which often use abstract language.[31] Boyer notes that the primary role of city planning is to preserve land values and regulate land uses.[32] To its credit, Viva Laredo prioritizes mobility, health, sustainability, and quality of life as opposed to the kind of myopic economic development that primarily conserves land values.

Viva Laredo is imagined as a living platform that begins an open-ended conversation about the future.[33] Each section describes underlying conditions and citizen concerns followed by strategies, goals, and policies. The Laredo Center for Urban Agriculture and Sustainability, tasked by the plan with inner city revitalization and historic preservation, is also located in downtown. The collective dream is to make Laredo vibrant and progressive. The ambitious plan, however, needs to be fully executed to turn Laredo into a dynamic municipality. So far the city has focused on new business development that has produced renewed nightlife in bars and restaurants but has been relatively negligent toward providing services for the residential section of downtown. The surest way to permanently rejuvenate the downtown is to improve the socioeconomic condition of the people who still live there. As *Felipe Calderon* notes, "The only way to have sustainable growth is to create well-paid jobs in Laredo." Similarly, *Elena Cruz* feels that "local businesses should be part of the solution to economic disparity that prevails in Laredo."

The proposed land-use patterns focus on walkability, mixed-income housing, and setting aside land in each neighborhood for civic purposes.[34] Part of downtown has already been made pedestrian friendly with brick-paved alleys and more parking spaces. The Aldo Tatangelo Walkway is a shaded pathway connecting Iturbide Street and San Agustín Plaza.[35] This plaza is now the heart of downtown revitalization efforts, with Iturbide Street being revamped as one of the main arteries of the arts district stretching to Laredo Center for the Arts. Before being moved to The Outlet Shoppes, the farmers market at Jarvis Plaza injected lively crowds in the forlorn square. St. Peter's Plaza, located in the historic district, is now surrounded by a few antique shops as well as the only bookstore in Laredo. A Texas Historical Landmark plaque to honor Jovita Idár has also been installed in St. Peter's Plaza. The restaurants and bars are all getting a facelift amid meaningful assistance from the city to attract local youth and tourists.

Restoring the downtown to its previous grandeur by preserving eclectic buildings, repurposing vacant structures by rezoning or by revising rehabilitation codes, and transforming downtown into a destination for entertainment with adequate parking and easy access to the inner city are the cornerstones of the citywide plan.[36] Community gardens and urban forestry have been included in the urban design, with emphasis on their relation to public transportation, walkability, and civic spaces.[37] Bike routes have been proposed, and future thoroughfare plans are focused on addressing traffic congestion as well as maintaining air quality.[38] Housing policies include not only new plans but also investing in "legacy" neighborhoods and addressing homelessness.[39] Creation and expansion of wetlands, diversification of the energy portfolio, and access to water supply are the goals for sustainability, along with the inclusion of neighborhood parks and schools in the planning process.[40] Health concerns include substance abuse, obesity and chronic illnesses, lack of access to health care, lack of proper nutrition, lack of mental health facilities, and environmental hazards.[41] An unprecedented emphasis has been placed on investment in parks and equity of access to green spaces.[42] Economic development policies include entrepreneurship incubators, the promotion of regional cooperation, and greater support for smart growth.[43] Recognizing local and regional arts and culture and making them a cornerstone of Laredo's identity is the embraced policy.[44] A key concern is to maintain the alignment between Laredo and Nuevo Laredo and create a binational council on education.[45] A detailed implementation matrix has been adopted to gauge the success and failure of each of the endorsed strategies and policies.[46]

Viva Laredo is in many ways a response to the input of citizens of all ages. While most new construction has been focused on warehouses, the master plan's aim is to restore downtown in a broader sense. The component of Viva Laredo that remains the most unfulfilled so far is poor housing in and around downtown. *Rodrique Taylor*, a resident of the Azteca neighborhood adjacent to downtown, relates that in the 1970s, 60 percent of the houses had owners residing in them while 40 percent had tenants, but twenty years later the proportions started reversing so that now owners stay in only 20 percent of the houses. Without ample job opportunities providing a living wage, the original properties have been transformed into smaller rental units. People who are economically successful want to leave while the neighborhood deteriorates. *Raul Muñoz* notes that Section 8 housing brings federal tax credits and is therefore tolerated in downtown. The low-income apartments are now in other parts of the city, and the new construction often consists of the type of mixed neighborhoods that have become popular in Laredo. The abject neglect of residential and commercial spaces in and around downtown was long inscribed in policy and budget calculations (or lack thereof) since this did not interfere with trade.

After the collapse of the downtown business center, cultural and social activity started moving northward, although even in dilapidated form downtown remained the focal point of revenue because of the international bridges. The bridges on the border continued to earn the bulk of the revenue at the same time as most of the residential neighborhoods became barrios for the working poor and some of the landmark buildings were preserved for affluent residents. Having worked at the Holding Institute for three decades, *Mike Socorro* has witnessed the level of poverty in downtown firsthand. There has been some drop in the official poverty level, currently 30.6 percent,[47] but working on the frontlines of poverty alleviation and providing assistance he realizes, "Statistics do not suggest substantial improvement. What has actually happened is that there are more people than ever who are one crisis away from being poor. People who work, often having two jobs, still need emergency food. During the government shutdown in 2018, federal employees got furloughed and had to show up for groceries in office attire." Socorro's institution supports about eighty local families (roughly two hundred and fifty individuals) with groceries each week.

The city of Laredo never focused on industries to generate revenues. Compared to other border cities that fomented the growth of small local industries after NAFTA, Laredo has traditionally lacked homegrown industries. *Erin Arroyo*, who leads a small manufacturing company, complains about the disconnection between policies and economic realities. As the owner of the oldest local industry, she feels she cannot compete with national producers if she has to raise the minimum wage to her employees. As discussed in the previous chapter, her industry supplies spices to the local market as well as other cities in Texas, but she has to compete with larger companies all over the country. Laredo may have a dependable customer base, but it is only one city. The transition to a trade hub allows large industries to sell their products in Laredo but does not help local producers in any substantial way. Arroyo observes that businesses on the north side already benefit from the city's investment and hopes that tax breaks will accompany downtown revitalization plans and help struggling businesses. She also complains about the apathy and lack of professionalism of workers in Laredo as impediments to business development.

The downtown revival plan also needs to be appraised thoroughly. The same firm that was responsible for the city's comprehensive plan was the one that designed the original North Dakota pipeline.[48] Backed by his experience as a city employee, *Alex Mead* notes, "The city lacks any vision connecting its history to revival plans. Most of the urbanism projects like housing or even added bike lanes were more of an expression of where private capital wanted to flourish rather than the needs of residents. The proposed bulkhead was about economic development and bringing in federal dollars with little sympathy for border crossers despite the racial homogeneity of the city. The implicit agreement is that criminalizing and detaining refugees and having a militarized border is acceptable as long as it is good for the local economy."

Mead grew up after downtown had lost its luster, and it was never part of his life, but going to Nuevo Laredo for nightlife continued as a matter of habit for young people until the seizure of the city by the cartels in the mid-2000s. As an adult he can appreciate the uniqueness of the vintage downtown and looks forward to the reprieve provided by its appealing features. He welcomes cafés, bookstores, and yoga studios but criticizes the lack of attention to the residential part of downtown. To him, "If revitalization leads to gentrification, then the whole purpose of downtown revival will be turned on its head. Downtown Laredo has many empty lots, and the city has to attract new businesses and also make sure that the businesses remain viable. Without safe, affordable, and pleasant housing, having only entertainment venues like bars will do little to sustain the downtown. The language of development often centers around revenues and misses out on the human element." If downtown is surrounded by the impoverished communities of Chacon Creek and El Azteca, it is difficult to imagine it being prosperous in the middle of the poverty zone.

By investing so heavily in infrastructure in north Laredo, the city played a role in making the north and south diverge sharply. On the northern outskirts, the Del Mar district became part of the I-35 corridor and a dominant part of the city, while downtown was confronted with the river on one end and poor residential communities on the other. Multiple stores in downtown shut down, and the inner city became an eyesore. *Mike Socorro* observes that the overemphasis on the installation of parking meters on all the streets (free parking taking effect only after 9 p.m. instead of 7 p.m.) suggests that the revival plans are far removed from the bustling and pedestrian-friendly downtown that had organically evolved as a cultural hotbed. *Ishmael Reyes* terms the downtown revitalization a top-down process because there is no emphasis on bringing back the affordable diners and cantinas where working people were comfortable. He would like to see the preservation of archival themes involving Chicanos as the mainstay of downtown.

Trade and economic growth following NAFTA did not improve the condition of the city center, but based on the stated goals of Viva Laredo, the city wishes to invest significant resources in revitalization. With the traditional close ties to Nuevo Laredo now strained because of security issues, Laredo has become two cities in its own territory. The increasingly prosperous north resembles flourishing U.S. metropolises, while poverty and lack of conveniences are as visible in south Laredo as in poor countries. Attempts toward a holistic cultural and economic growth plan rest their hopes on downtown revitalization, but while downtown Laredo serves as a reminder of past prosperity, its function as a brisk commercial center is no longer necessary for the global trade hub that Laredo has become. The present plan for downtown restoration views it as only a functional element to expand business and entertainment, not as a place for tenable habitation.

Laredo Main Street has been set up to connect with other agencies related to downtown recovery under the umbrella of the Texas Historical Commission. Their focus is on rehabilitation of significant buildings and economic development for businesses located in the area. The nonprofit organization is separate from the city but has worked closely with it for twenty years. A lot of momentum has appeared in the downtown area converging around Cultura Beer Garden and the bars and food trucks catering to millennials. Kayaking on the Rio Grande has become a popular form of exercise. The Uni-Trade Stadium for baseball,[49] constructed in 2012, is a reflection of these initiatives, although refurbishing rundown buildings remains a slow process. *Pamela Ivan*, executive director of the organization, mentions the Tax Increment Reinvestment Zone (TIRZ) as an economic development tool to stimulate partnerships. The TIRZ extends from Scott Street in the north to the Rio Grande to the south and Santa Isabel to the west, and it includes the LC campus. The board, which is appointed by the city, has developed its plan for the first $150,000. Private businesses are part of the collective plan to turn the downtown into a pleasant walkable space with cobblestone sidewalks and all the attractive bells and whistles. The privately owned Outlet Shoppes at Laredo has painted the adjacent businesses on city streets to provide a facelift. *Elena Cruz* discusses how the city has been very cooperative with private businesses, such as coordinating various events like the half-marathon Ride of Silence (to raise awareness about injured or killed cyclists) with nonprofit entities. *Alvin Travis* believes that Viva Laredo has provided a roadmap, "neighborhood by neighborhood, centering around the vision of how people live, work, and play." The sustainability of downtown is a major concern, which is why the residential and commercial parts should be interspersed to bring down transportation and other costs. *Ria Sandoval* is happy to witness the downtown renaissance efforts, which have brought a bakery and bookstore along with bars and restaurants, back to the heart of the city, reminding her of the Glass Kitchen restaurant in the old days, or La India Packing Company, which to her is "like stepping into a piece of southern history." *Jesus Castillo* has established his bookstore in downtown and is grateful for how the city went out of its way to ease the process, even to the extent of changing its ordinance about parking.

Residents such as *Cecily D. Vega* feel elated that the city is finally investing in blighted neighborhoods in the south. It has taken a long time for the city to realize that the smarter economic goal is to raise the standard of living in all the neighborhoods. Vega grew up in a spectacular residence (Mullally House, with a sculpture of two peacocks as one of its architectural show-pieces) that her grandparents owned in downtown long before it became rundown. Her grandfather engaged in currency trading and ran a taxi company from the building. She believes that "adding green spaces and quality-of-life incentives to poorer neighborhoods is the right direction, which the city seems to be pursuing."

Creating spaces of consumption through retail and restaurants was the main source of national urban revival in the 1970s.[50] Instead of the next phase of urban revival—creating cultural sophistication through museums, arts districts, and convention centers—Laredo's downtown catered to less affluent customers. The idea of urban renewal often includes changing zoning regulations to promote mixed-use neighborhoods where retail, residential, and entertainment functions can coexist.[51] This diversity, although not in pristine shape, existed in the city center from the very beginning, but the city was unable to take advantage of the well-rounded core. Viva Laredo offers the first official recognition of the ideal features of downtown and has forced the city to adopt policies to preserve and nurture its essence. The commitment of city leaders to revive the downtown may pass muster, but the nature of the undertaking cannot entirely escape critique. A multimillion-dollar Laredo Convention Center has been built in the San Agustín historic district in the heart of downtown to revive its centrality as the cultural base of the city,[52] but its very impressive design makes no attempt to pay homage to the city's architectural heritage.[53]

The quest for affordable housing, promised in the comprehensive plan, has not targeted any of the existing working-class neighborhoods in and around downtown but has surfaced in the southern tip of the city along Highway 83. *Sam Kornosky* joined United Independent School District (UISD) when it expanded in the south side's large expanses with impressive buildings catering to the new affluent neighborhoods rather than the needy ones in and around downtown. Laredo is now growing more on the neglected south side, which has enabled UISD to expand almost without restraint. South Laredo can now lay claim to a brand-new campus of LC and the second-largest high school along with beautiful parks. Students in UISD typically have less-educated parents, so one of the challenges is to get them involved in school activities and parent-teacher meetings. *Derek Perez* sees the housing growth in Laredo as taking place at an alarming rate and concludes that much of the growth on the south side is due to the low cost of land and housing. The city has also provided a motivation package to developers to establish mixed-income complexes in the north, which is populated with middle-class residents. In these large apartment complexes, some units are rented at market rates while other units are rented to people of limited means for a portion of the rent. They are already operating at peak capacity in relatively prosperous areas where waiting lists are long.

At the very juncture when the official city plan has at last responded to local needs, the efforts at downtown resurgence have collided with the border wall projected to slice through downtown. The mayor had already proposed an alternative to Trump's wall, an eighteen-foot-high bulkhead that could be beautified to attract tourists, evoking the River Walk in San Antonio, a project in which Nuevo Laredo would participate as well. The city never wanted to part from anticipated federal dollars while the federal government also wanted amicable partners. The compromise plan would have built a bulkhead along the river with federal dollars and created recreational activities surrounding it.[54] *Russell Garray* scoffs at the idea of the bulkhead, as he believes that the federal government is simply not going to take local wish lists into consideration. He thinks that the bulkhead will end up costing much more than the wall as it will have to be built on the riverbed.

Laredo has a sad history of missing out on unique opportunities to build public spaces that could have remade the entire landscape. Local folklore claims that the River Walk that ended up being built in San Antonio was originally planned for Laredo. Earlier efforts at a master plan included an ambitious proposal to build a huge Ferris wheel in downtown, evoking the memory of the World's Fair, without eliciting any feedback from the people. That plan in the early 2000s fizzled out once the reaction to 9/11 intensified surveillance in the border areas. As of today, however, there is an ongoing plan for a Binational River Park, which is as much about beautification as it is about inner-city revitalization. The original project, River Vega, was imagined as a riverfront between the two countries, an idea that the mayor of Nuevo Laredo supported as well. The two mayors remain in agreement about the prospective plan, and even in the middle of the heightened era of security and illegal crossings, it is coming to fruition. *Felix Rivera* categorizes the River Vega project as Laredo's River Walk, which could bring back residents and tourists to downtown. With 6.2 miles allocated for recreation, the other goal of the project is to regenerate and protect the Rio Grande.[55] While national policy aims to keep people out, this local initiative tries to unite the two sides of the river. This is an example of glocalization that confronts the strong sense of nationalism that has seeped into the border discourse.

FIGURE 22 Azteca neighborhood mural. Webb County Heritage Foundation.

Opening Up Spaces of Interaction

After Mayor Jarvis (1868), *Travis Mace* credits Mayor Aldo Tatangelo (1978–90) for having a vision for Laredo that included paved streets and green spaces. The new thrust toward viable public spaces is without doubt a manifestation of citizens' stipulations as articulated in Viva Laredo. Only recently Laredo stood at the bottom of Texas in terms of green spaces per capita. *Kayla Hall* asserts that Laredo now has more park space per capita than any other city in Texas. The city has been aggressive in buying land along the river from Laredo College South Campus to Father McNaboe Park. More than 80 percent of this land is owned by the city, which is creating the seven-mile-long Chacon Creek Hike & Bike Trail with great possibilities. The less affluent south side has made use of various grants for underserved populations. Residents have voted for a basketball stadium and a sports complex with their taxes. Bike trails as well as other options for exercise—such as walking, jogging, and yoga—were identified in Viva Laredo as key quality-of-life indicators. The master plan consists of thirty to forty miles of bike lanes around the city. Laredo College already has a hike and bike trail that will be connected to Chacon Creek. But trails across from LC near the border have lost the usual joggers. A Border Patrol officer suggested to *Jose Diaz* that he should not be at Father McNaboe Park because it is a dangerous place, which scared his wife.

Along with bigger parks, pocket parks with playgrounds are on the rise, and almost all such parks are experiencing heavy usage. The park at Independence Hills is located at one of the highest elevations in Laredo. *Alvin Travis* affirms that the city is investing a lot of money in public places, with one of the biggest budget allocations dedicated to the Parks and Recreation Services Department. *Sam Kornosky* gives the city credit for creating parks in different districts and says it is almost as if the council members were competing with each other to see which district can acquire the most. Relocating from a northern neighborhood to the Cuatro Vientos area, his quality of life has not worsened by any measure. He can bike and walk in the south-side parks, enjoying a healthy lifestyle and being able to go to safe areas for exercise and leisure. *Nina Vargas* is proud of Bartlett Park and its new amphitheater, the first one in Laredo. The covered basketball court was expensive but added an open space for both youth and adults so they can engage in different activities to express themselves. The quaint pond in the middle of the park attracts waterfowl. The city is actively trying to make these spaces more enjoyable for people to stay there longer.

At the heart of the new green spaces is North Central Park, a 125-acre floodplain that offers diverse recreational options and is widely used. *Gary Bell*, the county commissioner who spearheaded the project, narrates the complex story of motivating property owners to sell to the city as opposed to private developers. Acquiring the land for the park involved working with other commissioners and taking advantage of two landowners in conflict by persuading them both to sell to the city. The common ground he found with other officials, environmentalists, and private property owners was dedication to the public cause. The first tree planting ceremony in 2009 drew a crowd of two thousand people. A detention pond is being used for irrigation, and new aquatic features have been built around it. A dog park has already been added in addition to a monument for Vietnam veterans. A swimming club, a Boys and Girls Club, and bike rental facilities have sprouted on the grounds. Young people are much more interested in such outdoor spaces despite Laredo's weather. Residents enthusiastically attended the concert under the stars at North Central Park in 2019. Golondrina Food Park, adjoining the jogging trail, is a popular and packed destination for everyone in Laredo.[56] *Raul Muñoz* classifies North Central Park as the jewel of Laredo but cautions that it cannot be maintained without continuous funding.

One of the most exciting developments has been the farmers market, which started as a business incubator. The departed downtown H-E-B on Farragut Street left a void for senior citizens with limited mobility. The nonprofit Laredo Main Street had a mission to provide better food choices, and the farmers market emerged out of this concern. It brings people back to downtown and uses one of the historic plazas lending itself to an outdoor marketplace. Jarvis Plaza was chosen as the spot for the farmers market despite its rogue reputation and fears concerning homeless people. With the gazebo in the middle and the shade provided by trees, it has turned out to be the perfect spot for such an endeavor. Starting in May 2018, the farmers market takes place every third Saturday of the month. Locally produced honey, fresh eggs, fresh vegetables, cooked meals, and handicrafts are available. Social media has been the most useful tool to reach out to residents. *Samantha Taft*, who serves on the board, specifies that it was originally scheduled to be held in the first week of the month so that people with food stamps could use their resources.

When the farmers market could not attract enough agricultural vendors, Laredo Center for Urban Agriculture and Sustainability[57] was established at Canseco House, where an urban community garden had flourished on Chihuahua Street. A small garden at LC has been in existence for quite a few years and teaches people to install gardens in their backyards. *Travis Mace* grew up on a farm and appreciates the open spaces, speaking enthusiastically of the agricultural garden at LC. Progressive cities everywhere are creating such food consortiums, and he wants to connect LC's academic program with the farmers market and the food bank.

Katie Brown grew up in a family that was involved with Laredo Little Theater (LLT). She remembers going to rehearsals with her mother in the 1990s, when there were multiple shows each week. The theater slowly died out, but there was a resurgence around 2008–9 with four shows a year along with one big musical. About seventy to eighty people auditioned for *Mary Poppins*. Along with LLT, TAMIU and LC have their own theater groups. Brown explains, "Working in arts and culture in Laredo is a labor of love, not a professional gig. TAMIU and LC often share space for LLT performances. It was the Laredo Philharmonic Orchestra that brought Yo-Yo Ma to town. Laredo BorderSlam Poetry meets every month. Children now have opportunities to learn fine arts along with sports as extracurricular activities, and every summer they can enjoy shows geared to them." *Aileen Ramos* suggests that people need to leave their comfort zones and explore all the different parts of the city. There is a new flexibility with food trucks as well. Las Palmas Food Trucks & Park is an important addition. The Sisters of Mercy Water Park was intentionally planned for the south side. The north has the critical logistical base, which needs to be expanded to neighborhoods on the south side.

While there is emphasis on green and new spaces for public use, many of them are emerging as private entertainment venues rather than freely accessible public spaces. Instead of Lake Casa Blanca State Park, the Max A. Mandel Municipal Golf Course is now probably the most scenic spot in all of Laredo. Although no one is barred from the golf course or the restaurant there, it is not as inclusive and welcoming to everyone as the state park. The Sames Auto Arena (previously Laredo Entertainment Center and Laredo Energy Arena before Sames Auto Group purchased the naming rights) hosts most of the concerts, sports events, and graduation ceremonies, with even the WBC carnival having shifted to its grounds from the riverfront. In 2002 the arena started operating its 178,000-square-foot facility with a seating capacity of almost ten thousand people. The $36.5 million project was funded with a quarter percent sales tax approved by voters. The largest indoor convention space in South Texas can claim thirty-two thousand square feet of continuous open floor space.[58]

In Laredo, hot weather is the greatest obstruction to enjoying outdoor spaces. A convention center such as the one in McAllen with a music auditorium is on the wish list of many Laredoans. *Gary Bell* complains,

> The $12 million recreation center remains empty from 8:00 a.m. to 5:30 p.m. Residents often refer to such projects as white elephants. Different neighborhood schools, gyms, and library spaces are not always accessible to people who need these spaces the most, especially in the long summer months. Instead of being territorial, a lot more utility can be gained by sharing existing spaces. There is never enough shade around Laredo, so public spaces that are even partially shaded can attract many people and instill a greater sense of community.

The nonprofit City Makery grew out of Viva Laredo as an advocacy group that would carry out different parts of the comprehensive plan.[59] *Roxana Peel* headed City Makery, designed to serve as a pipeline for popular engagement and to channel the desires and frustrations of the people in a constructive way. Peel discusses organizing forty events throughout National Bike Month in May and in the process importing bike culture to Laredo. Each event created more opportunities and ideas and was well coordinated with other community events, such as urban gardening and art happenings, as well as with food trucks and both new and old spaces, such as Cultura Beer Garden or Gallery 201 at Pan American Courts or local restaurants such as Lolita's Bistro or El Capataz. The organization has succeeded in adding bike racks in front of city buses. It has also collected signatures for a petition for a skate park and coordinated political campaigns for progressive candidates who believe in transparent and accountable city government. Partly as a result of these efforts, the city is trying to be more walkable and bike-friendly.

The emerging public spaces do not lack their share of criticism. Often it is alleged that council members view their individual districts as fiefdoms, and each prefers his or her own park to hold events for the neighborhood. *Paul Cruise* complains, "The parks have turned into multifunction facilities that serve everyone, but what is needed are designated spaces for different activities like biking and birdwatching. Introducing a young person to nature has multifaceted benefits for the growth and development of young minds." A larger concern is competition between council members who focus only on their own districts. Moreover, parks are not the only needed public spaces. *Nina Vargas* ran for city council after joining a group that successfully fought against Laredo Municipal Management District, which would have increased taxes and favored large property owners at the expense of mom-and-pop stores. Vargas feels that one of the achievements for her impoverished district was to introduce BiblioTech Laredo Digital Library, enabling children to access information and check out devices and Wi-Fi cards.

Technology has expanded public spaces to the virtual format. *Erin Arroyo* highlights the Facebook page, "Remember when in Laredo, Texas (or Nuevo Laredo)," where people post memories and pictures of bygone eras. But *Rachel Lawrence* suggests that Laredo is so highly politicized that it is difficult for city employees to maintain social media accounts because they become bombarded with questions and comments regarding their work. It cannot be denied that virtual space in general is filled with mutually exclusive views and uncompromising conflicts. One such citizen journalist, Priscilla Villarreal, who calls herself Lagordiloca, has emerged as a local idol through her Facebook page.[60] She has one hundred and seventy thousand followers, more than the *Laredo Morning Times*. Her pledge is to inform the community with unedited and uncensored news. Because many residents feel that the established news media ignores real issues, her aggressive tenor against the powerful resonates with them. As *Karla Garcia* explains, "People see themselves reflected in her. The people who hate her are elitists overlooking a sector of the population that is often ignored and not valued or listened to or catered to for whatever reasons." Villarreal is very vocal about demanding transparency and accountability from city government. Her focus ranges from cartels to corruption to traffic accidents, all of it rendered with passion, her street cred deriving from her opinionated and fearless stature. There are plans to portray her as the protagonist of a television drama series who takes on the mainstream media with livestream street reporting.[61]

The *Laredo Morning Times* can take credit for being one of the only newspapers still making money for the Hearst Corporation. *Karla Garcia* highlights the local media group Sledge TV, which has started filming the underground punk rock scene in the city. *Grace Terry* mentions local musician Bob Beatty with admiration. She finds that people are trying to take welcome initiatives to create new opportunities driven by good intentions toward the city. These enterprises are often rooted in calculated market rationales rather than being spontaneous start-ups. In recent years, *Jesse Knight* has noticed a huge growth of nonprofits amid the informal citizenry. Outreach and fund-raising activities are now much more professional and corporate. Just as collective needs are coming to the fore, there is a generation of people who have come of age with the aspiration of making their own contribution, as with Kids Café, where children can eat for free in what has turned out to be a very successful program.

Sharon Zukin labels public spaces of art, along with restaurants, as con-sumption spaces that allow social interaction. The visibility of different groups of people and their depth of participation reveal the social mobility of the population.[62] *Trina Case* feels excited about Viva Laredo and appreciates the explosion of public art that has followed the downtown revitalization initia-tive. At the opposite spectrum is *Arthur Bailey*, a struggling artist who does roofing when he is not doing his art installations because the work from the city barely pays the bills. He feels the city council takes too long to make its decisions, and Laredo remains light-years behind Houston or even El Paso, so that it has nothing comparable to the El Paso Museum of Art. It is true that people with artistic talents have recently moved back, but he believes this is the time to make the most use of their skills. The city has started in-vesting in public spaces and acquiring street art and murals by local artists, but more needs to be done. Bailey, for one, believes that his mural at Blas Castañeda Park is "a window to the Laredo community."

Public spaces in Laredo are the few locations where one gets the feeling that the government is working for everyone. The new spaces have reener-gized residents' claims on the city. *Theodore Valenti* believes if you share a common interest with people and end up at the same venue that they do, then you may find you have other shared interests as well. *Matilda Roy* ob-serves, "Without public spaces, it is hard for real political discourse to take place and the voices of the people in the communities tend to fade away. The public spaces have generated more organic discussions about everyday life that touch on politics in a different way." The growth of "privatopia,"[63] or gated communities, is another trend to be understood side by side with reclaiming public spaces by groups such as Our Laredo or the #NoBorder-Wall Coalition. The forging of sentimental bonds between people and a place appears in the material formations on a geographic site and embodies new

FIGURE 23 MLK march. Rio Grande International Study Center.

meanings of engagement. Place attachment facilitates a sense of security and well-being, defines group boundaries, and stabilizes memories against the passage of time.[64]

Conclusion

The original plazas were designed to be accessible public spaces and served as social arenas of interaction in an elite-dominated society, but they lost their recreational utility when downtown was abandoned. The effort to rehabilitate downtown, the creation of new green spaces, and the revitalization of public spaces for art and culture have all engendered a new sense of togetherness and started a conversation about Laredo's border identity with urgency and vigor. A substantial part of this awakening revolves around basic issues such as the demand for safe water or more transparency from the city government. After successive alerts to use boiled water, despite the investment of substantial tax dollars to upgrade water treatment facilities and rising water fees, residents have become adamant about essential ser-

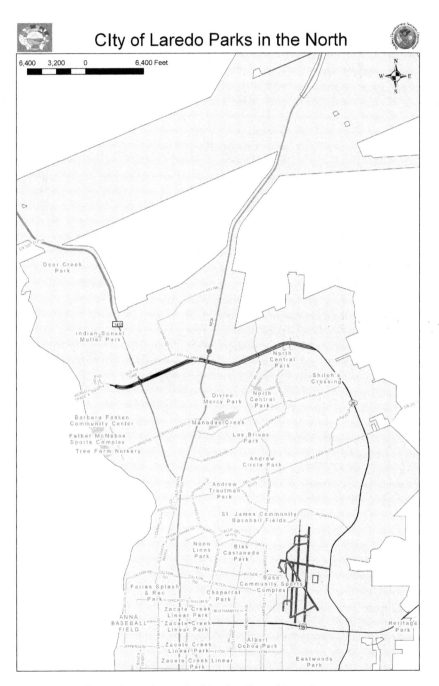

MAP 4 City of Laredo Parks in the North. City of Laredo.

City of Laredo Parks in the South

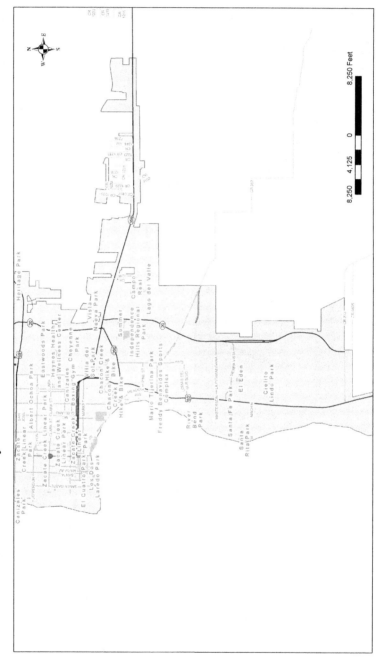

MAP 5 City of Laredo Parks in the South. City of Laredo.

vices. A July 2021 workshop on the city's Fifty-Year Master Plan for Water and Wastewater revealed that based on Laredo's population growth, the city will only be able to depend on the river for nineteen more years, or until around 2040, to meet its growing needs. The city council has to overcome a history of distrust, especially from poorer residents, because people do not trust what local government has been doing with taxpayers' money. The patron system may have ended, but trust has never been fully regained. *Jake Ruiz* complains that while the city charges for permits to hold garage sales, it is not maintaining water quality despite raising costs. *Kayla Hall* is more sanguine in believing that the empowerment of women as department heads is a much-needed solution for many city government problems.

Dolores Hayden has argued that public spaces are integral to memory and identity as they are keepers of the factual and emotional stories we tell about ourselves. When we pass by a particular landscape or neighborhood, we remember a lost time or forgotten part of ourselves. Urban landscapes thus contain more than the present, continuing to remind us of our past. It is in the past that identities are formed, and we understand ourselves better when we situate ourselves in the places where we have grown up and had transitional experiences.[65] Hayden has provided the examples of the women's and civil rights movements to illustrate how they are tied to particular spaces and have created collective memory, but on a smaller scale constructing a mall, opening a new arena, or closing a movie theater capture the essence of a community's collective memory by locating the identity of the people with the place where these events occurred. This connection is the essential element of social history, with the multisensory quality of open-ended spaces, sounds, smells, and textures forming the critical elements of sociocultural identity.[66] The inclusiveness and vitality of urban spaces are a reflection of the qualities of the environment where these spaces have been designed and preserved. Public spaces, which are amenable to different uses and can be claimed by various segments of society, have been called "loose spaces" in urban theory semantics.[67] Their quantity and extent of use, both by the absolute number of people and by the different strata of society, chronicle the presence of the community in urban places and the depth of engagement within a city.

The expansion of green spaces and reinvigorated public involvement have occurred simultaneously in Laredo and have a symbiotic connection. Public spaces bind people in a different relationship from consumption. The much neglected Los Tres Laredos Park has emerged as ground zero for political action, especially after repeated events held by the #NoBorderWall Coalition. The fight against the proposed border wall literally and figuratively is taking place on the banks of the Rio Grande, which has remained neglected and underutilized ever since downtown lost its luster. Just as there are Border Patrol agents manning noisy speedboats on the river, so are there more kayakers enjoying the natural beauty and claiming the river as part of life rather than needing to be defended to keep people out. Earth Day festivals organized by Rio Grande International Study Center (RGISC) now take place by the river at Los Tres Laredos Park, with the conscious purpose of initiating rapport between the youth and the river, because many believe that the primal bond has been tattered. These public events have aroused a new excitement, such as the insurgency of artists who have initiated BorderSlam Poetry and public art in the form of murals. Cafés, bars, and food trucks are extending the space for intellectual and artistic involvement. In this predominantly Catholic town where people have typically congregated around church activities, bike riding and cookouts along with golf and other outdoor activities have opened up new directions for conversation.

CHAPTER 5

Visions of the City

Institutions and Infrastructure

> You cannot have it both ways. If you really want a rise in federal law enforcement, you want to be in a war zone. If you want to show that you tamed the tiger, you have to give up federal funds. For some people, it is in their vested interest to picture this as a war zone or as the last bastion of security.
>
> *JESSE KNIGHT*, LAREDO RESIDENT

> We became the number one port but our roads are still totally torn up. We went two weeks without clean water. We have FBI raids of city hall every three to four years. At least one out of every three Laredo residents is living in poverty. So where is that money going?
>
> *ALEX MEAD*, LAREDO RESIDENT

A border city is a space of chaos that needs to be controlled in the national imagination. This perception is reinforced by diverse fields of inquiry, ranging from Gloria Anzaldúa's literary theory of the border[1] to Mike Davis's urban theory of the border,[2] in both of which the border is synonymous with anarchy and obscurity. This outlook is in stark contrast to the perceptions of those who actually live in the border regions. When people in Laredo are asked about their complaints, they point to internal power abuse and corruption as the source of disarray, much like other cities. The disorder that disrupts their lives stems from political, planning, and fiscal decisions that are local as opposed to any external mayhem. They identify the federal government's continuous interventions as the outlying obstruction to their lives. Contrary to the bleak image of the border, Laredo's residents view the city as a land of opportunity and identify the expansion of educational opportunities and social infrastructure as the path to advancement. Residents value the city's geographical advantages but are also aware of the corrosive impact of being a trade corridor, which strips downtown businesses and funnels enormous amounts of cash through the city, leaving very little for local development.

"Laredo is older than the United States, with such a fascinating history and culture and the fact that it can cling so tightly to its Mexican roots is extraordinary," notes *Trina Case*. Instead of highlighting its unique history, Laredo embraced the brand of "gateway city" in safer days when people flocked to Nuevo Laredo. With its new reality of being a transportation center, Laredo is struggling with its identity. How can the city reconcile its self-branding as "city on the edge" or even the more placid "the place to be together" with the fact of prisoners outnumbering college students? In the official iconography it projects to attract tourists, Laredo sells itself as two distinct products to two different markets in the United States and Mexico. While the focus on Mexican clients is strictly on trade and imports, for U.S. customers ecotourism and birding opportunities are highlighted. For U.S. visitors, Laredo is a Mexican culinary destination, whereas for Mexican visitors it offers the American experience. This fluidity in the city's image

FIGURE 24 Remembering Cesar Chavez. Rio Grande International Study Center.

corroborates its hybrid identity. The question for Laredo is which of these visions will dominate the future of this border city.

Chaos and Control

The evolution of Laredo as a border city is fraught with political power plays, but its development as an axis of trade is associated with a sense of coexistence, tolerance, and harmony. This duality of character is also evident in the incongruity of the binary interpretation of the maladies afflicting the city. For many local residents, concentration of political power resulting in corruption, skewed economic opportunity, and lack of infrastructure assumes priority when they think of disarray in the city, evoking issues that can only be resolved through an orderly political process. But in the national imagination the pandemonium on the border is mainly external, the result of the commotion caused by illegal people and drugs that needs to be controlled with the deployment of extraordinary forces of law and order.

The city of Laredo was dominated by the patron system of governance from the early 1880s until well into the 1970s. Fernando Piñon, in his treatise on Laredo, defines patron democracy as one "where the old Spanish families were to rule, the Anglo Saxon newcomers were to manage, and the Mexicans were to serve."[3] The end of the old system of Mayor Pepe Martin (also known as Joseph Claude Martin, or J. C. Martin Jr.) in the late 1970s is regarded as the beginning of a new era. However, many Laredoans believe that the patron system continues today, albeit in more sophisticated and less tangible forms. *Michael Factor* remembers how his parents fought against the political machine that ruled Laredo for forty years. There was active opposition to Mayor Martin in political rallies, paving the way for Aldo J. Tatangelo Sr. to become mayor of Laredo in 1978.

This was the first election in Laredo beyond the control of the Independent Club, the local elite organization, which exercised power over the city and Webb County. As assistant city attorney, Factor tried to change the city charter to prevent any kind of political machine from ever coming into power again and initiated term limits and single-member districts for more accountability.[4] This was the major political transition for Laredo, ending institutionalized corruption. *Justin Taylor* agrees that the fundamental political transformation in Laredo occurred in the 1970s with the collapse of the political machine. *Charles Vega* also affirms that the major shift in Laredo occurred after the patron system failed with the indictment of Mayor J. C. Martin Jr. The new mayor, Aldo Tatangelo, worked hard to build trust in Laredo and steered the city in the right direction. While there is more stability in the local government machinery now, the involvement of Washington, D.C., in the internal affairs of Laredo has escalated and brought in a new layer of complexity.

When Mayor Martin was in power, the level of corruption reached deep and wide. *Ishmael Reyes* claims that with his indictment, corruption took on a more subtle form. He recalls the story of how the Del Mar neighborhood, which was a utility district[5] on the edge of the city, got incorporated by city manager Marvin Townsend. While the city has been preoccupied with annexing wealthy neighborhoods, it has been quite negligent toward preserving poorer neighborhoods. Reyes took the city to court over a drainage ditch in a working-class neighborhood, citing the environmental impact, and won the case. As he muses, "Lawsuits do not stop projects forever, but only allow enough time for the community to come together and resist. The only way to stop these kinds of harassments is through a proper political structure. Political accountability increased when Webb County changed its election format to single-member districts." *Jake Ruiz* worked as a police officer and has seen the dissimilar way people are treated for the same crimes, depending on their economic background. He has seen how "corruption flowed from the very top of the system, from crooked judges to lowly officials."

The nuanced but prevalent forms of corruption are also highlighted by *Alex Mead*, who worked in city government and experienced the hypocrisy and lack of empathy for the very people the officials take the oath to serve. Mead points out how the El Pico Surface Water Treatment Plant was a $100 million investment with a tax-funded budget.[6] The water plant was supposed to provide safe water for fifty years, but it turned into a massive disaster, and the city levied another $50 million on taxpayers to get the same company, Dannenbaum Engineering, to fix the problem. The chairman of Dannenbaum committed suicide before the indictment, and two city council members were indicted as well. Meanwhile, the price of water had to be increased to address these bungled measures, and yet the plant provides water at only 20 percent of its promised capacity, and Laredo has repeatedly been under a boil water advisory.[7] Mead observes, "People who live on fixed incomes bear the burden while people who make millions of dollars get to dictate the growth of the city. Growth-centered urbanism prioritizes the wealthy while making the life of the poor harder with economic and planning measures." As mentioned elsewhere, the city has been subject to repeated FBI raids because of incessant charges of corruption.[8] One step to reduce corruption has been the practice of hiring city managers and planners from outside the local pool.

The status of Laredo as the largest inland port remains overshadowed by the depiction of the border city in terms of crime and lawlessness in the national political rhetoric. *Giselle Lamar* notes that her job is to prosecute people who break federal laws, and specifically she is assigned to a group that works on narcotics cases. In her words, "The cartel violence and corruption in Mexico have made the situation untenable. I see a spike in methamphetamine and heroin traffic since marijuana was legalized. I do not think the drug problem as far as usage has necessarily increased in Laredo, but it is shipped outward from here." What influences the drug business is the nature of the demand, the often neglected part of the commentary on drugs. The federal government has adopted many programs to discourage drug use, but their success depends on political support, so who is in office matters a lot. Citizens' voices are seldom part of forming policies such as legalizing marijuana. In Laredo there were programs like Operation Weed and Seed targeting middle school children, ages twelve to thirteen, teaching them to say no to drugs. It involved biking, camping, hiking, and finding mentors for kids. The funding for this successful federal program stopped when the Trump administration came to power in 2017.

The danger associated with trade and logistics as far as they involve frequent transactions with Nuevo Laredo is indeed high. *Alex Mead* recalls the firsthand story of an employee of a trading company who was kidnapped when he went to pick up goods on the outskirts of town. He was ripped out of his truck and beaten mercilessly, but thankfully his employer cared enough to pay his ransom and get him back. The chilling end of the story took place the next day, when the owner of the company complained to the cartel about the mistreatment of his worker. American companies often pay money to cartels for the protection of their employees who regularly travel to Nuevo Laredo. The cartel identified the two seventeen- to eighteen-year-old kids who were acting on their own and had kidnapped the employee for ransom money. The cartel murdered the two kidnappers and sent the video of the murdered bodies to the company within twenty-four hours. Mead emphasizes, "The forgotten part of such stories is how cocaine and other drugs are not only recreational but sustain the sixteen-hour shifts of drivers passing through the transportation corridor. The amount of money, $230 billion each year, that passes through Laredo can pave its streets in gold."

In Joseph Nivens's terms, the American state started with "despotic power" to conquer the borderlands, which has now been converted to "infrastructural power." The justification of despotic power is to bring order to lawless lands. Infrastructural power promises more security and opportunity and avoids the important question of who benefits from such measures.[9] Poor people in Texas, especially in the border region, have always been targeted by the state in order to establish unhindered authority over the troublesome borderlands. Andrew Graybill reminds us that both the Texas Rangers and the Canadian Mounties were the arms of the state to fight against labor protests and to crush disputes in favor of industry in the late nineteenth century.[10] It should be underscored that the Texas Rangers in El Paso were transformed into the Border Patrol to protect American workers from competing Chinese migrant laborers.[11] Nevins argues that Operation Gatekeeper at the San Diego–Tijuana border was a reaction to Proposition 187 and tied to California politics. The militarization of the border continues apace regardless of the rise and decline of illegal entries,[12] even as the priorities of the Border Patrol have changed from drug enforcement to apprehension of illegal border crossers. One goal that has ceased to exist is establishing public relations with local people, which was formalized with horse and foot patrols in 1984 for Laredo.[13]

The southern border has always been considered much riskier, and far more personnel and resources have been deployed there. The expansion of Border Patrol agents is useful during economic downturns and is achieved through lowering recruiting and training standards.[14] In 1980, 87.2 percent of Border Patrol agents were deployed in the southern sector compared to 9.3 percent on the northern border. In 2001, the proportion of Border Patrol officers rose to 93.9 percent on the U.S.-Mexico border, while the number of officers on the Canadian border shrank to 3.4 percent.[15] As Maril elaborates,

Within a relatively short span of time almost 20,000 border patrol agents, professionally equipped for the first time in their history but schooled for less than two months, patrolled the nation's borderline, with the vast majority of them stationed along the U.S.-Mexico border. CBP is now the largest federal law enforcement agency in the land. Congress also allocated funds for weaponry, vehicles, aircraft, and facilities. New apprehension policies also required a burgeoning and unregulated private detention system.[16]

The way the southern border has traditionally been controlled by the Texas Rangers and how this has influenced the present formation of the Border Patrol is important for deciphering who controls the border narrative. Cumberland analyzes how the Texas Rangers dictated law and order in the Lower Rio Grande Valley with the accepted practice of lynching and executions.[17] The killings were reported in newspapers as the hunting of bandits and outlaws as coyotes. State representative José Tomás Canales, the only state legislator of Mexican descent, called for a hearing, but it was difficult to get witnesses and evidence against the Texas Rangers. In 1918, fifteen residents of Porvenir, a small village in West Texas, were assassinated, and most of the 140 inhabitants of the village fled back to Mexico.[18] Between 1910 and 1920, hundreds of Mexicans were lynched, with three hundred killed in a 1915 massacre in the Rio Grande Valley.[19] Laredo, at least comparatively, was spared from this brutality, because there are records of only two victims, Pedro Gomez and Pablo Aguillar, who were lynched during this time span.[20]

In the past, the border for Laredo was just the river without restrictions, history professor *Justin Taylor* emphasizes. The limitations began in the aftermath of the Civil War to prevent smuggling and were gradually augmented by customs agents, police, and the Border Patrol. The biggest smuggling boom on the southern border occurred during the Prohibition era in the 1920s when Mexican border towns flourished because of illicit liquor. In 1925 the U.S. customs force had 111 officers, but by 1930 this had grown to 723.[21] Kelly Hernández describes the violent history of the Border Patrol that is erased in the national memory. Nightly gun battles during Prohibition obscured legal jurisdictions and allowed the Border Patrol to police Mexican nationals, which subsequently shaped politicized immigration policies, producing an unfair and uneven process of border control by the 1920s and 1930s. Harlon B. Carter, who led Operation Wetback in 1954, shot and killed Ramón Casiano in Laredo. Carter's criminal history should have prevented him from joining the Border Patrol, but instead it shielded him from legal consequences.[22] Racism and brutality always underpinned the narrative of border control. But now that the border and immigration have evolved into wedge issues in national politics, it is very difficult for a local perspective to capture national attention.

The relationship between the Texas Rangers, the Border Patrol, and the Laredo Police Department has not always been amicable. In 1927 several officers of the Texas Rangers and the Border Patrol attacked the local police station. Hernández states,

> The 1927 cleanup of the Laredo Station reflected the limits of Border Patrol disorganization that allowed for local management of immigration law enforcement. Although most local stations developed their own strategies, policies, and procedures, the Laredo Station was exempt until the infamously brutal racial violence of the Texas Rangers slashed away at the bonds between the Laredo Border Patrol and the local Mexican-American leadership. The cleanup transformed the Laredo Border Patrol into a refuge for white violence.[23]

Much of the mess stemming from the current asylum system is rooted in the ambiguous policies and mismanagement of the federal government. *Vera Gabriel* blogged about the caravans of Central American women and children who were released in Laredo in 2014. Frustrated by the lack of any official efforts, she arranged for people to join forces and form the Laredo Humanitarian Relief Team. This group bought heaps of apples and oranges and distributed them at the Greyhound bus station, shocked to see that people without any resources were being released on the streets. Gabriel ended up leaving her business to do work with the Holding Institute to respond to this calamity. Donations of food were collected citywide, and the Baptist ministry brought out its trailers for showers. As her research today involves trauma that affects immigrant women, she is well aware of how the number of detention centers is growing as well as the atrocities. She also serves as a volunteer doing translation work in detention centers. The stories of all these women—what they witness in terms of rape and murder—are traumatic. Children who have been separated and caged in prisons undergo profound changes in behavior and personality.

Robert Maril conducted ethnographic fieldwork for two years among Border Patrol agents along the Texas-Mexico border. He accompanied them to their work and interviewed them to get an understanding of their views on the border. Agents are either hailed as heroes or scorned as abusers, but his work takes into account the complexity of their jobs and their connection with the region. They may be committed to the immediate task of stopping illegal entries of people and drugs, but they are aware that their role is minimal in the intricate human and economic landscapes.[24] The amount of money invested in border protection, the profits made from illegal narcotics, and the funds lost to local jurisdictions paint a desolate picture of trying to control the border with a steel or concrete slab while ignoring the human consequences and attempting to quarantine larger social and political issues from their roots.[25]

Remarkably, the one-third poverty rate has remained static since the 1960s even though Laredo has grown so much.[26] The obstacle to reforming the city government is the strong control of the Democratic Party, according to *Van Vincent*. The patron system has only been replaced by a more labyrinthine system of fiefdom. Although the city and its people are friendly, the corruption, favoritism, and cronyism have never really evaporated, although they are not as blatantly transparent as in the past. According to Vincent, "There are probably eight different groups or tribes who control the entire city. Anyone who challenges power ends up paying a price. Any complaint to the Ethics Commission is almost guaranteed a retribution. Look at who is making the money!" In a recent case, a local organization active in holding the city accountable was fined ten thousand dollars in lawyers' fees for violating a rule of the commission. The same firm that manages the comprehensive plan owns unsafe and dilapidated apartment complexes throughout the city. Repeated raids by the FBI have convinced *Jack Hughes* that city hall is still corrupt. *Vera Gabriel* believes there must be more instances that need to investigated by the FBI that have not yet been brought to light and that people choose to ignore willingly.

Land of Opportunity

The population of the Laredo metropolitan area has surpassed three hundred thousand, with many residents able to claim family domicile for generations. Laredo offers unique opportunities both to sustain the hard-earned comfort derived from one's ancestors and to open up new avenues of growth. Historically, geography and location facilitated economic prosperity through owning ranches and trading. Like the rest of the country, Laredo benefited handsomely from federal investments in infrastructure development and policies that created avenues for upward mobility through education. The next wave of prosperity came with the explosion of transportation that sit-

FIGURE 25 Texas A&M International University. TAMIU online gallery.

uated Laredo in the middle of the global network. In recent decades, the establishment of institutions, especially those related to education, has created unforeseen opportunities for residents.

It is in Laredo where *Paul Sergio*'s American dream came true. Buying a ranch when land was cheap made it possible for his family to prosper. His father, who found his way to Laredo through the Bracero Program, was successful by dint of hard labor and was able to buy two thousand acres of land. This to Sergio is a Laredo story, because the American dream can be had here in Laredo. He remembers the time when workers would go back and forth seasonally instead of being permanently pushed here because of lack of safety in Mexico. *Bianca Frey* tells the story of how her father, the only one in the family who stayed in Laredo to take care of his aging parents, saved enough money to buy a thousand-acre ranch. He bought the ranch at seventy-five dollars an acre and was able to sell parts of it at $26,000 an acre. The belief in hard work and getting rewarded is rooted in the deep spiritual foundations of this Catholic community.

Land and family relationships are closely interwoven in living arrangements in Laredo. *Arthur Bailey* moved back to Laredo to be near his aging mother and to receive her help in raising his children as a single father. When *Samantha Taft* created a Mommy & Me group, which grew to 150 families and included women originally from England and Japan, the Parks and Recreation Department gave them space as they no longer fit in any single member's house. *Barry Rivers* also views Laredo as an opportunity to alter perspectives and bring value to activities that have typically been trivialized such as agriculture. He feels that because labor is abundant and available, there has been insufficient respect for manual work related to land. The emphasis on parks, soil conservation, and food production as enterprises worthy of attention is new to Laredo.

Deferred Action for Childhood Arrivals (DACA) recipient *Sebastian Fabian* is thankful for all the opportunities he has enjoyed in Laredo. Although he passed his young adulthood in constant agony over getting deported, he acknowledges that Laredo and the university have opened many doors to him. He was able to do research and serve in a leadership position in many student organizations, which he feels would be unlikely in a bigger and more cutthroat city. His volunteer and activist roles have enabled him to develop extensive professional and informal relations. He lived in fear of persecution by the Border Patrol but not under any social stigma. Laredo rewards initiative, so he never felt like a social outcast despite the lack of legal status. He was never punished or held back academically because of being undocumented. DACA approval allowed him his first set of legal papers, albeit temporary, as he chased his dreams beyond Laredo.

The first doors of opportunity that led to modern growth were catalyzed by World War II, *Margarita Gallellos* suggests, when residents of Laredo were exposed to racial discrimination and yet benefited from federal education and other policies targeting poverty alleviation. The interstate highways were a product of President Eisenhower's initiative, although many of the internal roads remained unpaved until the 1970s. Still, enough money from trade made its way to Laredo to flesh out the American dream. Following NAFTA, the World Trade International Bridge (also known as Laredo

International Bridge 4) was constructed to cope with escalating trade volume. When Texas Governor Ann Richards was capped as Mr. South Texas in 1994,[27] President Bill Clinton had already signed off on the bill for the bridge, but fifty-two other agencies still needed to approve it. As a gift to the people of Laredo, she obtained the permit for the bridge and brought it to the city, which eased the federal approval process. The transformation of the existing upper-level university to the city's first four-year university, Texas A&M International University, occurred in 1995 and propelled intellectual growth in the underresourced community.

Laredo College (the latest iteration of Laredo Junior College and Laredo Community College) was the first and for a long time the only higher educational institute in Laredo. Established in 1947 at the beautiful and monumental location of Fort McIntosh, it started out offering vocational education. Over the years, the range of degrees has expanded across two campuses. It certainly opened the doors for *Cesar Villarreal* to specialize in medical radiography and lead a middle-class life very different from his poor upbringing. He changed his profession to become an educator at TAMIU after completing his PhD in urban housing in Laredo. Laredo College shared its campus for twenty years (1969–89) with Laredo State University (formerly Texas A&I University at Laredo), until the latter became absorbed in the Texas A&M University system. These two institutions served as bookends to Villarreal's career, illustrating the advancement of educational prospects in Laredo.

Opportunities mean more in an insulated place like Laredo. *Sophia Brown* spent more than forty years in education as a teacher and administrator. She remembers how none of the teachers or principals ever attended the conference for public educators in Austin or even traveled on a plane. Within a few decades, however, Laredo opened its doors to immigrants such as *Sam Kornosky*, who reached his professional pinnacle as the principal of UISD. He believes in the value of enabling youngsters to get quality education beyond political boundaries, and he understands why the school district is strategically lax about residency requirements. *Trina Case* echoes that Laredo is finally catching up on progress with investments in higher education.

Laredo has been kind to *Travis Mace* as well. He has had a successful professional life as an educator, and he founded the Lamar Bruni Vergara Environmental Science Center (named after the local philanthropist who donated the money). The center has educated people about the biodiversity of the Rio Grande and has introduced students to animal habitats as well as persistent problems in the river basin and their impact on the city.[28] *Jonathan Everett*, another pioneer of the center, recalls discouraging his daughter from taking a canoe trip on the river because of pollution. He never planned to stay in the city but soon started relishing the opportunities that a small-town college offered: developing courses with total freedom and scheduling teaching blocs the way he thought would be most effective without having to answer to anyone. Starting with an interest in the beaver, he designed an environmental science course about the Rio Grande, leading to brainstorming about finding a solution to the raw sewage and plastic bags that were being dumped in the river. People were already worried about the erosion of the banks that had accelerated because of Border Patrol activities. Like-minded people wanted to take steps to save the river, which is the only source of drinking water for twelve million people, from ongoing pollution, and Rio Grande International Study Center (RGISC) was born out of these interactions.

Another founding member, *Theodore Valenti*, remembers the process of applying for nonprofit status for their brainchild, which initially involved only a few close colleagues. They made contact with other nonprofits and sought the help of what used to be the Texas Water Commission to safeguard the watershed. The Texas Water Commission had little authority over the Rio Grande, as it is an international boundary. It did not even collect regular data on water pollution, but monitoring water quality and retaining such data emerged as one of the most important agendas of RGISC. As in other parts of Texas, private property owners controlled land on the banks of the river, and the organization had to persuade private citizens for permission to get access to the river to sample the water. The Texas Commission on Environmental Quality (TCEQ) administers the Texas Clean Rivers Program on all the rivers in Texas. As per its requirement, RGISC expanded the collection of field data and started forwarding it to an EPA-approved laboratory for more in-depth chemical analysis. The key institution that persuaded the city of Laredo to ban plastic bags was RGISC, but the ten-year-long effort that culminated in an ordinance rare in Texas was overturned within three years by the Texas Supreme Court. It also pushed the city to adopt the Green Spaces Ordinance, which protects the wetlands and offers incentives to private developers not to build on imperiled land.

There was not a single sewage plant on the Mexican side, and Nuevo Laredo by itself was dumping twenty-six million gallons of raw sewage a day until 1996. Nuevo Laredo obtained the first wastewater treatment plant on the entire Mexican border, which was jointly funded by the United States, Texas, and Mexico.[29] Lobbying for this plant was RGISC, after starting the water monitoring program both downstream and upstream and maintaining records of the deteriorating water quality. *Jonathan Everett* recounts how RGISC also sought to stop the Laredo Town Center mall from being built right next to Lake Casa Blanca State Park, but all the efforts to engage citizens and fight the city council for months came up short against the private corporation that paid the city only $18 million for the land in a prime location.

The evolution of TAMIU reflects the existing social hierarchies, political negotiations, and economic prospects that constitute the story of the city. True to Laredo tradition, the legend involves philanthropy, community needs, and, of course, George Washington's Birthday Celebration (WBC). Former TAMIU president *Larry Sanchez* reminisces about the whole process with relish, as he believes that the university has provided much-needed advancement for Laredo. He was hired at Texas A&I University (Laredo State University until 1977), which was established in 1969 and shared the campus with Laredo Junior College. He succeeded President Billy F. Cowart, who had been ambitiously extending course offerings, the need for a proper university in the environs happily coinciding with such expansion. Laredo celebrates WBC extravagantly, and it was a tradition among Austin politicians to join the celebration, as political bargaining often become part of the merriment. To have an independent university on an independent campus hinged on a land grant and a lot of money. During a tête-à-tête at the luxurious La Posada Hotel, Lieutenant Governor Bob Bullock (1991–99) promised the money if the land was available. A group of university faculty met with Radcliffe Killam, the largest landowner in Laredo, who promptly promised two hundred acres of land. Laredo politician Judith Zaffirini, who had just been elected state senator, spearheaded the bill. The State Board of Education, however, required three hundred acres of land, to which Killam acceded, upon which the legislature duly provided the money for the construction of the buildings. The three hundred acres at the present location, formerly hunting grounds, was the preferred option, as this tract had suddenly become accessible because of the construction of Loop 20. The land where white-tailed deer abound, which Sue Killam loved to hunt, was donated by the Killam family for TAMIU.

An impending obstacle was whether the new university would join the Texas A&M or UT system, the two rival statewide institutions. The University of Texas was already in control of much of the border region, as it had a campus in El Paso and another in Brownsville. After disagreements and disputes, instead of handing the whole border region to one university system, the new university was made part of the Texas A&M system. Senator Zaffirini stressed the international aspect of the border; hence, the new campus was named Texas A&M International University. She continues to be the patron figure in legislative sessions for budget and other allocations to TAMIU. *Justin Taylor* views TAMIU as one of the great success stories of Laredo. Local residents claim pride of ownership and now simply call it "the university." The beautiful campus was designed in the Mission Revival style to reflect local cultural history, although during the planning phase there were warnings that the institution should not look like another hacienda. Out-of-state students started coming in after the expansion of the sports teams and have added a new, albeit still thin, layer of heterogeneity to the student population. The most diverse spot in the city is TAMIU, with out-of-state as well as international faculty and staff. Laredo's theaters and its arts scene have been able to regain much of their old eminence by working with TAMIU.

When he was president of TAMIU, *Larry Sanchez* was committed to gender parity and even called in the husbands of prospective students to convince them of the value of higher education. Thirty years later, the proportion of female graduates is higher than that of males at TAMIU, following the national trend. He was also adamant about joint program ventures with foreign universities in Mexico and Costa Rica, another mission TAMIU still seriously pursues. The university has been a beacon of light for *Matilda Roy*, who has been both a student and an employee at the institution. She remembers that during her graduation, 75 percent of students were of the first generation to go to college. The university is not the only convenient option anymore, but students choose to come here. A university in an impoverished area has a larger mission than providing pathways to successful careers. Roy hopes that the ripple effects of education will one day transform Laredo. People in Laredo now mention TAMIU as one of the landmarks along with representative buildings such as San Agustín Cathedral or the magnificent La Posada Hotel.

Opportunities in Laredo were not only initiated by the elites and the powerful but also bubbled from the ground up, such as the lawsuit against the state regarding the lack of four-year degree-granting institutions in South

Texas. The Mexican American Legal Defense and Educational Fund (MAL-DEF) and League of United Latin American Citizens (LULAC) lawsuit in 1987, *LULAC v. Richards*, was a response to the lack of universities and colleges in the border regions. The settlement from this long litigation resulted in $500 million for Texas border campuses.[30] *Sophia Brown* points out that before TAMIU was established, anyone aspiring to higher education had to leave town and seldom returned. Not only an avenue for higher education, TAMIU has slowly incubated intellectual progress in Laredo. The university, through formal programs of service learning and leadership development, attempts to prepare young people to be actively involved in public service. *Jose Diaz* believes that without TAMIU, it would be impossible for the city to retain its talent. More than providing educational opportunities, TAMIU offers the possibility to compete with anyone nationally, and this perception alone elevates the community. Arriving from a much more cosmopolitan city, *Yvonne Sims* felt most comfortable at TAMIU, with its diverse faculty and beautiful campus. She works at a magnet school and looks up to TAMIU as an opportunity for her own students. *Charles Fox* believes that the university has been transformative for the local population. Ties with Mexico have been strengthened, as many students from Nuevo Laredo attend TAMIU, and the executive MBA program explicitly targets career officials in Mexico.

The university serves as a base for sustained research and has attracted and retained many scholars interested in South Texas. As a researcher of local family history involving field visits to small towns, *Steve Griffin* has been able to carve out a niche where he can do border history with easy access to both sides of the river. *Jesse Knight* came to Laredo from snowy New England and remembers taking off his shoes and walking barefoot in his backyard in December and realizing that this was the place where he could make a difference. As he says, "I wanted to be a rock star when I was a little boy, but I played it safe, had a career and family, and lived a proper grown-up life. Laredo was the next best thing to my dream life. I love the slow pace of life and the many opportunities that keep happening. Laredo is where I have checked all the boxes for happiness."

Which Vision Dominates Laredo?

The contradictory narrations of decline and progress are interwoven in many city policies, complicating their implementation. The downtown rejuvenation

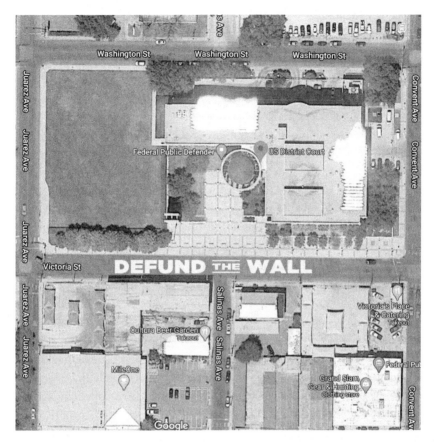

FIGURE 26 Defund the Wall mural. Rio Grande International Study Center.

plan is an excellent example, reflecting the contradictions inherent in the neo-liberal growth pattern. A profitable downtown and equitable distribution of resources within various constituencies are beneficial for the overall quality of life in Laredo but are not essential ingredients for advancement as a trade center. For the people of Laredo, a flourishing downtown is a continuation of history and a matter of pride. For the city, investment in downtown is a response to public appeals, but economically the sources of revenue from downtown are the tolls from bridges, which would be negligibly affected by downtown resuscitation. The national narrative promotes security measures that are inconsistent with growing tourism or even attracting local people to spend their time in downtown for entertainment. Laredo functions as a conduit for international trade, so it is irrelevant how prosperous or safe the downtown is. Neoliberal growth creates trade confluences across national boundaries that are connected, but the adjacent regions of these junctions are gutted to provide cheap and easy services for those who travel between these centers.

Laredo's residents typically had little say in the city's future unless they belonged to the top of the social and economic strata. The fall of the patron system and now the coming of Viva Laredo signal a change in the formal process, though the informal hegemony of the elites over decisions and investments is well acknowledged. In 2004 the city adopted the Green Spaces Ordinance in collaboration with RGISC, but the city itself has violated its own ordinance as it steadfastly refuses to obstruct any construction that promises more revenue, regardless of whether such promises can actually be fulfilled. Time and again, community organizations have challenged the city, and in some instances they have been successful. Most of these battles were lost, even though they paved the way for a more conscious citizenry and greater pleas for incorruptibility. In July 2021 the Laredo City Council adopted a resolution to post its budget online.

Clashes between residents and the city clarify who can have a voice in Laredo. The city was duly criticized for the Springfield road extension project linking two of the busiest roads, Del Mar Boulevard and International Boulevard, in order to ease the traffic that attempts to cut through the residential neighborhood. The land selected for the road consisted of wetlands adjacent to Manadas Creek. This was the type of land the city itself was motivating developers not to use because of increased flooding concerns. Moreover, water from Manadas Creek enters the river upstream to Laredo's wastewater treatment plant. City crews uprooted two hundred huge mesquite trees to build the 130-foot-wide roadway resembling an elongated S with sharp curves and safety concerns. The facts were that the road enhanced the value of one particular property owner and that city employees refused to attend public meetings, both noted by the community. *LareDOS*, the most popular Spanish-language newspaper at the time, had a number of its advertisements pulled out after it ran an article critical of the Springfield extension. When Laredo Superjail, one of the largest private prisons to house federal prisoners, was being built in adjacent Rio Bravo (the colonia mentioned in earlier chapters), there was hardly any discussion in the media or the public domain. The original plan for the prison had a greater provision for prisoners than TAMIU's dorms did for students at a time when Laredo was trying to market itself as a college town.

When it comes to larger issues that touch all residents, not just a handful, the city often prioritizes promises of development over the expectations of residents. The Laredo City Council approved selling an eighty-nine-acre tract to a private developer to build the aforementioned pedestrian mall, Laredo Town Center, on Loop 20 in the mid-2000s. A part of this acreage is wetland adjacent to Lake Casa Blanca, the state park enjoying federal protection. The wetland in question, even though manmade, is significant and has all the wetland characteristics: hydric soils, wetland plants, and significant inundation by water. The city applied for a Section 404 permit from the U.S. Army Corps of Engineers to build on the wetland. The location of the mall is within a couple of miles of TAMIU and just opposite Laredo International Airport. The Laredo Town Center was projected to have retail stores, restaurants, and a hotel, and it was to add $100 million to the city's tax base and create a thousand to thirteen hundred full-time equivalent jobs. Protesters gathered more than six thousand signatures under the leadership of RGISC, as mentioned earlier, but failed to stop construction. After a prolonged fight between environmentalists and the city, the new shopping complex opened with a few low-cost stores and seems to have had minimal effect on either retail or employment.

Vendors lost the right to sell their merchandise in the downtown plazas in the 1980s. Based on his experience of litigation against the city, *Ishmael Reyes* comments on the limits imposed on free zones allowing free speech, as he tells the story of how the vendors at San Agustín Plaza were barred after having been around for generations. They were first told that they were violating municipal ordinances. The priest at San Agustín Cathedral provided shelter to them when they were threatened with arrest. In the first round the hawkers prevailed on First Amendment grounds, but the charge was changed to illegal activity akin to soliciting by prostitutes. The unofficial explanation for removing small merchants from the plaza was that Hotel La Posada was worried about their presence near its facilities. Legally challenging the city becomes a necessary statement to show who has claims to it. Texas RioGrande Legal Aid (formerly Texas Rural Legal Aid) has sued the county many times along with the city, the U.S. Marshals, and the Border Patrol. Most of the cases involve civil rights violations: detaining people without reasonable suspicion, unreasonable search and seizure, police brutality, and use of excessive force.

The border and Laredo have been in the national limelight for immigration and drug trafficking, and more recently as a route for COVID-19 by way of asylum seekers. But within the city, the conversation about the future remains highly optimistic and ambitious. *Charles Fox* serves in the city's Planning and Zoning Department, and he would like the populace engaged in continuous dialogue about the future. Although policies that favor development at any cost seem to be the mantra of the day, *Trina Case* believes that the power of collective efforts remains undervalued. She recounts the story of a massive energy company that wanted to build a landfill for fracking waste a mile from the river, inside a hundred-year floodplain and close to the San Ignacio water intake pump. At the town hall meeting, the CEO got upset at local resistance and decided to abandon the project. The success of the #NoBorderWall Coalition in getting permission to paint the large mural at the entrance to the federal courthouse and motivating the city to join the lawsuit against the Trump administration is an example of the increase in the city council's responsiveness to the assertions of constituents. A founding member of the coalition, Carlos Evaristo Flores, has filmed *The Southern Front*, a documentary that narrates the fight with the Trump administration from the perspective of the people of Laredo. In the last few years, young and energetic new members have been elected to the city council on a very progressive platform unfamiliar to Laredo.[31]

Even as Laredo grows exponentially as a trade route, there is growing sentiment among residents to improve the regenerative aspects of life. Laredo has lacked a proper bookstore for decades. There are stores that sell children's books, but bookstores have experienced a terrible fate. The much-hyped Phoenix Bookstore opened in an important building in the pristine St. Peter's district but struggled because of the pandemic lockdown. Much of the intellectual vacuum is being filled with slam poetry, Little Theater, and concerts in the last two decades. To supplement this activity, film clubs have started in Laredo, holding shows at art galleries or Alamo Drafthouse Cinema. This grew out of the personal initiative of a nineteen-year-old, *Karla Garcia*, utilizing her Facebook page to reach out to like-minded aficionados. She was influenced by the example of guerilla filmmaker Robert Rodriguez,[32] who has been able to cultivate a self-reliant filmmaking community in Austin. Garcia believes that Laredo has the potential to become the cultural capital of Mexican American cinema. In the summer of 2015, an independent film production company based in Houston selected Laredo as the location for a film called *Journey*.[33] Laredo was picked because it was the only place they could find that looked very much like Mexico and very much like the United States. According to Garcia, this asset needs to be galvanized to showcase Laredo as a meeting place of culture and art, a huge shift from its familiar association with immigration and drug problems.

Along with history, geography has blessed Laredo in plentiful ways that remain underutilized. Laredo's topography is that of semiarid desert, but because of the river there exists a green ribbon of life that serves as either permanent or seasonal home to two hundred species of eastern, western, and neotropical birds. The stretch of river from Eagle Pass to Laredo is the most ecologically rich and diverse region in the entire Rio Grande Basin and claims to be the "the birdiest corridor in North America." A birding festival has been initiated by RGISC in Laredo in cooperation with the Monte Mucho Audubon Society, a citizen science organization, and the city. The Texas Ornithological Society has also helped with the vision and strategy of the Laredo Birding Festival (LBF). In the 1980s the U.S. Geological Survey's natural history survey identified half a dozen rare species of birds in Laredo and the Valley when enumerating the birds and mammals in the region. The Rio Grande Basin is one of the top ten places with the most biodiversity in the nation.

The rich and diverse ecosystem of the Rio Grande attracts many rare species of migratory birds, such as Morelet's seedeaters, scaled quails, gray hawks, Audubon's and Altamira orioles, green parakeets, Muscovy ducks, red-billed pigeons, and clay-colored thrushes.[34] Rare birds have been recorded by RGISC, including slaty-backed gulls, tropical parulas, black-headed grosbeaks, California and Iceland gulls, blue-headed vireos, dunlins, and canyon towhees. In 2010 and 2016 the female Amazon kingfisher made its first appearances in U.S. territory at the intersection of the Rio Grande and Zacate Creek. A rare sighting of a blue mockingbird also occurred at Riverbend.[35] A number of different locations where winter birds take refuge, ranging from local parks to distant ranches and small creeks to the riverfront, have all become vantage points to spot rare birds. Birders are accompanied by professional field guides and can select from a variety of full-day scenic trips. Birdwatchers come not only from different corners of the country (twenty-six states) but also from foreign countries (Canada, the United Kingdom, Brazil, Argentina). The festival is usually held over a weekend in February, a temperate and pleasant time. The birding festival started in 2013 with seventy-six visitors and has been growing steadily ever since. The peak number of visitors (161) was in 2020; the 2021 birding festival was virtual because of COVID-19 but still attracted 137 visitors. Starting with a loss of $2,525 in 2013, in 2019 LBF recorded revenues of $6,889, despite the fact that the festival is yet to get national coverage or even adequate support from the city.

Although Laredo reports the sighting of more species of birds, both common and rare, than in the Valley, there is less enthusiasm to take advantage of its natural retreats. The Valley has capitalized on its bird habitats, which are less diverse than Laredo's, to the tune of $350 million a year. The city is signaling more support as part of the commitment made in Viva Laredo. In 2021 the city announced natural landmarks at two scenic spots on the banks of the Rio Grande, a critical wildlife corridor for endangered species like the ocelot as well as the sighting location for the rare Amazon kingfisher. The city council voted unanimously to establish Riverbend as the city's first nature preserve and Las Palmas Nature Trail as its first birding sanctuary.[36] Newly elected council member Alyssa Cigarroa, District 8, led the motion, claiming that "our city's unique proximity to the river should be embraced as an eco-tourism opportunity—to protect our Rio Grande, conserve its environment, and share the beauty of its wildlife for generations to come."[37] This is a first step toward claiming an ecological identity for the port city.

Along with the Rio Grande/Río Bravo Basin Coalition, RGISC is promoting Día del Rio, made possible by a federal grant worth $100,000, to raise consciousness about watershed restoration.[38] The Paso del Indio Nature Trail was built in 1994 by a thousand volunteers putting in over thirty-four-thousand hours on the trail. The trail is a labor of love for those who built it. During Earth Day celebrations, nearly a thousand people visit the environmental science center at Laredo College. The Earth Day and birding festivals target different audiences and generate considerable income for the city.

Laredo as a bird sanctuary and a thriving trade port are to some extent mutually exclusive futures. While attention to enhanced road networks, reliable detection systems, ease of transport, and lack of bureaucracy is essential for a global port, a natural sanctuary requires legal protections that limit human and environmental damage. *Paul Cruise* cautions,

> The border ecosystem is fragile. The Lower Rio Grande has built bird sanctuaries which attract tourists to share in their natural bliss. Laredo, on the other hand, is expanding green spaces but is neglectful of protecting natural habitats despite the increased sighting of rare birds. Tangible entertainment

options like bike trails are prioritized, but the use of parks and public lands for walking, jogging, and biking is often detrimental to birdwatching.

The tasks of conservation and restoration of the precious riparian corridor will require heavy financial and political investment. The most challenging part will be working with Homeland Security and the Border Patrol, as these remote areas are subject to intense vigilance by the agencies. Ecotourism and control of the border are conflicting concepts, but Laredo is eager to dabble in both. One of the charges against the border wall is that Laredo will lose many winter visitors if massive construction erodes the habitats. The birds will steer away from the trees they rely on for food and shelter because of the physical and technological impediments that are on the way. The vision of elevating Laredo as a natural retreat and promoting the burgeoning industry of ecotourism clashes with the militarized border taking shape along the river.

The city has always focused on trade, to the point that promoting local industry was not even on the agenda. But trade in the globalized era makes distinct demands that are different from past national policies followed by industrial economies. Revenue from trade-related activities makes up more than half of Laredo's economy, but revenue from internal gross sales and thus sales taxes is negatively affected by global trade. The health of the local economy is dependent on Mexican shoppers, but local government has little power over regulations that obstruct the flow of such shoppers. *Charles Vega* is optimistic in feeling that Laredo has come a long way from the days of unpaved streets and the patron system, discerning policies that focus on common welfare rather than shortsighted political benefit. The irony is that when at last the city is responding to people's aspirations, the policies that impinge on Laredo are being shaped more than ever in Washington, D.C.

Laredo was tagged as the "Gateway to Mexico" for decades, but then new taglines like "On the Edge" or "Tour on the Edge of History" or "Rediscover Our Flavor" started to appear. James Bird discusses the concept of the gateway city to explain seaports, which function as links between the hinterland and the outside world. Trade is the lifeblood of gateway cities.[39] Although Laredo thrives on trade, it is a different kind of gateway city. What makes Laredo a gateway city is the image that it is a place to pass through. The image perfectly blends with the reality of having turned into a global corridor, and yet the motto of Laredo underwent changes to project the image of a tourist city precisely when the significance of its "gateway" characteristics became elevated. In 2020 the city opted for a rebranding—"The Place to Be Together"—underplaying its trade and tourism aspects and reimagining itself as a destination city. The new Convention and Visitors Bureau in the heart of downtown is refocusing on local crowds, both from within the city and from nearby ones, building on natural and cultural attractions along with identifying new commercial opportunities. It is the only agency funded by the city occupancy tax, which prevents it from pursuing local promotion and advertising. It partners with local organizations such as the Public Information Office, which in 2020 ran a civic-pride campaign called "Celebrate Laredo,"[40] now turned into an annual event.

According to *Trina Case*, Laredo has the potential to be a game changer on environmental issues and to take the lead in Texas, whose environmental record is paltry. She identifies the Rio Grande as ground zero for Laredo and the very center of its existence. She is happy that people are rallying around the river in different capacities, whether paddling or hiking or birding or using the trails, but Laredo needs to take the next step by preparing itself for the coming ravages of climate change. As mentioned earlier, it was the first city in Texas to ban plastic bags, which was featured in the documentary *The Story of Plastic*.[41] As climate change threatens agricultural capacity, Laredo can respond with the enviable advantage of adequate sun and wind all year long and put itself in a position to take the lead in renewable energy. These efforts can aid in the solar electrification of the port and set a new trend, which is a conversation RGISC is already trying to start with the city's policy makers.

After the Trump administration declared the border an unsafe place, Laredo steadily kept losing precious revenue from bridge tolls, sales taxes, and hotel and motel occupancy. The political brawl over the border wall has had a notable financial impact on the city. The local economy has felt the sting as fewer people cross the border, leading to declining revenue. While border security and reinforcements are important, the balance between security and trade has traditionally tilted in favor of the latter. *Alvin Travis* notes, "The amicable relationship with Mexico is an age-old tradition that people and politicians on both sides respect and are proud of. But the image of chaos, intensified by the Trump administration, has resulted in decreased bridge revenue." According to him, the guarantee of a secure border for commerce is essential for one of the busiest ports in the country to sustain its functions and develop further. The assurance of a secure logistical infrastructure cannot be overrated in trade, a dilemma made worse by the contradictory messages emanating from the resident population versus the national media. Working in local government, Travis is frustrated that the federal government does not understand the effects of its policies on local entities, and even worse, often does not care.

The dominant storyline of Laredo will continue to remain NAFTA. The Laredo Sector has almost five thousand Border Patrol and customs agents, all high-paying jobs. Many Mexican trade forwarders live in Laredo, and in the last decade oil and gas exploration has brought a lot of people to Laredo. *Raul Muñoz* notes that the new energy arena was built with taxpayer money but requires admission fees that may not be affordable to poorer people. He complains, "Taxes pay for transport infrastructure but do not benefit all neighborhoods equally. Being a border community prioritizing safety, more than 60 percent of general funds go for law enforcement. If the bridge were to be shut down for a day, Laredo's economy would collapse, but Washington, D.C., does not see Laredo as more than a conduit."

Laredo's economy is always oscillating between "feast and famine," claims *Samantha Taft.* During economic slumps, Laredo becomes more dependent on the Mexican economy, as Mexican shoppers take advantage of relatively cheaper goods and sustain the local economy. But a spurt in economic activity, such as the establishment of railroads or the discovery of oil and gas, brings out-of-town investors and provides an external boost. This dependable nexus is now being hindered as policies made in Washington, D.C., have eclipsed local networks of economic interdependence. *Roger Gordon* explains the conundrum thus: "The conflict over downtown is between people who want to preserve the architecture of the beautiful buildings and those who want to build a new image of Laredo. How can the city be a gateway to Mexico if it does not want people from Mexico?"

Despite ranking among the ten largest cities in Texas, Laredo still evokes a small-town feeling. It is very difficult to find skilled workers for existing jobs in the trucking industry even as biology and engineering majors are forced to leave home to pursue professional careers elsewhere. People from Louisiana or Ohio flock to Laredo for high-paying jobs as heavy equipment operators or truck drivers, but the large number of high school dropouts in Laredo could easily have been trained for such skills. Local entrepreneur *Erin Arroyo* highlights the challenge in finding skilled workers and reiterates the gap between local needs and opportunities. The city seems content with the large number of minimum-wage jobs created by NAFTA, when more infrastructure and development could move to south Laredo neighborhoods, where land is cheap and abundant, to allow the balanced growth of all neighborhoods to benefit everyone. Arroyo feels that revenue earned from bridges can be spent to improve the lives of residents by rehabilitating drug addicts, spaying and neutering animals, and most importantly, promoting local industries. *Raul Muñoz* notes that without a proper baseball stadium, competitions in Laredo are held in ten different fields, ensuring a logistical nightmare. Laredo hosts Pony League baseball for children aged three to five and all the way up to twelve, who come with parents, grandparents, and extended family. The potential to cash in on the significant economic impact remains unutilized. Meanwhile, the outdoor mall struggles to attract local shoppers who prefer to drive to San Marcos to frequent the same type of shops. The feeling of a robust community, with little traffic and stress, allows people more leisure time, argues *Aileen Ramos*. The city can enhance this atmosphere by arranging concerts and blockading downtown streets for events to bring people together. *Charles Fox* believes that the city's comprehensive plan is about recoding Laredo with balanced investments in downtown, but the implementation would require a mental shift that nurtures small business and enables links with the people. Fox believes, "Laredo should be seen as more than a warehouse. Local skills are needed to capture the full benefits of the important corridor, and people need to feel ownership of local businesses. Now that a reverse brain drain is occurring, TAMIU can help figure out various opportunities for the returning talents by initiating a benign space where policies concerning the city can be argued."

Jesse Knight summarizes well the entire paradox behind the conflicting subtexts of the border:

> The economic impact of one Border Patrol agent is at least a hundred thousand dollars [salary and overtime benefits]. So let's say we want ten more agents, that's a million dollars to the local economy. A hundred more, and it's a ten million dollar injection of federal funds coming in, eating at our restaurants, going to our shops, and buying houses and all that. We can get that by saying it's dangerous, we need help down here! But then that also harms the image of business. If we say everything is safe, then all of a sudden the agents move away. So how do we articulate it? Someone is going to make

a hell of a lot of money building those walls. And anyone who sits there and takes a strong stand against those walls is not going to get the contract for millions of dollars of work. So whoever speaks up and says that they're saving America is more likely to get the lucrative contracts.

The haphazard efforts at downtown revival are a reflection of what is remembered and revered in Laredo, but more importantly, what is forgotten. The Republic of the Rio Grande Museum, which occupies the first capitol building, is centrally located in downtown but gets very little attention despite its rich history compared, for example, to WBC. The forty-year-old Webb County Heritage Foundation, dedicated to preserving local heritage, operates the extraordinary museum, a landmark in Laredo, along with continuous exhibits in other historic buildings and tours for students and tourists. *Millie Allen* of the foundation notices the reflection of the city in its spatial formations: "Laredo retains a treasure trove of historic architectural structures in downtown, which should be a matter of envy to other cities. The oldest architectural units in town are still standing, even if they are not well preserved. The original architecture of commercial buildings from the second stories up is still visible, even if the ground floors may have been modified." Like its architecture, Laredo's history is remembered in tatters, not as the unbroken chronicle of a people who belong to the land and to whom the land belongs.

The attempt to overturn the negative image of Laredo, at least in music, materialized through local initiative in the award-winning PBS documentary *Rhapsody on the Rio Grande: A Confluence of Culture* (2017).[42] This exploration of how the Rio Grande has shaped its people has been constructed as a biopic of the river that is considered the soul of Laredo. The haunting musical score was composed by TAMIU faculty member Dr. Colin Campbell, who delineated the themes of U.S.-Mexico border culture and history from interviews with local residents. The language of music was employed for a conversation between the Laredo Philharmonic Orchestra and Mariachi Nuevo Tecalitlán de Guadalajara. It took two years of effort to plan, compose, and present the piece, which was much appreciated as the voice of Laredo.[43] Like the ebb and flow of the water, "the slow rhythm of the ballad, the double bass instruments of the classical orchestra, and the bountiful pitch of the mariachi songs" blended to create an imaginative portrayal of Laredo, "which stretches across languages and lands without boundaries." Campbell further explains, "The classical training of the mariachi singers served as the common core for the whole composition. Music in Laredo is almost superfluous, from local bands to trained mariachi ensembles. The music, following the river, starts with tunes about the mountains of Colorado and runs through the fallow lands of New Mexico to the lush landscape of Texas." He calls the composition "landscaping in music," wanting to capture the movement of the river with fifty-seven minutes of music. His rudimentary Spanish was not much of an obstacle as the vocabulary of music transcended all barriers and even different genres. By the end of the score, he felt he "could emotionally articulate the tune of the waterway that is rich in multiplicity and yet always flowing toward harmony." The different musicians were synchronized to capture the allure of the border. This documentary presents a very different frame to view Laredo, and it may well be a reflection of the claim of a new border identity voiced by people from the border itself.

Conclusion

The successes of Laredo remain mostly invisible beyond the persistent adverse narratives. Even the economic success of the port city is projected along with negative caveats about crime and mayhem. On all measures of violent crime—including murder, rape, robbery, aggravated assault, and property crime—Laredo lags behind state averages and those of bigger cities like Houston, Austin, Dallas, San Antonio, and even Corpus Christi. Any news regarding drug trafficking or illegal border crossing obscures the fact that two million commercial trucks legally transport merchandise between Texas and Mexico via Laredo each year, handling the bulk of the nation's trade with Mexico. The local economy depends on shoppers from Nuevo Laredo, especially the outlet mall, which has been quite literally built on the border. As the fight against the border wall escalated, the federal government adamantly erected a migrant processing center in the heart of downtown in 2018. *Paul Sergio* recounts how the Trump administration turned down the city's offer to lease a twenty-one-thousand-square-foot office space for just a dollar a year for reasons of inadequate space when their enormous facility is processing 46 percent fewer migrants than they had anticipated. The grotesque new structure built with shipping containers now thwarts the most bucolic view of Laredo overlooking the river and the bridge. Because of the risk of flooding, the federal government may yield to the city's offer and dismantle

FIGURE 27 Birding on the banks of the Rio Grande. Rio Grande International Study Center.

the eyesore after not getting much use out of it. The timing of resurrecting the paranoia toward migrants and border crossers unfortunately coincides with the city's multiphase effort to revitalize the downtown and attract both locals as well as neighbors from Nuevo Laredo to sustain its august center.

Laredo has always been associated with lawlessness, regardless of the actual violence that might or might not have taken place. The mayor of Laredo was chastised in 2012 for running advertisements on billboards all over Texas proclaiming that "Laredo is Safe."[44] He was, without a doubt, responding to portrayals of Laredo and fearing the loss of investment and tourism, but his reaction reveals how the image of Laredo is often directed from the outside. Border towns usually offer questionable merchandise (drugs) and services (prostitution), but instead of Laredo, the base of such taboo vices and pleasures happens to be Boy's Town in Nuevo Laredo, an enclosed bastion that is removed from the normal walks of life. The images that are repeatedly evoked for border towns haunt Laredo even though its disreputable entertainment options remain tame and scanty. The story of its transformation from a dusty town to the largest inland port rarely focuses on the positive aspects. The natural beauty and bounty of Laredo remain buried under security concerns. The downbeat national narrative is tied to federal dollars even though it harms local trade and tourism. The upbeat picture of the city and its successes seems to be mostly for local consumption, and although this makes Laredo more livable and enjoyable, the authentic voices are drowned out in the national cacophony of fear and insecurity. So far, the voices of the local people lack a sufficient outlet to define their own city.

CHAPTER 6

Border Identity

Remains of the Day

> When I go up to New York, I am Mexican, but when I am
> here, I am not. When I am in Mexico, I am American. So it
> is the special place where I can just be me. I am a border girl.
>
> *ROXANA PEEL*, LAREDO RESIDENT

> WBC is more of a political stunt. I think it is time to move
> forward. We need to counter with community events that
> are more representative of our culture, our roots.
>
> *JOHN LEE*, LAREDO RESIDENT

The element of pride in identity and belonging is a motif that remains constant for Laredo; the interesting task is to note the turning points of the account across generations and social change. Residents recount the growth of their cherished city with memories of compassion infusing the community and a sense of pride and comfort in who they are. Hispanic identity in this secluded space was able to thrive in the midst of intermarriage with white residents. The welcoming stance toward non-Hispanics created an inclusive vibe that Laredo has retained throughout its existence. Laredo does have a small non-Hispanic population, but it is seldom treated as a minority, and in that sense Laredo seems to better absorb differences that might otherwise have spurred conflict along ethnic lines. Class distinctions have formed people's privilege or lack thereof, yet the absence of ethnic or racial rivalries has been treasured, and injustices rooted in economic divisions have been largely accepted and ignored. Many residents choose to live here or have even moved here so that their children can grow up never feeling like a minority. An interesting aspect of Laredo's history is how people from diverse ethnic and racial backgrounds (although much smaller in number), not just from next-door Mexico, have made it their home. Localism in Laredo is tied with connections to the city, not necessarily race, ethnicity, or nationality. This phenomenon has always allowed the integration of Anglos, Mexicans, Tejanos, and non-Hispanic settlers within the landscape without much problem.

One of the striking components of Laredo's culture is its celebration of George Washington's birthday. Laredo exalts it with much pomp and splendor over more than a month, making it the most boisterous such event in the country. The beginnings of the ceremony show a racist cast, an attempt to Americanize the Hispanic population, yet this Hispanic town has given it paramount importance. The changes in the ceremony over the decades and its sudden disparagement by the new generation encapsulate the evolution of identity formation and conflict in the city, a history that started with relative calm but has recently been disturbed by neoliberal economic polarization. This chapter is about the construction of border identity, driven by the awareness that in Laredo's collective memory few of the controversial historical issues have cast a long shadow, and instead there has always been a tendency to smooth over differences and discard critical memory. Laredo's much beloved identity, which never needed to be defined sharply as long as the city remained in its small and safe comfort zone, is now being redefined in the national limelight as the emerging generation claims the mantle of minority with pride and absorbs it within the salient but silent border identity that has always existed in the lives of Laredoans.

The Border as the Blending Point

The physical border between the United States and Mexico failed to leave a permanent nationalistic mark on Hispanic bodies in Laredo. Newcomers like Anglos or African Americans or people of Middle Eastern descent folded into border communities made up of Hispanics, Chicanos, Mexicans, Native Americans, and mestizos. Hybridity is a key characteristic of the border, sparking ethnic and racial mingling even at the height of well-established racial hierarchies and the prevalence of ethnic prejudices. Scholars agree that the very construction of Chicano identity has been hybrid.[1] The term *hybridity* has a postcolonial connotation with Homi Bhabha labeling it as the space where identities collide and come to terms with opposing elements. There is always an undercurrent of resistance in hybridity as its different parts compete to overpower each other.[2] This "in-between space" or "thirdspace" also

FIGURE 28 The Republic of the Rio Grande Museum. Webb County Historical Foundation.

demonstrates a spatial dimension where identity conflicts produce responsive spaces that are continually being reclaimed. The status of privilege in the hierarchical segments of hybridity is always in flux and has to be captured in a specific time and context. The process of globalization has added another intricate dimension to the ongoing production of hybridity.[3]

In the contested terrain of such thirdspaces, what sets Laredo apart is how little of its hybridity was constructed in friction. In place of strife, a peaceful arrangement occurred almost organically between Hispanics and Anglos, diverging from the mode of battle between Hispanics and Native Americans. I would argue that the border region, especially Laredo, provided the space to blend the contesting aspects of hybrid identity. Instead of the Hispanic body being situated in American history, Hispanics in Laredo make a claim on history while being rooted in the land of their ancestors, where they have prevailed throughout the formation of different nation-states. The spatial marks of Mexican heritage abound in the older parts of the city. From the days going back to when Laredo joined the Union, newcomers arrived and assimilated as they learned Spanish and adopted certain mannerisms (greeting people with an embrace and kissing the cheeks). The pliability signifying the border is the essential aspect of border identity that has soothed the edges of hybridity and produced a synthesis rooted in its own chronicle of land, language, and local sensibility.

Gilberto Hinojosa claims that Spanish social structure in Laredo prevailed because of Laredo's geographic location, relative isolation, and comparatively large population marked by steady growth through the years.[4] Growth and struggle both continued during the Mexican War of Independence (1810–21). By 1820 Spaniards constituted 57 percent of Laredo's population, as mestizos, *mulatos*, and Indians were unable to keep up with the new entrants.[5] Hinojosa notes the rigid social hierarchy of Laredo, where a quarter of the land was owned by two of the elite members of society and a tenth by two other residents while the rest of the people owned land worth five hundred pesos or less.[6] The economy of Laredo added a variety of new occupations through the 1860s, including real estate, although half the people were common laborers, servants, washerwomen, and shepherds. In the land of Mexicans, Hinojosa recorded the presence of twenty-two Anglo-Americans and eleven Europeans among the population, six from France, four from Ireland, and one from Germany.[7] Fred Rippy documents the clashes along the Rio Grande between Americans and Mexicans over tariffs, smuggling, and runaway slaves,[8] but it is important to note that after the Civil War, many African American soldiers chose to settle in the Rio Grande Valley, where they felt more accepted in the Hispanic society.

The five families that owned the most land in Laredo were not only Anglo-American but also mixed race, tracing their origin from Spain to Mexico. Laredo was warm and welcoming to merchants, whether they were Spaniards, or Jews from Eastern Europe.[9] Railroads expanded the wealth and influence of the merchant class as well as the sheer number of settlers (mostly white) in the region. On the social front, instead of the distinction between nobles and ordinary citizens, the contrast that was clear and understood from the beginning was between rich and poor. At a time when mixed marriages were common, the differences between Spaniards, mestizos, and *mulatos* were never that prominent.[10] American immigrants to Laredo entered into marriages with local elite families to secure their status in the new city.[11] Hinojosa mentions that the census before 1824 distinguished between Spaniards (Españoles) and Indians (mestizos, *mulatos*); although with time these classifications were expunged, the social title of Don prevailed to provide a clue about elite status.[12] Wealth and status in America have always been intertwined with race and ethnicity, but in this Hispanic-dominated city it was social class that overshadowed racial status.[13]

Although Anglo-Americans owned most of the land in Laredo, instead of dominating the local elites they became part of the social strata through intermarriage. Laredo has always been an immigrant town, heavily Mexican and with Spanish as the first language. *Richard Andrew* narrates, "Until the Union Army took Laredo in 1848, Laredoans had hardly ever seen any Anglos even though Laredo had supposedly been part of the Republic of Texas. There were never any Anglos in Laredo before Texas became part of the Union. Instead of crushing the local elites, the Union Army made a deal with them, allowing them to run the city but taking over the county, which was the new political subdivision." Clashes along ethnic lines seldom emerged as there were hardly any attempts to take over the political reins of the city. Hinojosa confirms that Webb County government was ruled by Anglo-American judges, as municipal political offices were often left undisturbed with local elites in power.[14] The only disruption was the clamor for landholdings by white settlers, but with twenty new land titles, a truce was reached between the Anglo and Hispanic communities.[15] This trait of collaboration rather than confrontation has been predominant since the nineteenth century. American nativist sentiments feed off minorities and foreigners,[16] but the expression of racial and anti-immigrant prejudices has been rooted in class differentiations in this heavily Hispanic city. This twist has also effectively hidden conflicts within the city. Throughout different turbulent historical moments, such as the Civil War, this peaceful arrangement between the two ethnic groups remained intact. Laredo actually sent soldiers to both the Confederate and Union armies. At the end of the war, many black soldiers decided to settle in the Rio Grande Valley, lured by the absence of tangible bigotry.[17] Instead of racial discord, the war brought unprecedented prosperity to Laredo as trade grew exponentially following its brief role as a primary channel to smuggle cotton for the Confederate army.

Even though ranches were populated on the other side of the Rio Grande all through history, Nuevo Laredo emerged as a city much later, in 1848, formed by those who left Laredo and opted to remain Mexican citizens. Family and business connections on the two banks of the river continued as seamlessly as the flow of the river. This congruence formed the foundation of border identity, prioritizing cohesion over conflict. Social and ethnic harmony has remained a constant theme for the city. The usual prejudice against mixed-race people or mulattos was almost nonexistent compared to cities like San Antonio. Old-time residents like *Thomas Jeffrey* remember listening to stories about how the KKK in the early 1900s was going to descend on the city for a march, but the locals stopped them even though the KKK had a formidable presence in Texas, in places as close as San Antonio.[18] As an Anglo shop owner in downtown, he has never felt out of place despite being an ethnic minority in the city. Racist and anti-Semitic feelings are not entirely absent from Laredo, though this has never evolved into ethnic animosity. The drive for profits always enjoyed prevalence over any friction in Laredo, which permitted newcomers to settle in the city without facing much prejudice.

Despite Laredo always having been a port, the lifestyle of its residents was mostly monochromatic, at least until the 1950s. *Bianca Frey* first encountered white bread with her classmates who lived at the air force base. Her regular lunch had only been tortillas with beans. The children were curious about each other's foods and started exchanging lunch. Frey remembers selling her lunch to her classmates and making a profit. *Martina Russo* remembers that the first time she felt she was different was during a road trip to San Antonio when she begged her father to stop at an unfamiliar restaurant, and her army officer father told her that they would not be served in many eating establishments. This incident took place in Cotulla, just sixty miles north of Laredo. Russo had so far enjoyed her sheltered life and was shocked to learn that "they didn't serve Mexicans and they didn't serve blacks either in certain places on the other side of the checkpoint."

Laredo was not immune to the larger political shifts that occurred nationwide after World War II. *Margarita Gallellos* recalls, "When my father was serving in the military in Nevada, he ran into signs that said no dogs or Mexicans allowed. But the officers of his unit left the restaurant where he was denied entry." In his exposure to the world outside Laredo, both loyalty and identity emerged as intricate issues. He recounted his war experiences in a notebook. Laredo's boys came back from the war as men, facing discrimination to which they were unaccustomed. After the war, Gallellos's father wanted to go to Columbia University but lacked the financial resources and was unable to get government funding despite having served in the war. There was an enhanced emphasis on education in the family, not only to acquire better skills and jobs but also to be treated equally. This was the era when unequal treatment of minorities was a widespread norm, especially in the South, but for men from Laredo the awareness of being a minority came as a rude shock when they first ventured outside their hometown.

Oscar Martínez claims that Mexican Americans historically remained second-class citizens along the U.S.-Mexico border territory. His categorization of Mexican American identity is situated in political change in America, which paved the way for more people (read white Americans) from other parts of the United States to come and settle in the borderlands. The border identity that evolved came about through interaction and confrontation between indigenous Mexican Americans and Anglos who claimed cultural and political hegemony.[19] This is the point of divergence between Laredo and other border territories. Not only did the proportion of white settlers (and other minorities after NAFTA) never outnumber the ethnic majority but also most of these newcomers were associated with major institutions (Fort McIntosh, Laredo Air Force Base, TAMIU, Laredo Medical Center) and thus esteemed by the public. The process of acculturation in Laredo was turned on its head as it was the Anglos (and other minorities) who had to assimilate into the thriving Mexican American culture. Martínez finds a "relaxed and tolerant atmosphere" in Laredo and Brownsville as opposed to domination and confrontation in San Diego and El Paso.[20] His categorization of "mixers," which denotes hybrid identities in the borderlands, exhibits racial tolerance, an ubiquitous comfort level within the social sphere, and a self-deprecating sense of humor, all of which he finds in evidence in Laredo.[21]

Border identity is a strong if somewhat intangible notion outside border cities. *Kayla Hall* attests that before leaving for an out-of-state university, her daughter was not even aware that she was a minority or had an accent. *Katie Brown*, a young professional, had never heard anyone use a racial slur against anyone Hispanic in her life. She confirms, "Laredo is a bubble where I led a sheltered life amid the comforts of familiar culture and close-knit family. Instead of the teenager's life depicted in films like *American Pie* or *Varsity Blues* where students party at a frat house, I went across the border to party and have drinks and fun with my friends. Mexico was a lot safer when I was growing up." She remembers friends who were undocumented or only had student visas but could easily sneak into the bars of Nuevo Laredo as the Border Patrol officers turned a blind eye to these harmless practices.

The city often felt like an extension of the family, and the sanctuary was taken for granted. Growing up in Laredo, *Samantha Taft* did not value her culture or care to learn Spanish. Her role models were blonde women on television, so she colored her hair to look like them. The only Hispanic characters she saw on television were prostitutes or crooked people. When she went to college in Austin, she was ashamed of her heritage and worried about Hispanic stereotypes, imagining that people were perceiving her in that light. A turning point for her was the Tejano singer Selena's death, as she observed people from every ethnicity mourning for her. She was astounded to find that so many people admired the girl on the poster in her room. In her twenties, she started working at the U.S. Embassy in Nuevo Laredo in the international department. She could barely speak Spanish and ran into incidents such as when she mistook a check for a thousand dollars for a million dollars (misreading the Spanish word *mil*, which stands for thousand). This changed her attitude toward her culture and home even more, as they started to reveal their beauty and she began accepting who she was. She is proud to note that her daughter, also raised in Laredo, has high self-esteem as a Hispanic.

Taft claims that the patriarchal element in Hispanic culture is more relaxed at the border. Her father always told her she could be anything she wanted to be. Perhaps this was the benefit of being part of American culture. *Matilda Roy*, who immigrated to Laredo in her adolescence, has a contrasting experience. She feels that her gender stood out in high school in Laredo much more than in her native Mexico. Even when she joined the ROTC, she had to fight all the way to the top of the chain of command to get permission to do what her male colleagues were doing. She was warned not to demoralize her male colleagues with aggressive behavior. Although Mexico is perceived to be very traditional, her experience is that it was easier to grow up in Mexico City without a strict gender identity. She feels that there exists a schizophrenia in Laredo when it comes to self-identification: "We believe ourselves to be neither American nor Mexican, but Mexican and American at the same time, and then on top of that Texan, so you have both cultures feeding these gender roles and all of them push toward conservatism."

Based on her own life journey, *Samantha Taft* offers the prognosis that Laredo has a personality conflict, the same one she experienced as a child when she was embarrassed about her culture: Laredo is embarrassed to be too Mexican. For her, the paradigm of Laredo is this personality disorder, as being neither Mexican nor American. *Sophia Brown* also perceives a split personality in Laredo. As a Mexican American with Italian heritage, she grew up without ever feeling discriminated against and was rather self-assured. *Karla*

Garcia, on the other hand, never felt any conflict about her identity. She is thankful that she is able to experience both an American and a Mexican side to life, but she was not conscious of the border growing up in Laredo. Until fifth grade, she did not comprehend that she lived an existence that extended into two different countries. She loves being able to go to Mexico to visit the doctor or to get food, and misses hearing Spanish even when she travels to San Marcos. The violence that has restricted the border is most unfortunate to her. Laredo, for Garcia, is a warm place defined by family.

Many residents express their ease with being both American and Mexican. *Millie Allen* feels "equally Mexican and American, and the two parts don't feel conflicted but interlinked." *Rebecca Park* remembers a poem about not being American or Mexican but having the color of caramel, a mixture of white and brown, that perfectly captures Laredo for her, especially the line where the poet describes feeling like a puppet pulled by two cultures with allegiance to both. "When I sing 'The Star-Spangled Banner' I get teary, but when I hear 'Mexicanos' that makes me equally emotional," Park notes. Even though she is not a Mexican citizen, Mexico means family to her. She now only visits Nuevo Laredo for funerals and weddings. It breaks her heart not to be able to go across as she pleases, because in the past the city was not removed from her life but was simply an extension of her backyard.

Laredo is unequivocally home for *Martina Russo*, as the city allowed her to become the person she is by offering her solid opportunities. She, too, believes that the social order is welcoming to strangers and not judgmental. Not only did people grow up without feeling defensive like most minorities, they were not even aware that they were poor as they lived in a homogeneous and harmonious society. The significance of family was clear to *Katie Brown* when she lost her brother to a drug overdose, and the whole city lent her its shoulders. As a Latina growing up in Missouri, *Pamela Ivan's* first exposure to Hispanic culture occurred in Laredo, but she only started appreciating this after she left town. She started relating to the city and saw how her identity was entrenched in different modes and mannerisms manifested in everyday life from grocery stores to architectural styles. Now she feels committed to keeping the historical integrity and vibrant culture alive through her professional role while running a nonprofit to revive the downtown legacy. *Viviana Cortez* feels that experiencing both American and Mexican celebrations has enriched her life and considers herself fortunate to enjoy music in two languages.

The bilingual and bicultural character of the city enticed other Hispanics to make it their chosen home. *Ishmael Reyes* wanted to experience what it would be like to live in a place where Chicanos were in control, and Laredo happened to be that place. It stood out to him because, as he explains,

> The assimilation pattern in Laredo was in reverse. Anglos assimilated into Hispanic culture and not the other way around as in other communities. What was it that made this type of reverse assimilation possible? Hispanics had retained the capital, the land, and the economic power because of their sheer numerical strength and intermarriage with Anglos.[22] They did not surrender to Anglos like they did in other parts of South Texas. The power of Hispanic wealth was not only rooted in land, but also in the intelligentsia, because of the presence of the professional class among local Hispanic people.

Reyes wanted his daughter to flourish in just this type of cultural ambience. Residing in Laredo, he has realized that if it was wealth that safeguarded Hispanic identity and culture, then this same wealth has separated them. The process of marginalization occurs in Laredo not along the usually visible race lines but along class lines that often remain invisible in America. Reyes feels that even with existing class differences, it is difficult to imagine such a tight-knit "Chicano nation" anywhere else in the country. There was a zone for the privileged class, whose very existence created a cultural schizophrenia or dual personality that celebrated the cultural heritage while oppressing people of the same heritage. Reyes discovered Laredo in search of a roadmap to fight against social injustice, and while Laredo offered him a place to prosper and raise his child, he is also disillusioned about making it a working-class haven. He realizes that "if we cannot make it happen in a place like this, then we cannot do it anywhere else."

Laredo is a place "where our identity is a little bit lost," feels *Roxana Peel*. Like her city, she is neither fully Mexican nor fully American. Laredo is a special place that allows her to be both without any questions being asked. She identifies completely with the border and calls herself a "border girl." The border has been a safe haven for her, where people are genuinely curious about her accent. She loves switching back and forth between English and Spanish, since that is how her brain works. She believes she can enjoy the best of both worlds on the border, explaining, "I have Mexico at my fingertips and I have the great food, but I also have the amenities of the U.S." When she interacts with nonprofit organizations in New York, London, and similar places, she feels they do not really grasp the concept of the border. She marvels that her office is just a mile away from Mexico, and many of her coworkers cross the bridge daily to come to work. She believes people are becoming genuinely more intrigued about the border because of the news, even though most of the issues are presented negatively. One of her friends in New York helped produce a documentary about the aforementioned baseball team, Tecolotes de los Dos Laredos, the only professional sports team that played in both countries. The ironic movie title *Bad Hombres* comes from President Trump's derogatory labeling of Mexican immigrants.[23]

Washington's Birthday Celebration (WBC)

Laredo exhibits a highly idiosyncratic feature, the six-week-long celebration of George Washington's birthday spanning all of February, an eminent event for the founding father who had no connection with Laredo's history. The initiation and renovation of this ceremony contains many aspects of border identity. It began in 1898 in Laredo as a two-day ceremony with reenactment of the Boston Tea Party by the Improved Order of Red Men (IORM) Yaqui Tribe #59 fraternity. A hundred-foot-long ship was placed in front of city hall, where the Red Men, dressed as both Indians and white Americans, fought with each other, as Indians were scalped and overthrown along with boxes of candy labeled as tea.[24] The *Laredo Times* reported the event as an endeavor to awaken patriotism among Hispanics and to deliver the message that they lived in the United States, not Mexico.[25] The narrative thread of the play *One Night with the Red Men* was about claiming Laredo as part of America, establishing a civic religion of patriotism to overshadow all other identity orientations.[26] *National Geographic* recently did a feature story on WBC in Laredo, highlighting the exotic features of the celebration and connecting it to upper-class aspirations.[27]

Elaine Peña has deconstructed the original ceremony described in the official documentation of *Improved Order of Red Men's Official History* (1893), where the group narrates its history and strategy of constructing an American sprit by usurping Native American rituals and ceremonies to demonstrate the superiority of European heritage.[28] She also notes that several members of the IORM Yaqui Tribe #59 settled in Laredo in the early 1880s and prospered economically. They headed industries like Coca-Cola and

"Embracing Traditions"
120th Washington's Birthday Celebration 2017

FIGURE 29 Washington's Birthday Celebration poster. Washington's Birthday Celebration Association.

Budweiser, wrote for the *Laredo Morning Times*, and served as county sheriff, county treasurer, and even mayor of Laredo.[29] As Peña notes, "Walking downtown along streets named Moctezuma, Matamoros, Hidalgo, Juárez, Iturbide, Santa María, San Bernardo, and San Agustín that intersected or ran parallel to Washington, Lincoln, Farragut, Houston, Davis, and Grant, for example, heightened their sense of purpose."[30] Her recent book, *¡Viva George! Celebrating Washington's Birthday at the U.S.-Mexico Border*, is based on how the celebration evolved in Laredo, the backroom dealings of various stakeholders, and the meanings of such a ceremony for the city.

There is not a person in Laredo who does not have some memory of or association with WBC, but despite generally pleasing recollections, their views of it as a hallmark of Laredo are varied indeed. *Alvin Travis* remembers looking forward to the only month in the year that really provided activities for people to come together. He remembers making sure to get a seat in the front row of the parade because he wanted to view every float and display. He is now conscious of the dubious origins of the ceremony, but as a child he associated it with carnivalesque fun. He has noticed that over the years the organization has done a much better job of including diverse groups with affiliate events. Although some events (such as the Society of Martha Washington Colonial Pageant and Ball) are still run by the elites, the inclusion of a variety of events (such as the Laredo College Family Fun Fest and Musicale) now offers something for everyone to participate in. It is understood that not all events signify the same prestige: the Princess Pocahontas Pageant and Ball created much later is not on a par with Martha's Ball.[31]

Elliot Young explains the origin of WBC as part of the conscious construction of racial harmony on the border. The rituals started out as mock fights between Indians and Americans amid the conquest of the south, projecting the former as stereotypically barbaric.[32] The irony is that Laredo actually had relative racial peace, but the story of nation making seldom resorts to rapport and affinity. Laredo was known as a melting pot, and despite land transfers to white settlers, elite Hispanics retained much of the control over the city. The IORM[33] was an offshoot of the Sons of Liberty formed during the American Revolution. The exclusive white male organization claimed to be following the Iroquois League, a federation of six Indian nations, yet one of the rituals of WBC in Laredo was the street theater consisting of an Indian attack on city hall where war-painted Indians were vanquished by white Americans protecting the city.[34] The Pocahontas Ball was added to the ceremonies much later. Although it may appear incongruous, it is a nod to a more inclusive display of American history, and probably not an accident that the Hispanic part of history is missing from the construction that took place in their own land.

By 1905 WBC had become a regional event attracting tourists with the street drama of the city hall attack as a pivotal draw.[35] Young notes that real racial discord between African American soldiers and Hispanic residents emerged in the early 1900s, after "uppity" African Americans settled in South Texas.[36] This was not a concern for Laredo as the handful of African American residents came to the city much later, mainly as officers at the air force base, and therefore were not targeted for discrimination. Rather, it demonstrates a long-standing tradition of inclusion. Hispanic elites were included in the fold of white Americans as long as their cultural symbols remained invisible. The lower-class citizens of Laredo were really the audience for this nation-building exercise. Young categorizes WBC as part of the process of the Americanization of South Texas, whereby patriotism was redefined as national identity rather than connection with land.[37] For the elites in Laredo, whether white or Mexican, it was explicitly demonstrated who the "others" were and implicitly understood who was in charge. Although WBC claimed to project racial unity, it was actually projecting class unity. Battles between Mexicans and Americans are not part of the ceremony. In this allegory bringing forth a new identity construction, Washington crosses the Rio Grande rather than the Delaware River to bless the Mexican turned American patriots.[38]

Events for WBC have evolved into a six-week-long celebration, from the middle of January to the end of February, although preparations and planning stretch across the entire year. City officials cooperate in every possible way, and some organizations, such as the League of United Latin American Citizens (LULAC), use it for fundraising. The events bring in a large number of people, filling hotels, beauty parlors, and spas. It is the busiest time of the year and by far the most festive occasion for Laredo. *Viviana Cortez* of the WBC Foundation claims, "We generate millions of dollars in our community. Because of all the fiestas, lots of people come to Laredo. They come repeatedly to our celebration, and families have their reunions planned around Washington's birthday. It's a really good opportunity for our kids to show off their talents." Laredo truly becomes the center of the universe in these weeks, at least for South Texas, especially as the weather in February is perfect for outdoor engagements. Cortez believes that something must have been done right, otherwise the ceremony would not have existed for a hundred and thirty years. More and more businesses contribute to the celebrations; for instance, the fireworks are now donated by H-E-B. For a mere twenty-five dollars, children can experience a top-notch spectacle like the air show. Cortez believes, "The core of Laredo's identity as a city is in WBC when everyone is on the same wavelength. Mexican school bands play in the event and march in the parade, and corn dogs and fajitas are cooked side by side."

Until the 1960s only the elites were part of the ceremony. While *Margarita Gallellos* vividly recalls her own presentation at the Society of Martha Washington, *Cesar Villarreal* only saw photographs of the Martha Washington pageant in the newspaper because he did not belong to such rarefied circles of Laredo society. The elite aura of the WBC diminished over time as more people, especially from the schools, started performing in the parades. *Bianca Frey* remembers participating as a Girl Scout. The scouts were the hostesses of the big banquet held at the hangar of the air force base. In February debutantes wore fur coats to escort guests to their seats. As a little girl, she was in awe of the grandeur and fanfare. Another highlight was the citywide parade in which people from Nuevo Laredo collaborated, as the bridge was thrown wide open for unrestricted passage. As a Girl Scout, she remembers feeding band members who came from Mexico. *Michael Factor* remembers marching in the parade and regularly competing as part of the ROTC drill team.

The engagement of schoolchildren in the WBC parade made the celebration less restrictive. *Martina Russo* remembers preparing at school for the athletic talent show as well as the parade. When *Mimi Rose* was in charge, she brought over famous Mexican singers, with real cultural blending taking place as opposed to the symbolic exchange of garlands on the bridge. As a teacher, Rose takes pride in recollecting how her students participated in the events side by side with professional artists. She also remembers Christmas and New Year's dances of a bygone era when courtship took place in social spaces, not commercial spaces such as bars. She believes that such subtle interactions were filled with romance. *Matilda Roy* came to Laredo during high school and remembers feeling proud of wearing her ROTC uniform during the parade and experiencing warmth at the thought of serving so many people.

The current president of the Society of Martha Washington, *Kayla Hall*, narrates that the association was started in 1939 by civic-minded upper-class ladies. Her great-great-grandfather, Samuel Jarvis, founded WBC in 1893 with a party at his residence. It took off on a larger scale much later as a public event. Washington's Birthday Celebration has evolved and grown over the years as has the Society of Martha Washington, with debutantes joining in from San Antonio. The selection of Martha and George is a key event, and the pair is the crown jewel of WBC, certainly in terms of the money spent on colonial costumes for the dance floors. People from all over the country participate in the commemoration, with hotels being sold out. After Laredo Civic Center closed down, Laredo Country Club was the venue for a number of years. Now Sames Auto Arena is the only space large enough to accommodate the swelling participants and audience. It is not only about economic revenue but about the cultural aura that joins together people from different worlds.

Washington's Birthday Celebration Association (WBCA) is a nonprofit organization with five paid staff members, six executive committee members, and thirty-two members of the board of directors, who are elected to serve three-year terms. An additional eight hundred volunteers serve in the months of January and February, and funding and support from the city are bountiful. Almost half a million people come down to visit the festival, which has a multimillion-dollar economic impact. The WBCA advertises in San Antonio, Houston, Corpus Christi, and the Rio Grande Valley, and the event is routinely covered by media such as CNN and the *New York Times*. *Gill Taylor* appreciates that in the months of January and February the city becomes transformed, and everybody unites for the celebration. She started as an intern at WBCA in 2012 and now serves as its digital marketing manager, handling thirty-seven events in forty-six days, explaining,

> We kick off the celebration in January with a Commander's Reception held at Sames Auto Arena. Then comes the gala, wine tasting, Jalapeño Festival, Martha's Ball, and Pocahontas's Ball. The LC Fun Fest and Musicale is also an affiliate event. We recently added the week after for Laredo Open, our golf tournament, which is a new event. The Sunday air show draws twenty-five-thousand people, while tens of thousands of viewers gather along the route from San Bernardo to downtown for our Saturday parade.

The day of the parade during WBC also evolved as the day of freedom, when bridges were opened, no questions asked, and indeed no visas checked for people from Nuevo Laredo to enter Laredo. The border was much more fluid then, as it allowed people to come and also go back. In 1957 the Laredo Chamber of Commerce requested the American consul general in Nuevo Laredo and the director of the Immigration and Naturalization Service (INS) for a temporary open-door policy to allow Mexicans to visit Laredo for ninety-six hours during the WBC ceremony. Péna records these deliberations in detail and mentions the commercial prospects of the International Bridge traffic.[39] As *Jake Ruiz* reminisces,

> Until the late 1970s, the day of the parade was the day of libre, or free entry pass, with no questions asked at the checkpoint. A lot of people seized the

opportunity and headed to Chicago or some northern city to get a job. This was not considered an issue at the time because the reputation of Mexicans was mostly as hard-working people willing to strive. Thousands of people from Nuevo Laredo would walk across the bridge and celebrate together. The grand parade created a space of interaction among young participants from different corners of Laredo and Nuevo Laredo.

The tradition of *Paso libre* ended in 1977.

While WBC may have long dominated the social landscape of Laredo, the city was successful in adding its own distinctive features to it. Instead of only emphasizing American identity, the events expanded to include the people of Nuevo Laredo, while *Abrazo*, the garlanding ceremony on the bridge, emerged as a symbol of friendship and common identity. The political significance of *Abrazo* has now overshadowed the communal spirit, and the exchange on the bridge is showcased as a gesture of political harmony. *Martina Russo* distinctly remembers the day Lieutenant Governor Bob Bullock was crowned Mr. South Texas, his strong voice making an impact on her. She also has a vague memory of President Nixon coming to Laredo. When Ann Richards became governor, a huge delegation went in a caravan from Laredo to Congress Avenue in Austin to witness her being sworn in. She was chosen as Mr. South Texas and visited Laredo many times. The ceremony acquired national significance, which persists to this day. Security on both sides is tighter, but it is still possible to shake hands with important people like the Mexican ambassador or former U.S. House Speaker Nancy Pelosi, who frequently visits the *Abrazo* ceremony.

While the staging of Americanization remains the tangible part of WBC ceremonies, the more nuanced claims of binational and bicultural identities often do not receive adequate attention. *Charles Vega* recollects, "It's surprising that a lot of people don't know that the only time they admitted the armed forces of another country to come in armed into the United States was during WBC. Mexican troops would walk into the United States to participate in the parade and they had weapons." Behind the laid-back attitude of the two governments was a real cultural convergence. The distance to San Antonio or Houston made it expensive and time consuming to catch a Spurs or an Astros game, but any event in Nuevo Laredo was like visiting the backyard. Laredo returned the favor by opening the door to Nuevo Laredo during WBC. Mr. South Texas would visit Laredo, and political horse-trading would take place. The whole saga of selecting Mr. South Texas was fraught with political, economic, and cultural dealmaking. People from Mexico City would come and negotiate about making movies or exporting tequila. Vega remembers that a certain Mr. South Texas gifted the city twelve hundred bottles of tequila. He wanted to invest in tequila production and market it in the United States. The cold February mornings on the bridge for the *Abrazo* ritual drew many key political and cultural figures and instilled pleasant memories of striking conversations for Vega.

The expansion of WBC from being a weekend affair to a six-week-long bash has helped numerous nonprofit organizations grow and make money, which in turn makes it possible for them to carry on operations for the entire year. The ceremony has largely moved away from downtown with the exception of the parade route. It was only after a tête-à-tête with his girlfriend in Houston that *Arthur Bailey* realized how bizarre the celebration was. Growing up in his comfort zone in Laredo, he looked forward to the parade as it was the only boisterous time for a city that did not even have a McDonald's until 1975. Fine local restaurants like Glass Kitchen or Julep's were often out of reach for poor residents, and cruising the streets or heading toward Nuevo Laredo were the only options for entertainment without spending a lot of money. In this context, the long celebration opened up avenues of social interaction for different strata of people, which were as important as the commercial dealings and political significance marking the event. From a social stage for debutantes of elite families, the ceremonies evolved into more of a popular fiesta.

It is also possible to view WBC as the embodiment of a cumbersome identity problem for Laredo, as *Charles Fox* does. He explains, "While Laredo has deep Mexican roots, it also has enough space to accommodate American heritage. Regardless of why and how it [WBC] started, it is now part of Laredo's culture. I welcome a deconstruction of the problematic aspects of the celebration but also recognize the benefits for the community. Its benefactors bring in millions of dollars of outside investment to Laredo." Although the lavish debutante ball is certainly an elitist ceremony and does not reflect Laredo, one cannot disregard the commercial opportunities it brings. *John Allen*, on the other hand, cherishes the tradition of WBC regardless of its roots. He notes that debutante culture was very strong in Mexican culture and is at the root of quinceañera. Allen realizes that a large city like San Antonio did not have a Hispanic mayor until Henry Cisneros in the 1970s,

FIGURE 30 *Abrazo* ceremony. Washington's Birthday Celebration Association.

so the inclusiveness of WBC needs to be celebrated rather than denigrated. More and more young people, however, are voicing their disagreement with this sanguine view.

Washington's Birthday Celebration constituted a conscious formation of American identity for the Hispanic population of this border town. Although this method of constructing an American self-image for the borderlands started with obliterating Native Americans and silencing Hispanics, people in Laredo were able to insert their own version of history as one of peaceful coexistence by revising the ceremonies. Instead of a mock battle between cowboys and Indians, Pocahontas rides along with George and Martha Washington in the parade. Although the historical misrepresentation cannot be overlooked, it should also be noted that Pocahontas now has her own debutante ball. The *Abrazo* ceremony on the bridge is a nod to Mexican heritage that slipped through the cracks of Americanization and has emerged as a political symbol of utmost significance. This was the implicit bargain whereby locals participated in the official delineation of American citizenship but in their social lives proudly held on to Mexican heritage.

Deconstructing Hybridity

The question of identity for Laredo is not only bicultural, biracial, and binational but is also drenched in the much longer history of its seven different political affiliations. Many of the ancestors of the Hispanic or Anglo families had European lineage (Bruni, one of the prominent elite families, was from Italy).[40] In his landmark research on border people, Martínez observes that Hispanics in Laredo never identified as a minority and were almost unaware of ethnic discrimination. In the incessant social and cultural interaction between the peoples of Laredo and Nuevo Laredo, the sense of "othering" remained absent.[41] Martínez confirms the lack of racial discrimination in Laredo and identifies geographic isolation and the dominance of the Hispanic population as the foundation for secure border identity. Instead of ethnic rivalry, intermarriage between Anglos and Hispanics solidified class hierarchy. Laredo at one end of the spectrum may appear as a utopia of racial harmony, but the scars of deep class prejudice are still visible in social settings.[42] At the same time, though the Arab and Jewish population in Laredo may not be ample in number, their success as merchants (and later as business tycoons and key real estate developers) solidified their status alongside the elite Anglos and Hispanics. Residents would be shocked at being treated as a minority when they crossed the perimeter of the city. Even white inhabitants felt uncomfortable with the lack of tolerance when finding themselves in other cities.[43] Martínez specifically notes that people in Laredo are accustomed to mixed marriages. Spanish first names and English last names are a common indicator of such interracial conjugal relations.[44]

Many local residents who could not wait to leave Laredo started pining for their hometown once they were out of it. Even San Antonio sparked culture shock, forcing them to acknowledge their minority identity. *Charles Fox* only cherished a relationship with the city as an adult, after he had left and returned. As he claims, "I could see Laredo's beauty only after I could not experience it." After moving to San Antonio, he was listening to a radio station in Laredo, and the same music that he had shunned as being lower-class filled him with joy. He felt a deeper bond with his Mexican roots after he left Laredo. Growing up in a mixed ethnic household, *Katie Brown* admits that she was not able to appreciate the border before she grew older and moved away. She was not fluent in Spanish as a child, but working in the theater she now appreciates her Hispanic heritage and has embraced her city and identity. *Margarita Gallellos* acknowledges that Laredo allowed her not to think of herself as a minority. Moving back from Dallas and Austin, she ran a newspaper and courageously exposed different levels of corruption that were common in Laredo. Her exposé on Laredo Independent School District (LISD) earned a lot of praise,[45] and a few enemies, too, who tried to tarnish her image in the conservative society with salacious information about her private life. A large number of Laredoans have preferred to come back to their venerated community and decided to raise families here despite better economic opportunities in other places.

Laredo offered its residents a place to claim with pride in their self-perception. People could cherish their Mexican heritage in the comfort of their homes and neighborhoods. This sense of security and confidence in their own personality has always manifested in the attitude toward outsiders. *Rosalie Wright* arrived in Laredo in 1976 to make it her home. She found Laredo a little insular but friendly, and was impressed by the absence of interethnic rivalries. She provides the example of a special celebration at the San Agustín Cathedral after a rosary for Our Lady of Guadalupe. She was surprised to find Jews, Hindus, and Muslims in the large group of people who had come out to honor her. The dual sources of national identity often astound newcomers. *Sam Kornosky*, an immigrant who moved to Laredo, is awed by the enthusiasm shown during Cinco de Mayo and Diez y Sies de Septiembre and often wonders which team Laredoans cheer for when there is a soccer match between the United States and Mexico. Despite being an ethnic minority who stands out in the predominantly Hispanic city, Kornosky has no experience of facing prejudice. As he claims, "I am an outsider but I have great interactions and a wonderful level of camaraderie with my colleagues. I am the only one who is from a different race in the entire UISD administration, but I walk in peace with everyone." *Roxana Peel* views outsiders as having more of an appreciation for Laredo because they are intrigued by the rich history and do not take the quality of life for granted. Friendliness within the Laredo confines seeps into newcomers who arrive here. With fewer things to do, they tend to convene with professional colleagues and have barbecues. They form their own groups such as knitting circles, arrange cookouts, and nurture bonds during major celebrations like WBC. People do not have to drive back and forth forty miles between home and work and instead have the time to relax in the easy mood of the city.

A distinctive way to decipher identity paradoxes in Laredo is through the various ceremonies quite aside from WBC. Noche Mexicana, introduced in 1925, deserves special attention, as it exhibited a formal celebration of ethnic and national solidarity, perhaps to combat the American nationalistic narrative infusing WBC. Elaine Peña discusses the roots of the celebration, which was started by a Mexican citizen, Matias de Llano, who was serving as the acting president of WBCA. Instead of the mock clash between cowboys and Indians, San Agustín Plaza was decorated like the floating gardens of Mexico City. Mexican music and dances were showcased to evoke a very different cultural identity. It drew record crowds from both cities, as it was held in a public setting, free for everyone to attend. People would meander around the plaza at night from food stand to food stand, socializing with each other and strolling to the churches. After soaring success, it was dropped from the WBC program within a year, ostensibly over cost concerns.[46]

Peña notes the importance of the timing of Noche Mexicana, occurring right after the Mexican Revolution, and why it was deemed dangerous to allow elements of Mexican nationhood and budding Mexican identity into the borderlands.[47] Noche Mexicana was a festival that implicitly challenged the construction of American identity then taking place and therefore could not be permitted to coexist with WBC. For a number of years, however, Noche Mexicana was observed as a separate event, in a truncated form in the civic center, but still featuring famous artists, movie stars, and singers from Mexico, all of it rivaling WBC. Many older residents remember these events as a true exchange of culture, an assembly more public and welcoming than debutante balls or political networking galas. It slowly withered away, and it has only been in the last decade that LULAC has revived this event, which now serves as its major fundraising platform.

Washington's Birthday Celebration was fabricated to tarnish Native Americans, their history, and their Indian bodies in opposition to the continuing American nation-building enterprise. It was impossible to caricature Mexican culture and present it in a thoroughly negative light to the Laredo audience. This was probably why WBC made room for Pocahontas but evaded anything associated with the Hispanic ethos. When it came to a public ritualization like WBC, a more nationalized and commercialized space for identity emerged where the elements of Hispanic culture remained symbolic and were overshadowed by American mystique. To excavate the roots of identity in this border town, we have to look at the whole range of components in the city's festive past. It is often forgotten that while WBC may have been the main attraction, it was not necessarily the only show in town. The timing of the expansion of WBC is also noteworthy. In the 1970s, when Hispanic identity blossomed on the broader political scene, it was precisely during this period that WBC started to devour all other cultural and religious celebrations that constituted the tradition in Laredo.

May was the longest festive month at San Agustín Catholic Cathedral when *Sophia Brown* was growing up. She also remembers dressing up in white for Holy Communion, cutting flowers from the garden for the Virgin Mary, visiting the seven churches on Holy Thursday (the day before the crucifixion), participating in the *posadas* during Christmas, and enjoying garden parties where they ate homemade pimento cheese, chicken salad, and cake and cookies and drank punch and hit the piñatas. The first Holy Communion for girls was an important social marker. Religious ceremonies were longer and more inclusive of the entire community, remembers *Ria Sandoval*, who was a regular at Our Lady of Guadalupe Catholic Church. Her favorite was the twelve-day-long celebration for the virgin in December, accompanied by mariachis and *matachines*.[48] She loved dancing outside and the food, particularly tamales and *champurrado* (Mexican thick chocolate). She grew up with her grandmother and great-aunts close by, and they would have their family *la merienda* (afternoon snack) with coffee and pastries around 5 or 6 p.m. Playing *lotería* (bingo) with the family was an enjoyable pastime. She participated in all the Catholic religious events, which also happened to be the leading social events. There was *tamaleras*, communal cooking, where her great-aunts and the women of the church would get together to make tamales. Sharing different recipes and methods created camaraderie among the women. As Sandoval reminisces, "The month of May was dedicated to Mary Our Blessed Mother, and all of us who had made the communion would dress up in our little communion dresses and take flowers to Mary with hymns playing all around us."

During Christmas, *posadas*[49] took place in barrios where people would walk and sing and end with a party at someone's house. In the true *posada* there is a reenactment of Mary and Joseph looking for a place of refuge from Nazareth to Bethlehem, with songs and dramatic portrayals. Two people dressed as Mary and Joseph, along with a donkey, would go from house to house singing. At the end of the event, children had hot chocolate and broke piñatas. *Rosalie Wright* also loved celebrating *posadas* during Christmas, because in Laredo these turned into large social gatherings, with food like tamales, *pozole*, and noodles. These religious festivals were the heart and soul of Laredo. Fireworks were always lit on Easter, Christmas, and New Year's Eve. People would go for picnics, usually at Lake Casa Blanca, on Palm Sunday, and the state park would get full, while some people went to the ranches. People who did not have ranches or could not find space at Lake Casa Blanca would start picnicking on the grass along the road.

Back in the 1960s the Day of the Saints in September was as prominent as WBC. All the Catholic celebrations dominated the social life of Laredo. People would perform the Seven Churches Visitation on Easter to redeem their souls, recalls *Mike Socorro*. The whole day would be a huge treat, as the churches were full of flowers, and people chatted with each other on their way in or out of church. *Felipe Calderon* remembers the dance before Our Lady of Guadalupe, which he claims was unique to Laredo. They still perform it at the Holy Redeemer Catholic Church in the "lotería neighborhood" on December 12, the Virgin of Guadalupe's birthday. Calderon's grandfather grew flowers and sold them to churches and individual devotees from October to December. All Souls Day was an occasion for tremendous flower sales. Día de los Muertos was another day of coming together. *Samantha Taft* remembers visiting the cemetery with flowers and huge sugarcanes in the traditional Mexican manner. *Rosalie Wright* recalls Cinco de Mayo being celebrated in Laredo with more emphasis than in various parts of Mexico. Until the 1970s an equally prominent celebration was Border Fest, which depicted life in the nineteenth century with gunfights and other performances accompanied by storytelling. In contrast to the elite-dominated WBC, Border Fest was held outdoors at the civic center in the summer. With plenty of food stalls, vendors selling crafts, and mariachis singing and dancing, it was a weekend full of liveliness. Border Fest was revived in the early 2010s, first as a beer festival, and has grown impressively in the last several years,[50] drawing crowds from Nuevo Laredo.

The public events are all commercialized now, more broadened and inclusive, but the spirit of the traditions seems to be diluted. Few people visit the cemetery during Día de los Muertos. Affiliations within the society were often created through ongoing religious celebrations, and while the people are still very family oriented, the space for common activities has become smaller and sparser. *Grace Terry* remembers being entertained at the Life Downs Carnival, which had a rodeo and menudo bowl competition. It used to be held in January on the field adjacent to the civic center. *Martina Russo* recalls that dog or horse races were considered family events. *Justin Taylor* recounts that the biggest game in town was always the Martin-Nixon football game, and people would go crazy on Fridays and Saturdays. It was difficult to get students to class, so he scheduled his exams on Fridays. Jamboozie has now evolved as a big annual musical festival, while Laredo International Sister Cities Festival each July showcases Mexican artifacts and draws crowds from both cities.

Laredo's people demonstrate a sense of nostalgia for WBC that the troublesome origin story cannot eradicate. Washington's Birthday Celebration was about creating an American identity that could absorb the distinct contours of Hispanic identity, but to its credit Laredo has over time added different elements of Hispanic identity (the opening of the bridge and the *Abrazo* ceremony), allowing the citizenry to claim the event as its own. The transitions in border identity reveal a symbiotic relationship with the transmutations of WBC. *Millie Allen*, who works at Webb County Heritage Foundation, categorizes WBC as an artificial part of Laredo's history. Although it is rooted deep in Laredo's culture and memory, it was a celebration she believes was dropped on Laredo. She regrets that the history of the Republic of the Rio Grande, the ten-month-long independent country with Laredo as its capital, garners much less attention. Washington's birthday might not have any factual connection to Laredo, but its significance as a key ritual defining Laredo is well established. The cultural and political life of Laredo has been centered around WBC for a long time. *Michael Factor* remembers having a debate with a friend of his about when life begins, and his friend blurted out, "when the carnival comes to town."

The transformation of WBC from an elite display of power to a popular event, the singular dominant one absorbing a diversity of celebrations, is a resonant story of constructing American identity in the border region. The debutante balls are still restricted to the elite (the tickets cost a few hundred dollars each), but new additions have opened up social spaces to the common people. The commercial prospects of WBC have spilled over into elite power plays and extended the spectacle to everyone in the community. *Trina Case*, who moved to Laredo from San Antonio, initially reacted, "WBC is funny," but now thinks, "I find a parallel between the transformation of WBC and the growth of Laredo. Like the city, the elite still has a secure place at its core, but the celebrations have expanded to make room for everyone." The amplification of WBC to a six-week-long celebration gradually took shape in the 1990s when the commercial significance of WBC in the rapidly growing city took center stage.

It bears emphasizing that WBC succeeded in eliminating most of the Hispanic cultural and religious ceremonies by usurping the landscape of communal entertainment and capitalizing on the commercial potential. The construction of an American identity was based on the explicit cultural hegemony of white America and deeply ingrained in the economic system. Yet the extinct celebrations linger on in the collective memory of older inhabitants. The fact that many of these forgotten events (Border Fest, Día de los Muertos, Noche Mexicana) are being revived points to the excavation of the roots of Hispanic identity in this border town. The way these traditional Mexican festivals are being restored also shows a new commercial dimension to the lost celebrations. Noche Mexicana, as noted above, serves as a major fundraising driver for LULAC. The timing of both the eradication and resurgence of these spectacles is noteworthy. Mexican ceremonial rituals finally faded from Laredo in the 1970s just when the political presence of Hispanics on the national front began flourishing, which suggests a weak affiliation between Hispanic and border identity. On the other hand, the resuscitation of cultural and religious festivals is occurring just when the border is being redefined as a danger zone. This time, the articulation of the conscious relationship with Hispanic heritage is markedly dissimilar from the earlier quiet presence of border people in the inauguration of their American identity. Laredo's residents are fighting the derogatory sketch of their homeland and themselves through a much stronger proclamation of their ethnic identity. All these interactions reveal the convergent points of border identity, which overlaps with Hispanic identity and yet is distinct because of its deep roots in land and language as well as a political orientation founded in citizenship claims rather than minority pleas.

New Identities in the Border City

Laredo is what *Jose Diaz*, a researcher of South Texas history, defines as an "American feeling place," suggesting that people feel like they belong and have no fear of repression. People feel very American here although outsiders might imagine that this is not what America looks like. It is like a giant ethnic neighborhood on its own instead of being part of a city like New York

FIGURE 31 #NoBorderWall Coalition protest. Rio Grande International Study Center.

or Los Angeles. Diaz notes that Laredo was part of New Spain, then in 1821 became part of Mexico, and finally in 1848 the United States. Between this time, Texas was a republic. The Nueces Strip, from south of San Antonio to the Rio Grande, was always part of Mexico, not Texas. Even though Santa Ana had conceded that the Rio Grande would be the boundary between Mexico and the Republic of Texas, this was not accepted by the Mexican government. It was only when U.S. General Zachary Taylor invaded Corpus Christi in 1845 and threatened to invade Mexico City that Mexico gave up the land north of the Rio Grande. Laredo has a long and winding history of being in New Spain and Mexico. The quirky phase of being the capital of the Republic of the Rio Grande is another odd part of its existence. It is no wonder that it still feels different from other places that are not border territories. People in Laredo lived in relative peace and harmony, even though after the Mexican Revolution Mexicans were perceived as bandits and from 1915 to the 1930s were lynched across the South. This history of oppression was not experienced in Laredo, so residents often experience culture shock when they travel north of San Antonio or Austin.

The claim of being natives along with having experienced harmony with other races and adjacent lands seems to be the main ingredient of border identity. People from Laredo encounter the feeling of being a minority not within the city but when they leave it. Being on the border and having grown up with bilingualism and biculturalism influenced *Nina Vargas* in a positive way. She used to be scared at law school that she would flip-flop all of a sudden in the middle of an argument because she was used to switching rapidly between English and Spanish. She also experienced her first discrimination in San Antonio when she became acutely aware of her ethnicity. Even with its strong Hispanic presence, she did not find San Antonio Hispanic-centered in its culture. Vargas felt like a minority beyond the borders of Laredo. The realization of a minority identity for *Martina Russo* took place in the halls of the capitol in Austin. She was trying to persuade a legislator on a budgetary issue and pleaded, "When are we ever going to catch up?" The elected representative stopped in his tracks and responded, "Your people have gotten more than they deserve." She was speechless at the insensitivity of the statement and the way Hispanics were being defined by elected officials at the state level.

Astonishment at being treated as a minority signifies the distance between Hispanic identity and border identity. In the 1970s Hispanics were claiming a national political space for their ethnic identity, and yet Laredo remained locked into its own world. Fernando Piñon, who grew up in the barrios of Laredo, has penned a memoir that testifies to how the poor segment of the population was socially "sealed off" from the elites and the sense of marginality was rooted in class differentiation rather than ethnic identification.[51] The fact that Laredo was ruled by the same few privileged families for more than a century was much more of a political reality than the national politics far removed from the lives of most people.[52] The major political event of the 1970s in Texas was the formation of La Raza and fifteen of its candidates winning seats on city councils and school boards in Crystal City, Cotulla, and Carrizo Springs. For the Hispanic population of South Texas, this constituted a watershed moment of political visibility and newfound claims in the national realm.[53] The parallel turning point in Laredo was the end of the patron system in city government, which took down an elite Hispanic mayor and ushered in democratic governance by an out-of-towner, also Hispanic. Laredo's polity in the 1970s was galvanized by transformation in the city council, which was not driven by ethnic or political identity at all.

Although Laredo has always remained predominantly Hispanic or even Mexican American, in-migrants and immigrants have felt free to share the peace and bliss of the community. *Rachel Lawrence* moved to Laredo from Colorado and feels quite at home, especially since her work as a librarian requires her to know so much of local history. Her husband, though Mexican, is not from Laredo, but they have lived in the city and raised their children here. She does not feel like an outsider but recognizes she is a little on the periphery of the society. As a newcomer to town, she experienced the strange dichotomy of being in the United States yet being completely surrounded by Spanish-speaking people. She faced a barrage of questions, yet everyone was always gracious toward her. She was also struck by the superstitions people seem to abide by. Her first feelings were of incongruity toward finding herself in America but not in America and living in an urban environment that showed a kind of naivete unfamiliar to her. As a non-Hispanic minority, *Yvonne Sims* feels less questioned and more accepted here, as people have easily welcomed her in their homes. As she notes, "I've been to other places where I felt I had to hide my identity. Here I feel like an outsider mostly because I don't know Spanish." She was active in several student groups and was a founding member of the Muslim Students Association at TAMIU. *Christopher Cartin*, on the other hand, found it difficult to make friends in the community, with its established family and friendship networks. Although people have been extremely welcoming, inviting him to family gatherings, he feels they have had to deliberately leave their comfort zones to include him and his family in social goings-on. In his words, "The city feels like it has a very strong spectrum of differences, it's like a patchwork quilt."

Instead of an insider/outsider division, a more meaningful way to understand the perceptions of Laredo's residents is through their connection to the city. *Derek Perez*, who did not grow up in Laredo and yet made the city his home, thinks that Laredoans live in a self-constructed bubble with like-minded people holding similar beliefs. The drawback of feeling all-American is that people in Laredo always live behind their protective shield and are never on the defensive. He feels that this comfort zone, along with the social hierarchy, makes Laredo apathetic and acquiescent toward oppression and corruption as ways of life. This explains to him why people might be reluctant to question authority or show up for protests. *Trina Case* is also sad to see Laredo lacking in progressive thinking, but after living in the city for more than two decades, she is finally noticing like-minded people taking initiatives that hold the promise of having a lasting effect.

Rediscovering their connection to the city is a leitmotif for many people. *Giselle Lamar* had no intention of moving back to Laredo from the much more glamorous city of Dallas. She had a close connection with Laredo because her grandparents lived here, and she spent holidays and even a few years of her childhood here. One of her friends mentioned a job opportunity to which she applied only because she felt stuck in her entry-level position in Dallas. When she was offered the job, rather than saying no, she asked for a salary too high for a brand-new prosecutor just out of law school. Although the district attorney's office declined at first, within a week they offered her the position. She took the job reluctantly with the intention to come to Laredo to learn and move up and then go back to Dallas. She teased her grandmother that she must have prayed with a candle in every Catholic church to get her granddaughter to move back with her. Once she got to Laredo, exciting opportunities opened up for her. She loved being with her grandparents, and she met her future husband here. Her sister jokes, "You were a little fish in a big pond in Dallas, but in Laredo you became a big white fish in a little Mexican pond."

Alvin Travis, who chose never to leave Laredo when his cohorts left for San Antonio, Austin, Dallas, or New York for university, echoes the sentiment that Laredo has provided him a great window of opportunity. He serves on the city council and believes that a good life for his family has only been possible because of the many avenues that were available to him in Laredo. He feels validated in his life choice as more and more people who left Laredo for New York or California are deciding to come back to their native city. Austin is experiencing a huge migration from the West, but the new professional positions in Laredo are occupied not only by newcomers but also by natives who have returned from other locales. *Barry Rivers* came back to Laredo because of family reasons but was drawn to its cultural possibilities, where he found a niche for his love of entrepreneurship and gardening. *Sophia Brown* feels excited as the feisty new identity is more conscious of political rights and is changing the long history of low voter registration in the region.

It is clear that quite a few residents have discovered love for their home after they were away and chose to come back. *Roxana Peel* left her job at Goldman Sachs in New York City to relocate to her hometown because she wanted to create something tangible with her efforts rather than just earn money. Having initiated a new nonprofit organization and having worked on political campaigns, she feels satisfied with her life, although at first she questioned her decision a lot. Her high-pressure finance job on Wall Street had not felt rewarding at all, so on a whim she quit her job, traveled to Russia to watch the 2018 football World Cup, and moved back to Laredo. At first she worked remotely from Laredo, but she soon decided to be more fully present rather than just reside here. An encounter with a family friend opened the door to the nonprofit, which she gladly entered because she wanted to enrich the cultural features that she appreciated in Laredo and make them part of her own journey. *Alex Mead* ties the quest for identity with the new trend of the return of many original residents. On the one hand they are much more cosmopolitan, but on the other hand they are much more conscious of their Hispanic identity as a minority, which represents a marked difference from earlier generations. He also notes skeptically that the lack of affordability in cities like San Antonio or Austin is driving people back to Laredo. Whatever the reason, the reverse brain drain is serving Laredo well, with a higher proportion of college-educated people now patronizing the bars, thrift stores, local artisans, community gardens, and public events.

The lines of division in this city have typically followed class as opposed to race, but now a new element has been added to the demographic breakdown. *Raul Muñoz* views Laredo as more progressive but much more divided than in the past. The division is not only with respect to liberal or conservative philosophy but also with respect to age. Cooperatives and nonprofits focusing on different lifestyles (City Makery, which promotes civic engagement, or Red Wing United, which supports single mother households) have cropped up alongside sophisticated eateries (Lolita's Bistro, Tabernilla), which cater to the young and cosmopolitan sensibility. Border Foundry Restaurant & Bar was a boring small-town establishment but has now become cool and trendy. *Grace Terry* remembers local musician Bob Beatty, who proclaimed that anyone who thought Laredo was boring was in fact a boring person. After living in Laredo for two decades, *Jesse Knight* knows he can go anywhere and fit in, and believes it is the city that is teaching him how to change from within and learn to adapt.

Another important component of border identity is self-confidence, which is the opposite of a victim mentality stemming from a history of oppression. *Bianca Frey* recounts how ABC newscaster Peter Jennings (Canadian by birth) was struck with awe at seeing how easy it was to communicate and resolve problems with the Mexican side of the border. The strong undercurrent of cultural pride as Mexican Americans has revived and culminated in the new Hispanic identity. Young activist *John Lee* confirms the sentiment by noting a stronger feeling of identity cropping up. It might only be the new generation struggling to define itself, but it seems to him more than a coincidence that the brown beret, symbolizing the Chicano radicalism of the 1960s, only came into fashion in Laredo in the last few years. Its presence is now palpable at marches and protests, in line with the new insistence to have a bust of Cesar Chavez in the downtown area. A generation ago the Chicano movement left almost no mark on Laredo because political activism, especially around Hispanic identity, seemed redundant or unnecessary. The legendary Jovita Idár's resurrection, mentioned earlier, can be viewed in the same vein.

Perhaps the most enlightening discussion is again taking place around WBC. Lee finds WBC demeaning because for him it diverges from history and operates as a political stunt. He thinks there needs to be more public occasions tied to Laredo's roots and culture to counter the lack of representation in the overpowering symbolism of WBC. *Ishmayel Reyes* is also highly critical of WBC: "It's an excuse for the upper class to flaunt their wealth at the poor. The thousand-dollar dresses worn by debutantes are far removed from the common people's lives. The individual chosen as Mr. South Texas is invariably the least progressive politician. George Washington has zero connection with Hispanic heritage and culture, so it feels like occupied territory during the celebration." Reyes is bothered that public buildings are named after politicians or public officials who have recently served in office and done nothing significant for the city. Laredo even has a school named after a Confederate general, but there is no memorial to Chicano resistance during the period of lynching.

Alex Mead holds such a disapproving view of WBC that he began collecting signatures to petition to abandon it. He notes that the average cost of the colonial costumes ranges from twenty-five to thirty thousand dollars, more than the yearly income of many families. It was the landowning, light-complexioned, elite families who started the tradition, and they still control the performance. The Princess Pocahontas Pageant and Ball is contradictory to the mestizo spirit, the acknowledgment that Laredoans carry Indigenous bloodlines. Mead reiterates, "We are actively participating in the erasure of our own culture. George Washington was a signatory to some of the most violent massacres of Native Americans in American history. If you unpack American mythology, we are actively celebrating the same man who in all likelihood killed lots of Native Americans." He emphasizes that border residents are a mixed race but have lost their sense of history. His own DNA testing revealed 45 percent Native American ancestry, the part of history that is neither preserved nor celebrated. He resents that WBC was started by a fraternity that usurped the tribal name of the Order of Red Men and rewrote Laredo's collective memory with the staging of the massacre at city hall by Native Americans with white Americans rescuing Laredo. This embodies the implicit rite of passage of being an American, shunning Cinco de Mayo while embracing colonial racist and classist history. Washington's Birthday Celebration brings in a lot of money, but Mead wonders where the money is being spent. Similarly, $230 billion passes through Laredo every year,[54] but the city is only able to retain a fraction of it through taxes and tariffs on the bridges. Laredo remains one of the poorest cities in the entire United States even after being elevated to the rank of largest port of entry.

The national political discourse about Hispanics and Mexicans has opened up new ground to discover an identity that is both Hispanic but unapologetic, tied to the land and the history of the border yet eager to claim individuality for border residents who desire more control over border policies. This relatively unruffled space has recently been distressed with a repurposed barricade of the idea of America as the Trump administration moved ahead to rapidly fabricate an enemy and recreate the border as a shield. With time it has become clearer that more than identity issues, what undergirds WBC is the commercial and financial enterprise that enriches Laredo's economy. The border identity of the Hispanic community thrived in local harmony as long as it was removed from the national spotlight. The solace of being both indigent and the prominent race, at least within the compartmentalization of Laredo, is difficult to sustain in the midst of the rise of identity politics as well as the anti-Mexican backlash.

For a substantial portion of Laredoans, especially among the elites, the deconstruction of WBC is a source of discomfort, challenging a tradition they feel is as ingrained as their Mexican heritage. *Charles Fox* provides the example of the president of the Society of Martha Washington who, while promoting the debutante dance, also heads the highly profitable firm that creates so much opportunity for Mexican Americans to practice law and become leaders in local legal circles. The neat categories of oppressor and oppressed seldom apply to Laredo, especially in current socioeconomic conditions. Of course, the lived reality of poor people, recent immigrants, and those who have been poor for generations is a different story. They find it difficult to depend on state infrastructure for medical needs. They provide essential services but are barely able to survive between the twin cities, forever oscillating between footholds to stable economic opportunity. They can hardly claim to be part of the political dialogue in Laredo. Fox remains hopeful that "Laredo can be more inclusive and compassionate toward everyone who contributes to the economy. When it comes to the economic opportunity America provides, there is still no comparison to any other country, even if globalization has shrunk and dispersed many of these opportunities."

Fox defines the border as its own place with its own identity, with Laredo having its own version of the border. Residents like him do not view themselves as a minority because they grow up with high self-esteem as Hispanics or Mexican Americans. There is a historical pride in being older than the United States that is ingrained in people's identity. Most families can claim that their ancestors were on this land before Laredo was part of America. Fox notes that Donald Trump's family has been in the United States for a shorter period of time than his family has been in Laredo. He distinguishes Laredo from El Paso, where he spent his adolescence, with its large Anglo-American population. Hispanic identity in El Paso had to be constructed in contrast to Anglo identity. For his mother, growing up in a small town adjacent to Laredo, the overriding reality was the patron system. The others were those with power, who were mostly Hispanic. Before the provocation of the border wall and the Trump administration's explicit anti-Hispanic and anti-immigrant rhetoric and policies, Laredo's people felt little urgency to define themselves or question their place in the national fabric.

What motivated a nonminority identity in Laredo is the absence of a white versus Hispanic power struggle. The Union army, railroad builders, and traders mostly chose to settle in Laredo and become part of the local experience without trying to change it. The shifts that did occur came about through economic expansion that most people believed to be good for the social order and embraced enthusiastically. The contemporary drift in the national political conversation regarding the border has created a challenge to the inhabitants who have gone so far as to sue a sitting president over the estrangement of their homeland. Whereas earlier conflicts in the city involved selected stakeholders, the community as a whole has now experienced negative stereotypes that can no longer be ignored. The new quest to redefine identity has been influenced by contemporary social justice movements and expressed in solidarity with conventional modes of minority politics, which is a departure from the claim of a unique border identity.

FIGURE 32 Washington's Birthday Celebration parade. Photo by author.

Conclusion

Oscar Martínez perceives border identity as a manifestation of the cultural interactions that take place between the people who inhabit the space.[55] As interaction between the two cities has shrunk, border identity has shifted to repositioning itself within national political discourse rather than continuing to emphasize only the bicultural and biracial elements. According to *Charles Fox*, "Laredo has certainly not been a border town for my children. I grew up in a proper border town where I would travel to Nuevo Laredo every weekend. My children never experienced that. Many people still go back and forth regularly, but it is mostly for functional reasons." When Laredo was disjoined from its cultural counterpart and became a trade center, it lost its allure for him. Being at the economic pinnacle does not necessarily encourage quality of life if cultural richness is missing. Fox feels that the city has been forced to rearticulate an identity of its own amid the new tangibility of reduced reliance on Nuevo Laredo. The essential factors that have under-girded border identity—namely, interdependence and harmony with Nuevo

Laredo—might not be too distant in the past, but they might be impossible
to recapture in the era of the globalized and criminalized border. The new
elements of identity are forged not only from the altered definition of the
border but also because of political swings on the national stage.

The refashioning of the border after NAFTA is also a source of economic
as well as cultural reorientations that have disrupted border identity.[56] The
population growth of all the border cities has accelerated because of trade,
and new entrants to the cities are often from varied ethnic or even national
origins, adding diversity to the traditionally biracial societies. In Laredo, people from diverse racial backgrounds work for TAMIU, the Border Patrol, and
the medical sector. Cities like El Paso have experienced the common phenomenon of white flight, but Laredo's 95 percent Hispanic population seems
to be pretty stable. Still, it is impossible not to identify with the negative
portrayal of Hispanics or Mexican Americans elsewhere in the country. *Jack
Hughes* is saddened by the fact that locals use the term *illegal* unflinchingly,
forgetting their own past relationship with Mexico. When he was young, he
was under the impression that Chicanos were united but slowly discovered
it not to be true. He admires African Americans for the unity his people lack.
The self-doubt regarding Chicano bonds is also a reflection of the feeling of
contracting interconnection with Nuevo Laredo. In the midst of the anti-
Hispanic national mood and withering interdependence with Mexican people, border identity is relocating its crux in the Hispanic American experience, which is distinctly different from the history and culture of the border.

People in Laredo were always comfortable with the identity supplied by
the city, surrounded as they were by family and friends. Now there is renewed conversation about what it means to be Mexican American in the
aftermath of the Trump regime. For the first time there is a palpable threat,
and a new definition is bubbling up. Laredo's identity is evolving with a
strong sense of Hispanic pride. In the past the Hispanic majority produced
a snugness that made most people apathetic and even apolitical. People
had a tendency to be disengaged because the history of oppression did not
resonate with them. Laredo always fell under the softer oppression of corruption, except for sporadic violence. People in Laredo never had to define
themselves as the other or against any other ethnic group. There were always
just a handful of power players at the top, so the potential for conflict was
narrow to begin with. With a large proportion of poor residents, survival and
acceptance of power dynamics were the norms. Conflict had always been

well managed, as the small group of people at the apex tightly controlled the city. Until recently, the more intelligent and sophisticated members of society tended to leave Laredo. The Trump-era policy of justifying the border wall by demonically painting the Hispanic population with a broad brush and depicting the border in its essence as unsafe and lawless territory, along with the national protest movements against civil rights violations affecting minorities and on behalf of social justice, have served to ignite a new spark in Laredo so that people are reclaiming their Hispanic identity with pride, fighting to protect their land from the intrusive border wall, and reflecting on their city beyond its economic growth potential.

Conclusion

The population of Laredo has a cultural DNA that is very self-sufficient, intrepid, problem solving, and determined to go forward at any cost.

MILLIE ALLEN, LAREDO RESIDENT

Laredo is the future of Texas, as Texas is becoming more Hispanic and starting to show more of the characteristics of Laredo. This is where America is going to be forty to fifty years from now.

JESSE KNIGHT, LAREDO RESIDENT

Laredo is not only a border city but also a city that celebrates its ancestry. The city experienced the rise and fall of opulence decades before it evolved into one of the busiest ports in the nation. The different aspects of identity—the border, distinctive history, being a global node—compete with each other to form the central narrative arc of Laredo. Border regions are usually ambivalent about holding on to their past since the border is associated with continuous change. In contrast Laredo demonstrates affinity with its bygone era through a series of living links that encompass national boundaries along familial, racial, cultural, and economic bonds. The geographical location of Laredo is generally credited for its economic prosperity, ignoring the annals of history, the rich cultural heritage, or even the blessings of the Rio Grande that provides the city with water, much-needed vegetation, and enduring association with Mexico and its past, all of which are disparaged in the neoliberal economy.

Laredo's residents consider their city to be unique by referring to its antiquity, bicultural heritage, and lasting significance to national and international trade. This is in stark opposition to journalistic and literary depictions that often paint a desolate picture of border cities as brimming with clashes, restless and ever-changing sites where no one can be trusted or fully known because the border is inhabited by shady characters. Even in urban theory, the border is supposed to be an out-of-bounds place where anomalies are tucked into the regular way of life, allowing exploits and escapades to flourish. It is the isolation, both with regard to culture and landscape, that allows the border to develop as an unregulated space where anarchy and adventure prevail over order and rationality. The border is supposed to be an in-between space shot through with confusion and perpetual evanescence. Gloria Anzaldúa refers to the U.S.-Mexico border as an open wound, and border culture as a response to the ongoing conflict and sense of invasion felt by the two nations.[1] She speaks of multiple identities propelling the struggle of forever shifting from one to the other and constantly embracing the feeling of not belonging and never reaching home, since the borderlands can never be home, as Edward Soja also poignantly elaborates.[2]

Laredo, however, appears as a nourishing community that has opened the doors of opportunity to economic and intellectual progress in the eyes of its people. After becoming a settlement, Laredo functioned as a frontier where Native Americans, Spaniards, Mexicans, Tejanos, and Anglos collided, fighting to subjugate the enemy at hand and tame the wild land, and served as a hotspot of territorial confrontation between nations. Situated along a key trade route, the imagined midpoint between New York and Mexico City, Laredo rapidly broke free of its rogue reputation and evolved into a major trade center. The Anglo settlers were woven into the social and political fabric of the dominant Hispanic population through intermarriage and power-sharing arrangements. Laredo takes joy in a rich history older than the American nation. What makes Laredo's history distinct is that even though the city has been under seven flags, its people can determine their predecessors across generations and national formations. The history of the people and their land never got lost during the transformations that demarcated Laredo in different countries. The land in Laredo is considered almost sacred because it is the ranches that sustained the community with agriculture as well as oil and gas before it became a trade center. Like their ancestors, the people of Laredo today display a solidarity with land that is rare in urban settings.

Laredo operated as a frontier when conflicts between Native Americans and Hispanic settlers erupted or during the later military conflicts that took place between Mexican and Texan or Mexican and American soldiers. The frontier characteristic of wild and rowdy elements is not absent from Laredo's history, but it can be seen as nominal compared to its relatively peaceful progress as a trade hub. The notion of the frontier where continuous fights occur between stakeholders is the new element of global cities, according to Saskia Sassen. Instead of arms and ammunition, the new tools of modern (or postmodern) battles are various monetary and fiscal policies, including deregulation and privatization. In the past cities tended to resolve conflict through civic means while the nation-state used military power, but a crucial body of regulations derived from neoliberal economic philosophy is constructing new borders around global cities.[3] The new rules promote ease of transformation of capital and guaranteed service and information flows, but for Laredo they have destroyed the old synergy that existed within the city as well as with Nuevo Laredo.

Laredo and Nuevo Laredo were called twin cities (though they were founded nearly a century apart) because they complemented each other in land-use patterns and offered different conveniences to people residing in either city. The same families owned land on both sides of the river, typically ranchland or at least a homestead to the south, and a house on the northern side of the river where education, employment, and business opportunities abounded. Laredo became detached from its southern half only after Mexico conceded the land north of the Rio Grande. Nuevo Laredo evolved as a Mexican city, but both cities, belonging to separate nation-states, remained interlinked economically and culturally well into the 1990s. The more efficient infrastructure of Laredo formed the basis of the financial sector, while Nuevo Laredo offered cultural and entertainment facilities. Instead of feeling isolated, Laredo's residents keep harping on the interconnection with Nuevo Laredo and its recent loss because of rising drug traffic and crime there. Laredo has retained its language and nurtured its Hispanic heritage throughout this passage of time. Residents personify the nostalgic picture of a city conjoined with its Mexican counterpart and consider both parts their home. Social class hierarchy and political patronage were dominant throughout Laredo's existence until globalized trade ushered in a new educational infrastructure opening novel paths to upward mobility.

The map of the United States marks Laredo as the border in the form of a concrete line, but for those who live in Laredo the line has always been abstract or symbolic rather than an obstruction to their lifestyle, which has included "going across" the bridge to Nuevo Laredo as easily as crossing the street. This definition of the border, derived from the lived experience of Laredoans, presents a glaring opposition to the contemporary signification. The border is expressed as culture and beauty, as opportunity and enrichment, by the people actually living there. Instead of an edge or endpoint, the border denotes to them a gateway and connector between cultures. The border for Laredo has been a thoroughfare between two worlds that are equally treasured by the people. *Barry Rivers* explains how he feels lucky to be part of the richness and warmth of Mexican culture, such as the way people greet each other with an embrace or a kiss on the cheek, mannerisms conveying a sprightlier worldview and mode of relating to each other. The friendliness and closeness are the most valuable aspect of Mexican culture and integral to border culture. People are proud to call where they live a border town while challenging antagonistic preconceptions by reciting their strong community ties, cultural legacy, and economic vitality.

While national and political discourse heats up over the uncontrollable border and security obsessions, border residents cite crime statistics that are much lower than major cities in Texas. They see drugs and crime violence as spatially limited to particular zones beyond the river and the national boundary. Even drug cartels down the river are invested in preserving a "safe zone" in Laredo for commercial traffic. As the number of trucks carrying merchandise has escalated, the system of oversight for drugs or illegal entries has undergone a marked change. Companies that pay for the Fast Pass buy the right to have their trucks pass through the border unsupervised, while noncommercial and human traffic is subjected to agonizingly long scrutiny. Most drugs pass the border through legal means, inside a truck or car, while monitoring the border focuses on lone transgressors crossing illegally or smuggling small amounts of narcotics.

Creating a tangible obstacle such as a border wall on the southern periphery has been rendered as a deterrent tool for decades in parts of Texas, Arizona, and especially California. The Rio Grande flows as part of the Texas and Mexican border, making the construction of the wall not only highly expensive but also logistically daunting because the wall has to be built along the riverbank, causing the loss of a million acres of land and access to the river beyond the self-imposed barrier.[4] The Trump administration resolved the convoluted funding obstacle by declaring the border a war zone and moving money from the military budget to build the wall all along Texas. The Biden administration has canceled all contracts in Laredo, as well as the adjacent Lower Rio Grande Valley. What has driven the migration crisis is gridlock in the legal immigration system as well as cumbersome asylum procedures. A genuine political solution seems implausible, resulting in ad

FIGURE 33 Local voices. Rio Grande International Study Center.

hoc systems that actually make the border less safe, much to the chagrin of residents. The alternative to a concrete physical barrier is a virtual wall incorporating big stadium lights and other technological deterrence. Such mechanisms would render the night sky bright, hinder birds and bats, and put an end to the tradition of watching meteor showers in the dark skies using telescopes at the ranches. The fact that the boons of a quiet ranch lifestyle will be upended by border security apparatuses is a serious local concern, but has been considered too trivial to be included in the larger political debate over the border.

The river was once full of life, often flooding the twin cities with force. Now the pacified topography welcomes winter birds, but a manmade impediment like the wall can result in floods and loss of the bird and animal habitats, robbing Laredo of its precious natural bounty. The river is the boundary according to international treaty, but local lifestyle patterns have always viewed the river as a shared resource and living connection with a common ancestry. It should also be remembered that the Rio Grande has sheltered Laredo from outside transgressions. The river is not an inhibition to anyone in Laredo, but to an asylum seeker in Nuevo Laredo the river constitutes a significant barrier. Unlike a host of border cities, Laredo never declared itself a sanctuary city. Despite general empathy for the large number of undocumented people who reside here, the absence of a symbolic political stand points to the city government's prioritization of trade and transportation over social and cultural values. The power structure in Laredo has always been reluctant to rock any boats, as good rapport with the federal government is considered essential for smooth commercial flow through the port of entry.

When the border is defined as the river, the overtone of the border becomes attachment rather than division. To understand the border, we need to delve into some unique characteristics of the Rio Grande. *Jonathan Everett* points out that the land on the riverbank, instead of being viewed as valuable real estate like most other places, tended to be the domain of the poor. This is usually how it is perceived in developing countries, where land that is vulnerable to flooding or natural calamities is left to the impoverished. Usually in American cities proximity to the water has meant real estate that is more valuable. Although the Rio Grande offers pleasant secluded spots, wealthy people have built on the hilltops and the poor in the lower regions. The land-use pattern may have been influenced by the history of Indian attacks, as the interior of the city was considered safer for wealthier inhabitants. There are a few areas where the elites live near the water, but generally they tended to move away when the river was considered a risk.

While the border appears raucous and uncivilized in the national paradigm, local residents are preoccupied with fragility. The Laredo border is blessed with the ecological gift of the riverfront. The people of Laredo nurture their contact with the river just as they do with the community. The river was customarily viewed as a resource shared in common, a space that sustains wildlife and winter birds and contains lush green swaths of public parks deserving protection. Everett notes with sadness, "The worst thing to do to a body of water is to make it an international border. As soon as it becomes an international boundary line, two different nations that can be so different in what goes on in their respective parts of the watershed with the tributaries draining into it assume charge of all its problems." It becomes difficult to resolve river pollution issues with two separate entities in control. Often there is a false dichotomy between prioritizing the environment versus development. In reality they go hand in hand, but sadly Laredo has made itself vulnerable by not focusing on the environment. *Theodore Valenti* explains the role of the river in Texas jurisdictions by noting, "What makes Texas unique is that almost every bit of land is in private hands. Texas was a country before it was a state, so there was no public land available for the federal government." It is no surprise that Laredo has a large number of public parks along the river. If these lands were to be walled up, all access points to the river would be lost. The Border Patrol slashes away at the cane and brush, their actions contributing to riverbank erosion, while residents harp on the importance of green spaces and trees.

The homegrown environmental nonprofit organization Rio Grande International Study Center (RGISC) has established itself as the de facto guardian of the river. Working as an environmental investigator sampling water quality on a 300-mile stretch and living on a ranch 150 yards from the river, *Erica Hall* perceives the border as her lifeline. Her personal, professional, and recreational lives revolve around the river. As she explains,

> I have formed a deep connection to it, kayaking with my daughters and enjoying the beauty of the flora and fauna. The river feels like a calm lake after the rain and is perfect for paddling around, watching the deer and the waterfowl, the different varieties of egrets and ducks. I have come face to face

with a large coyote holding a rabbit in its mouth that just trotted away. It is a blessing to expose my children to nature and get them to appreciate it and the planet that needs to be taken care of.

The natural beauty of the southern border, with its centrality in the folkways of border people, is rarely recognized in the national political conversation about the border.

Having the border open to trails and horseback riding while leaving it in its present condition is important to *Giselle Lamar*, who views the land and its management as part of her heritage. She asserts that "the culture of South Texas is raising horses and cattle." The presence of the border wall on ranches at the edge of the river has been a thorny issue between landowners and law enforcement agencies. Border control has escalated regardless of different political regimes, so that retired veterans from various parts of the country now dwarf the proportion of local recruits, initiating a warlike enterprise along the southern border. While the focus of discipline always converges on the edge, spaces of restriction abound within the city as well. There are seven checkpoints outside the city limits of Laredo where people are questioned about citizenship and asked to show documentation. These layers are imagined as protective shields against criminal transgression, but they also mean that the resident population is constantly under scrutiny. The most tangible example of such vigilance is the growing visibility of the private prison industry, which is notorious for its poor treatment of migrants. This is the new profit-making venture that has become one of the largest donors to Texas politicians. The colonias—neglected neighborhoods in the vicinity of the city where the working poor reside—are segregated from urban niceties yet are close enough to provide labor. It is well known that many colonias residents are undocumented but are allowed to work, buttressed by occasional raids or stricter supervision by the Border Patrol when it is felt necessary.

While Laredo's economy was always centered on trade, this activity in the pre-NAFTA era brought local abundance, as both capital and revenue flowed through local traders. Affluent downtown businesses boasted of native owners while the spatial centrality of the downtown plazas provided social spaces for friendly residents. The rise of chain stores and malls shattered the organic city center and made the divide between the rich and poor spatially discernible in the north and south neighborhoods. This kind of spatial division caused by urban redevelopment as well as economic polarization is a common feature in American cities. The hollowed out downtown neatly fit into the neoliberal economy, where its cultural appeal or even local economic opulence became redundant. Edward Soja has studied the intensification of social and spatial control brought about by privatization, policing, governance, and the design of the built environment. Soja's encapsulation of the model of urban growth, "cosmopolis," captures the impact of globalization for cities that prosper because of their location within geopolitical boundaries.[5] Location has historically been a significant indicator of growth for cities, but powerful economic and trade networks have unnaturally accelerated Laredo's development. Laredo was engulfed by the shadow of urban decay in the 1980s, but after NAFTA its downtown became one of the most important thoroughfares in the global marketplace.

Laredo is a border city where every resident has to confront a checkpoint when leaving the city to enter the interior of the country, and it also happens to be a hotspot in the array of prisons dotting South Texas. The concept of the carceral archipelago, which originated with Foucault and has been applied to urban spaces by Soja,[6] emerges as another framework applicable to Laredo, especially in the context of the incessant contention regarding the border wall. As the debacle of the asylum seekers continues on the southern border, the political rhetoric over the border sweeps away the important nuggets of interdependence between the U.S.-Mexico border cities along with the failure of the asylum policies of the U.S. government. Because the federal government has redefined the border as a "security" problem, all aspects of immigration have become fixated around this obsession, departing from human or even economic considerations. Border cities have the least sway over the political framing of their own reality, and yet their destiny is molded by such narratives.

Laredo never lost its ethnic homogeneity, and its Mexican American culture remained preeminent in social settings. At the same time, impressive growth has been unable to eradicate the high poverty level (30 percent), income disparity, and class prejudice that have been omnipresent in the otherwise friendly community. The forces of globalization foment inequality through new economic norms that legitimize existing socioeconomic disparities with singular focus on profits, which can be detrimental to local stakeholders. Contemporary theorists like Sassen[7] and Soja[8] have drawn attention to global processes that exert enormous power over local jurisdictions and transform their spatial and cultural systems without taking into

FIGURE 34 Poster from Laredo Center for the Arts. Photo by author.

consideration the interests of the people who reside there. The global trade route through Laredo links Canada and Mexico in seven days of road transportation. The irony is that Laredo was far more conjoined with other cities, such as Chicago and Mexico City, through the railroad, at least from the perspective of human mobility, before it became a trade node. Laredo lost its deep umbilical tie with Nuevo Laredo after the initiation of NAFTA. The new rules of global profits replaced interdependence with the sister city, and the economic emptiness left in Nuevo Laredo was swiftly satiated by the rising drug cartels. Lawlessness and crime in Nuevo Laredo function as validations of the strict supervision of the border and bolster zones of disorder around the territory that is being controlled. Only a small percentage of the billions of dollars that pass through Laredo benefits local citizens, while money and merchandise tied with drug trafficking and crime enjoy easy transit through the superior infrastructure of the city.

The Viva Laredo comprehensive city plan, based on input from Laredo's residents, identifies habitat preservation and downtown revival as top priorities. People are cognizant of the indifference toward quality-of-life indicators and want to cultivate parks and other green spaces to reenergize the public sphere. The newly established farmers market and the prospect of beautiful parks in previously neglected neighborhoods reflect this vision. Entertainment options, both indoors and outdoors, have increased in contemporary Laredo. The socioeconomic hierarchy in this border town was always pronounced rather than subtle, which has manifested spatially in the north–south divide between the elites and the poor. The comprehensive city plan is the first attempt to invest in the growing communities in the south, where land is relatively cheap and where working-class communities are seeking more services after enjoying moderate upward mobility.

While the downtown evokes romantic nostalgia for the glory days, in its current iteration it is only a channel for trade and is surrounded by warehouses. The bulk of local government revenue comes from the bridge tolls even as businesses in downtown struggle to survive. The current city plan targets the revitalization of plazas and downtown businesses, while the trucking industry gobbles up land in the vicinity of downtown as well as southern neighborhoods along I-35 and the proposed I-69 (transforming Highway 59). It is important to note that Laredo has not attracted any corporate headquarters despite being such a large port of entry. The expansion of the trucking industry is inevitable, but it has not yet been accompanied by the growth of small-scale industries linked with transportation. The educational institutions have not developed degrees or courses needed for the local economy. It needs to be underscored that the enormous revenue from the bridges has failed to put a dent in the stable statistic of a third of the population living below the poverty line.

The contradictions between the national and local perspectives seep into any blueprint for the future. While cities compete with each other to sell their "authenticity"[9] to attract business and tourism, in Laredo the magnificent plazas are forsaken and the historic buildings suffer from decay. Sharon Zukin suggests that separation between sense of self and experience of space leads to the longing for authenticity.[10] Both border identity (discussed in chapter 6) and the cultural significance of downtown (discussed in chapter 4) continue to be momentous for the city, and yet the genuine characteristics of this historic city remain buried under its economic explosion as a trade nexus. The transnational process of relentless transportation has altered the centrality of downtown. While the economic significance of downtown has been enhanced because of global commerce, it has been stripped of its pivotal status of being the sociocultural magnet.

Residents show worry about Laredo's future trajectory. Entrepreneur *Samantha Taft* believes that Laredo is going to become even more commercial as a junction of trucking and transportation. People dream of a faster route between Corpus Christi, the nearest seaport, and their own inland port, in order to benefit both cities. But global nodes are not about augmenting any particular locations, they are about the maximization of profits. Laredo remains torn between local, national, and global stakeholders and is unable to raise its voice against wider macroeconomic forces. The border is meant to implicate the experience of economic growth and upward mobility in the local experience, but it now evokes a sense of frustration and sadness when it comes to the plight of migrants pushed around by national policy.

As the city grows economically and spatially following the increase in trade, internally the focus has shifted to quality-of-life issues that have spurred new organizations holding the city council accountable and presenting a vision diverging from the official mission. The new parks and public places such as the farmers market have initiated a novel discussion about the future direction, especially among younger residents. The new generation is more expressive about Hispanic roots and more likely to identify with minority groups nationally, which their forefathers evaded as they were always at the

FIGURE 35 Mural on Tres Laredos Park. Photo by author.

helm of power. When the Trump administration was agitating for the border wall, the city was at first reluctant to part with the flow of federal dollars until the #NoBorderWall Coalition compelled the city to join its lawsuit
against the administration. The first march to celebrate Martin Luther King
Jr. Day took place in January 2019, and Red Wing United, a local organization
formed to forge racial unity across the usual divisions, held a protest rally
in front of city hall following the murder of George Floyd. A bust of Cesar
Chavez is planned to be installed in Bruni Plaza, while Jovita Idár is in the
middle of being extracted from the archives of local history. The #NoBor-
derWall Coalition has injected the Hispanic cause in the recent movement
for social justice for minorities with its massive street mural called "Defund
the Wall/Fund Our Future" in front of the federal courthouse.[11] Public art
embodied in murals and on food trucks represents sites where transformational conversation about the community is beginning to supplant past
apathy toward national and local legacies.

In the past the underserved communities fell under the patron system,
and even today complaints of corruption and power abuse against the city

and county governments top the list of residents' grievances. They are wary of unsafe drinking water, the poor quality of education in the school districts, and the lack of bookstores and museums for children. The broader narrative of the border is ingrained in problems stemming from crime, drugs, and border crossers. People express love for the city by citing stories of generational struggle that led to economic success, while the opportunities they discern are rooted in key educational and cultural institutions. In its quarter century of existence, RGISC has initiated cleaning the water and continuous measurement of its quality, the passage of city council ordinances to protect wetlands, and even the prohibition of plastic bags, although the last measure was overturned by the Texas Supreme Court. The leading Hispanic-serving institution in the state is TAMIU, as identified by philanthropist MacKenzie Scott, earning the university its largest-ever endowment of $40 million.[12] The successes of border cities are often concealed behind the paranoia associated with the broken border. Although the classification of the border as an anomaly is offensive to locals and results in less tourism and revenue, this same classification paves the way for the steady flow of federal funds. The city has attempted to strike a fine balance between normalcy and unruliness to attract federal funding without sacrificing revenue from bridges and hotels originating from visitors and traders, but in the heated political blowup over the border narrative the balance is always difficult to maintain.

Laredo has historically enjoyed more than the usual autonomy because of its seclusion, being located 150 miles from the nearest city in each direction. City leaders were never under any pressure to compete with other metropolitan areas and instead developed a patron system vulnerable to abuses of power. Although politically and administratively the extreme concentration of power has been squashed, the remnants of centralized bureaucracy and corruption that draw routine FBI raids have resulted in continued distrust in city government, which also demonstrates a lack of leadership. Efforts to make the city government more transparent, accountable, and responsive have been taken up by a few local groups that regularly clash with the ruling factions and cliques. It is hoped that Viva Laredo will operate as the much-needed long-term vision since it is based on an extended participatory and inclusive process. Laredo became transformed into an international trade center without diversifying the economy or bringing well-paying jobs to residents. The problem with overreliance on international trade is that the city has no control over its operations. The largest employers in town are currently the school districts, the Border Patrol, and the freight companies. There may well be unexploited opportunities to promote small manufacturing connected with transportation, such as auto parts, or to develop renewable energy, capitalizing on the scorching heat of the long hot summers.

The paradoxical priorities informing the future trajectory of the city are reflected in the simultaneous effort of guarding the border and implementing strategies that harm the riverbank and create clashes with local ranchers while also promoting the annual birding festival and preserving sanctuary areas for birds and animals on the same waterfront. Laredo appears tough when the topic of discussion is trade and commerce, or even elections, not to mention crime and drugs. This veneer hides the rich yet fragile ecosystem that has nourished the region. The river is obscured by bridges that are essential for economic survival (providing much of the city's revenue through tolls) but remains indispensable as the only source of water for the two cities and for the wildlife on its banks as well as a living reminder of cultural lineage. An unexplored niche for Laredo is to develop itself as a bastion of ecotourism. The fear is that the current brawls over the border will derail any efforts at natural preservation for fear of migrant crossings. Although awareness about environmental protection is increasing, people worry that the dream of developing ecotourism in Laredo will follow the example of the missed opportunity of the River Walk. As long as the prevailing image of Laredo remains dominated by crime and violence, internal commercial and environmental aspirations are in peril.

Laredo has never really marketed itself as a tourist attraction or seriously tried to lure retirees to settle down as do many cities across the Sunbelt. Even in the heyday of the 1950s and 1960s, the tourist attraction was Nuevo Laredo, while Laredo was happy to lend safe space to visitors who would stay in Laredo but enjoy wild nights of adventure in Nuevo Laredo. Laredo used to be the gateway to a sophisticated world of cultured and rich Mexicans enjoying live music and drinks before Nuevo Laredo succumbed to the cartels. There was no attempt to fill the void by highlighting Mexican culture for tourists to experience in relatively safer Laredo. Compared to the large and brimming El Mercado in San Antonio, the small strip of shops that carries Mexican artifacts on San Bernardo Avenue is pitiful. Food trucks or even taco trucks arrived years later than in Houston or Austin. While the city was trying to boost its image as a college town, it was constructing a prison with more beds than dorm rooms. The flux of taglines—Gateway City, Rediscover

Our Flavor, City on the Edge—captures the hesitancy about how it wants to project itself to a broader audience. In 2020 the city adopted its most recent logo, "The Place to Be Together," invoking a sense of permanence that departs from its earlier projections of transient fantasy.

The lack of decisiveness about the image of the city is in contrast to the strong sense of identity of the people. Even when they are critical of the city, people express a strong and stable notion of themselves as residents of the borderlands rooted to the land, ethnic ancestry, and a sense of pride that mirrors national identity formation rather than a marginal identity in the American political context. The 95 percent Hispanic majority rarely underwent any minority experience inside its own territory. Geographical distance from other cities and the historical affiliation with the Mexican side also resulted in an independent and self-driven streak in Laredo. While the border might feel like the edge from the national standpoint, this location has provided comfort and safety to people who have enjoyed the advantage of concurrent vistas to both the north and the south. The border in Laredo was never a point that cut off anything—commerce, ethnic ties, or even land-use patterns—before NAFTA.

The vibrancy of the town, the only survivor of the five original settlements on the Rio Grande, may not mean much to outsiders, but it has instilled in the people a sense of self-dependence and survival amid economic or other crises. This has manifested in a new identity, namely border identity, which may overlap with ethnicity but ultimately stands apart from racial overtones. Laredo has been marked by class prejudice but rarely a history of minority suppression. Instead of oppression causing a sense of victimization, the people have always experienced the privileges of the majority. Secure in their identity in relative geographical isolation, they have been welcoming to outsiders who choose to reside in Laredo. The definition of the local in Laredo is neither ethnic nor geographical (people still live in Nuevo Laredo and go to work or school in Laredo) but is understood in terms of the relationship to the city. *Bianca Frey*, a former elected city official, recounts the story of a coworker who made stickers called "Laredo: Love It Or Leave It," and wanted the city to hand them out. Cooler heads prevailed to stop him in his tracks.

People who could not wait to leave Laredo in their youth report falling in love again and appreciating the city the minute they live somewhere else. The peace of mind that once prevailed inside city limits has been shattered by the increasingly anti-Hispanic and anti-immigrant tone of national politics. The new quest for a border identity is reflected in political participation, both locally and nationally. This border identity is not just a dual identity that houses two cultures but is instead an identity that allows for easy interaction between cultures and takes pride in the resulting amalgam. Border residents are intrinsically trained to navigate between two worlds. Some grow up speaking both languages, as one or several family members might be monolingual. But the cultural pride has rarely been cherished in any formal setting. Laredo's children do not learn about Jovita Idár in the classroom, nor are they exposed to birdwatching as an extracurricular activity in one of the most welcoming locales for winter birds.

The miniscule Republic of the Rio Grande Museum commemorates the eccentric history of the short-lived country with Laredo as its capital. It may not have left a big mark on history, but it definitely embodies the signs of self-sufficiency, independence, determination, and even a quest for identity. This part of history is treated more like an aberration than rejoicing in unconventional traits. In this Hispanic city, the biggest celebration happens to be Washington's Birthday Celebration, conducted with much pageantry throughout the month of February. The racist origins of the ceremony have turned off some younger people, but most Laredoans express pride and nostalgia regarding deference to a colonial grandeur that never was part of their own heritage.

The border has turned into a hot issue when living on the border should be a cool thing, *Grace Terry* feels, as she experiences the palpable fear that is often exaggerated and overshadows the cultural treasures that exist in the borderlands. "Laredo is culturally significant on its own terms, but to the outside audience it has always been defined in terms of what it lacks, never in terms of what it offers," she laments. The predominant image of Laredo is constructed by a media influenced by stories of crime and violence, stories that sell. The perception of the border is dominated by illegal crossings and arrests, whereas a leisurely stroll by the river or the sighting of rare birds has never been part of the image. Laredo is featured as a cartel-dominated, low-IQ city to the outside world. It is always staged as a space of violence and tumult on the silver screen. In country music, Laredo features as a place where people are trapped and await their brutal end, diverging from the sensibility of peace or home or even nostalgia typical of that particular musical genre.

The neoliberal economy desires a border city that contains tangible lines for delimitation and yet is malleable enough to be overseen according to commercial requirements. Laredo is a misfit in this scheme, with the porous border of the Rio Grande and a strong identity rooted in history and territory. It is the bridges and roads that are the conduits of international trade, while the river functions as the site that needs to be enclosed for tracking purposes. The Rio Grande is still the only source of drinking water, the life source for Laredo's vegetation, and the heart of its ecosystem. The history of this binational and bicultural city is intertwined with the river. The people may have lost rapport with the downtown and the river for a short period, but a new awareness about global warming and environmental concerns has recharged the commitment toward all of the natural and manmade bequests Laredo has inherited. The downtown revival process continues even as warehouses occupy the adjacent landscape. The national spotlight on Laredo is both desired and dreaded as federal dollars pave the way for the disrepute that the proud border town vehemently combats.

Location has been the greatest asset of Laredo, but if it becomes just an unremitting warehouse along the long corridor of international trade, it will end up becoming its greatest drawback. It remains to be seen how Laredo can negotiate economic (trade revenue) and political (national security) rationales by inserting its uniqueness into the conversation to return the focus to benefits to the local domain. In the post-COVID reality, location itself has accrued new meaning. Young people feel that the prevailing zeitgeist is the preference for a location where people feel most in control. The structural flexibility of the workplace is going to be beneficial to small and midsize affordable cities all over the country. This goes well with local efforts to revive the downtown by creating opportunities for vibrant nightlife and tourism. The norms of American political discourse offer little meaningful space for local concerns, but they do record minority anguish. Different factions are forming that either prioritize the preservation of the city's cultural and environmental dynamism or fall in line behind all the security measures so as not to hinder trade flows.

Saskia Sassen labels complex urban centers the new frontiers of globalization. The unstable quality of border zones is vulnerable to renewed territorial combat over economic power as fresh stakeholders emerge in the lush landscape of profit maximization. The new processes of production and exchange manifest in new norms and identities. All of these take place in urban regions that are shaped by global trade and in turn reshape the authority structure, spatiality, and rights of the people of the particular locality.[13] Just as the transnational neoliberal system propels a city to reorient its economic, social, and cultural preferences, the affected locality can push back against the process by choosing the interests of immediate stakeholders and the needs of the population. As discussed previously, this method of rescaling economic activities has been characterized as "glocalization," where local concerns are folded into the broader dynamics of globalization.[14] By positioning its downtown as the cultural center, Laredo has implicitly challenged the spatial reorientation of the city. The direct confrontation with nationalistic and neoliberal definitions of the border is perhaps most visible in the proposed Binational River Park, which would create a public space for the people of both cities and preserve their only source of drinking water. What sets this urban planning apart is the local initiative that evolved organically and succeeded in defeating the more powerful political options of the wall or the bulkhead to claim the land for the benefit of the people as opposed to economic or national interests.

Paasi identifies boundaries as analogous to institutions and points to the relationship between territoriality and the production of identity.[15] In Laredo, the transformation of trade practices has manifested not only in the obvious economic growth but also in the inevitable unevenness of urban investments, which, to be fair, predated NAFTA. Nevertheless, the expansion of the inland port has opened up new horizons for border identity by connecting parochial grievances to the larger issue of social injustices pervasive in minority communities, which Laredoans were not familiar with in their own city. It is generally accepted that class constituted the most dominant (possibly the only) line of separation within Laredo, but now the population is fractured with competing visions for the city. These rival claims to the city exhibit the political sensibility of the border city that aspires to counter the undertones of the border as well as explore border identity beyond the local context.

NAFTA unequivocally changed the spatial and mental landscape for the inhabitants of Laredo. There is no path to return to the self-sufficient days of local ownership when the border remained abstract or invisible in everyday life. One sad way forward is the neoliberal track of escalating new networks of bridge and road infrastructure while ignoring endemic inequities, perhaps accompanied by token investments in social infrastructure like education. Another road is the one rarely taken, where local priorities emerge at the forefront of national and international consideration. The clash of local, national, and international primacies is actively shaping this border town. Laredo's rich history goes back generations, all the way to nation-state formation, but it also displays a living concordance with land, language, and self-pride that is yet to be severed. The millennial generation, estimated to be half the population, is asking for a very different set of quality-of-life improvements from the city, which has historically only focused on trade and growth. This is the culmination of a new identity that taps into local cultural heritage but also assimilates the racial political identity prevalent on the national stage.

Laredo is in fact at the crossroads of a border city and a global hub. As the largest inland port, Laredo is expected to channel a mammoth volume of trade speedily and efficiently, but it is now under the kind of strict scrutiny that deviates from its own legacy. This ongoing tug-of-war between the local population and national authority is a new phenomenon for a city that built its sustenance around trade and its image around self-sufficiency. From passive national neglect, Laredo is now basking in the spotlight of a noxious mix of crime, drugs, and transgression by undesired immigrants. For all of these reasons, Laredo embodies fertile ground for continued research to study the evolution of the border in American political economy as well as the resilience of local communities against the forces of globalization.

This research points to several key areas that are crucial to comprehend a border city. Along with geographic and economic advantages, border cities need to be examined in their historical and cultural contexts. Without the knowledge regarding the organic growth patterns of a city, it is very easy to follow a myopic model of financial expansion that can end up stifling and even subverting its possibilities. As shown in this book, Laredo was better connected with other cities, both in the United States and Mexico, before its iteration as a global port. Laredo's local entrepreneurs have been swallowed up by national and global corporate conglomerates because of its international significance. These are the areas where border studies must focus attention, shifting from macroanalyses of globalization to actual impact on citizens and communities. The existing purposes and roles of the border, especially its monitoring mechanisms, need to be analyzed by taking into account all of these conflicting factors. Fear seems to be inscribed in the totality of border discourse, a discomfort that has been explained very differently in literary or cultural studies (ambiguity and/or failing to belong) and theories of globalization (crime and/or illegal trespassing of people and merchandise). These different threads of scholarship demonstrate some overlap but so far have not engaged with each other to provide a well-rounded discourse about the border. Most importantly, in border studies the local voices defining their own abodes have remained marginal. Studies on other border cities can benefit from the framework that has been used here to analyze Laredo. Future research on border cities might incorporate the issues manifested in Laredo—local versus national interests, the obstruction of people's mobility while promoting trade, the shifting gaze from illegal transactions to illegal pathways, the aspirations of the community, and the transformation of border identity—to decipher the actual meanings and functions of the border in the current global context.

As long as Laredo was insular, the luxury of not entering into a national dialogue over the real implications of the border was accorded to its people. As a result, the meaning of the border city in lived experience has been far removed from the official delineations of the state. The international demarcation of the border is inconsistent: it needs to be immaterial for ease of trade and transportation but palpable or even corporeal for the purposes of efficiency and safety. It is the mechanisms or rituals of efficiency and safety that are important, as these can easily be recorded regardless of whether or not they achieve their objectives. The most problematic aspect of the international border is that its importance is overwhelmingly economic; when softer cultural and social issues come into play, the border is treated as symbolic. For people who live in the borderlands, their cities amount to much more than symbolism or the edges of political boundaries. The nation-state considers the border as absolute, while the people have always regarded it as more abstract because it has never interfered with their real mobility. Even at the height of the crime and drug violence, people in Laredo are scrutinized when they travel toward other parts of the country but not when they are going to Mexico. If local voices fail to put their imprint on how the city is categorized, Laredo will be headed toward a glorified warehouse district with its downtown as a relic of the past. Laredo has much more to offer, and the new discussions regarding the problems and possible futures of the city have the potential to move growth and investment strategies toward more equitable distribution along socioeconomic lines. The city is in need of this, and it deserves spatial and environmental planning that respects both nature and culture and is people oriented rather than being only profit centered.

Notes

Introduction

1. Throughout the book, each interviewee's name is italicized upon first mention in a passage.
2. Julia Wallace, "Laredo Becomes No. 1 Trade Port in the US," *Laredo Morning Times* online, May 22, 2019, https://www.lmtonline.com/local/article/Laredo-becomes-No-1-trade-port-in-the-US-13871740.php.
3. "Port of Entry: Laredo," comptroller.texas.gov, https://comptroller.texas.gov/economy/economic-data/ports/laredo.php.
4. Saskia Sassen, "The Global City: Strategic Site/New Frontier," in *Readings in Urban Theory*, 3rd ed., ed. Susan S. Fainstein and Scott Campbell (Malden, Mass.: Wiley-Blackwell, 2011), 55–72.
5. "Streets of Laredo (song)," Wikipedia, https://en.wikipedia.org/wiki/Streets_of_Laredo_(song).
6. Johnny Cash, "Streets of Laredo," Genius.com, https://genius.com/Johnny-cash-streets-of-laredo-lyrics.
7. Warren Zevon, "A Bullet for Ramona," Lyrics.com, https://www.lyrics.com/lyric/2674046/Warren+Zevon/A+Bullet+for+Ramona.
8. Flaco Jiménez, "Ay te dejo en San Antonio," Lyrics.com, https://www.lyrics.com/lyric/1182223/Flaco+Jim%C3%A9nez/Ay+Te+Dejo+en+San+Antonio.
9. Bronco, "La hechicera," Lyrics.com, https://www.lyrics.com/lyric/1173849/Bronco/La+Hechicera.
10. Los Alegres de Terán, "Los pilares de la cárcel," Lyrics.com. https://www.lyrics.com/lyric/4652411/Los+Alegres+de+Ter%C3%A1n/Los+Pilares+de+la+C%C3%A1rcel.
11. Joe Ely, "Letter to Laredo," Lyrics.com, https://www.lyrics.com/lyric/314653/Joe+Ely/Letter+to+Laredo.

12. Frankie Laine, "Wanted Man," Lyrics.com, https://www.lyrics.com/lyric/3539 028/Frankie+Laine/Wanted+Man.

13. Pat Smith Nickell, "Postmodern Aspects in Larry McMurtry's *Lonesome Dove, Streets of Laredo, Dead Man's Walk,* and *Comanche Moon*" (PhD Diss., Texas Tech University, 1999), 61–63.

14. *Laredo* (TV series), Wikipedia, https://en.wikipedia.org/wiki/Laredo_(TV_series).

15. "Fox News Reporter Roasted over Tiny Vest at the Border," NowThis News, April 8, 2019, https://www.youtube.com/watch?v=UyUP5il21BY.

16. Norma Elia Cantú, *Canícula: Snapshots of a Girlhood en La Frontera* (Albuquerque: University of New Mexico Press, 1995).

17. Daniel D. Arreola, "Border-City Idée Fixe," *Geographical Review* 86, no. 3 (1996): 359.

18. Robert D. Wood, *Life in Laredo: A Documentary History from the Laredo Archives* (Denton: University of North Texas Press, 2004), 16.

19. Gilberto Miguel Hinojosa, *A Borderlands Town in Transition: Laredo, 1775– 1870* (College Station: Texas A&M University Press, 1983), 123.

20. Hinojosa, 59.

21. Hinojosa, 96–97.

22. John A. Adams Jr., *Conflict and Commerce on the Rio Grande: Laredo, 1775– 1955* (College Station: Texas A&M University Press, 2008).

23. Adams, 85–9.

24. Adams, 99.

25. Adams, 106–8.

26. Adams, 191.

27. Kathleen Da Camara, *Laredo on the Rio Grande* (San Antonio, Tex.: Naylor, 1949).

28. Wood, *Life in Laredo.*

29. Milo Kearney and Anthony Knopp, *Border Cuates: A History of the U.S.- Mexican Twin Cities* (Austin, Tex.: Eakin Press, 1995).

30. Daniel D. Arreola and James R. Curtis, *The Mexican Border Cities: Landscape Anatomy and Place Personality* (Tucson: University of Arizona Press, 1993).

31. Daniel D. Arreola, *Postcards from the Río Bravo Border: Picturing the Place, Placing the Picture, 1900s–1950s* (Austin: University of Texas Press, 2013).

32. Setha M. Low, "Cultural Meaning of the Plaza: The History of the Spanish-American Gridplan-Plaza Urban Design," in *The Cultural Meaning of Urban Space,* ed. R. Rotenberg and G. McDonough (Westport, Conn.: Bergin and Garvey, 1992), 76–93.

33. Carl Grodach and Daniel Silver, eds., *The Politics of Urban Cultural Policies: Global Perspectives* (London: Routledge, 2013).

34. John Hannigan, *Fantasy City: Pleasure and Profit in the Postmodern Metropolis* (London: Routledge, 1998).

35. Hans Krabbendam, Marja Roholl, and Tity de Vries, eds., *The American Metropolis: Image and Inspiration* (Amsterdam: VU University Press, 2001).

36. Anssi Paasi and Kaj Zimmerbauer, "Penumbral Borders and Planning Paradoxes: Relational Thinking and the Question of Borders in Spatial Planning," *Environment and Planning A* 48, no. 1 (2006): 75–93.

37. James Anderson and Liam O'Dowd, "Borders, Border Regions and Territoriality: Contradictory Meanings, Changing Significance," *Regional Studies* 33, no. 7 (1999): 593–604.

38. M. Coleman, "U.S. Statecraft and the U.S.-Mexico Border as Security/Economy Nexus," *Political Geography* 24 (2005): 185–209.

39. Anssi Paasi, "Boundaries as Social Processes: Territoriality in the World of Flows," *Geopolitics* 3, no. 1 (1998): 69–88.

40. Paasi, 75.

41. Edward W. Soja, *Postmetropolis: Critical Studies of Cities and Regions* (Oxford: Blackwell, 2000).

42. William Sites, "Primitive Globalization? State and Locale in Neoliberal Global Engagement," *Sociological Theory* 18, no. 1 (2000): 133–34.

43. Fernando Romero and Laboratory of Architecture Staff, *Hyper-Border: The Contemporary U.S.-Mexico Border and its Future* (New York: Princeton Architectural Press, 2008).

44. Romero and Laboratory of Architecture Staff, 42.

45. Sophie Body-Gendrot, *Globalization, Fear and Insecurity: The Challenges for Cities North and South* (London: Palgrave Macmillan, 2012).

46. Cari Lee Skogberg Eastman. *Shaping the Immigration Debate: Contending Civil Societies on the U.S.-Mexico Border* (Boulder, Colo.: FirstForumPress, 2012).

47. Joseph Nevins, *Operation Gatekeeper: The Rise of the "Illegal Alien" and the Making of the U.S.-Mexico Boundary* (New York: Routledge, 2002).

48. Sylvia Longmire. *Border Insecurity: Why Big Money, Fences, and Drones Aren't Making Us Safer* (New York: Palgrave Macmillan, 2014).

49. Ronald Rael, *Borderwall as Architecture: A Manifesto for the U.S.-Mexico Boundary* (Oakland: University of California Press, 2017).

50. Robert Lee Maril, *Patrolling Chaos: The U.S. Border Patrol in Deep South Texas* (Lubbock: Texas Tech University Press, 2004).

51. Robert Lee Maril, *The Fence: National Security, Public Safety, and Illegal Immigration Along the U.S.-Mexico Border* (Lubbock: Texas Tech University Press, 2011).

52. Ray Ybarra Maldonado, *Born on the Border: Minutemen Vigilantes, Origins of Arizona's Anti-Immigrant Movement, and a Call for Increased Civil Disobedience* (Phoenix, Ariz.: Hispanic Institute of Social Issues, 2013).

53. Bill Broyles and Mark Haynes. *Desert Duty: On the Line with the U.S. Border Patrol* (Austin: University of Texas Press, 2010).

54. Dale Squint, *My Border Patrol Diary: Laredo, Texas* (Bloomington, Ind.: Authorhouse, 2007).

55. Two essays that summarize theoretical advancements in border studies are David Newman, "The Lines That Continue to Separate Us: Borders in Our 'Bor-

derless' World," *Progress in Human Geography* 30, no. 2 (2006): 143–61; and Vladimir Kolossov, "Border Studies: Changing Perspectives and Theoretical Perspectives," *Geopolitics* 10 (2005): 606–632.

56. Emmanuel Brunet-Jailly, "Toward a Model of Border Studies: What Do We Learn from the Study of the Canadian-American border?," *Journal of Borderlands Studies* 19, no. 1 (2004): 6–7.

57. Erik Swyngedouw, "Globalisation or 'Glocalisation'? Networks, Territories and Rescaling," *Cambridge Review of International Affairs* 17, no. 1 (2004): 25–48.

58. Alan Klein, *Baseball on the Border: A Tale of Two Laredos* (Princeton, N.J.: Princeton University Press, 1997).

59. Mike Davis, *Magical Urbanism: Latinos Reinvent the U.S. City* (London: Verso, 2000), 26.

60. Joseph Nevins, *Operation Gatekeeper*, 5–6.

61. Nevins, 7.

62. Patricia Price, "Inscribing the Border: Schizophrenia and the Aesthetics of Aztlán," *Journal of Social and Cultural Geography* 1 (2000): 101–16.

Chapter 1

1.   "Texas Is Home to the Country's Largest Inland Port," Authentic Texan, https:// authentictexan.com/texas-home-largest-inland-port/.

2.   Daniel D. Arreola, *Tejano South Texas: A Mexican American Cultural Province* (Austin: University of Texas Press, 2002), 150–54.

3.   Kathleen Da Camara, *Laredo on the Rio Grande* (San Antonio, Tex.: Naylor, 1949), 12.

4.   Gilbert R. Cruz, *Let There Be Towns: Spanish Municipal Origins in the American Southwest, 1610–1810* (College Station: Texas A&M University Press, 1988), 87–89.

5.   Seb. S. Wilcox, "Laredo During the Texas Republic," *Southwestern Historical Quarterly* 42, no. 2 (1938): 84–86.

6.   Gilberto Miguel Hinojosa, *A Borderlands Town in Transition: Laredo, 1775–1870* (College Station: Texas A&M University Press, 1983), 12–13.

7.   Oscar J. Martínez, *Troublesome Border* (Tucson: The University of Arizona Press, 1988), 53–79.

8.   Robert D. Wood, *Life in Laredo: A Documentary History from the Laredo Archives* (Denton: University of North Texas Press, 2004), 82–83.

9.   Milo Kearney and Anthony Knopp, *Border Cuates: A History of the U.S.-Mexican Twin Cities* (Austin, Tex.: Eakin Press, 1995), 51.

10. Kearney and Knopp, 30–31.

11. Da Camara, *Laredo on the Rio Grande*, 14.

12. Wood, *Life in Laredo*, 78–79.

13. Wood, 3–9.

14. Kearney and Knopp, *Border Cuates*, 182.

15. Hinojosa, *Borderlands Town in Transition*, 48–53.

16. Wilcox, "Laredo During the Texas Republic," 99–105.

17. Wood, *Life in Laredo*, 30–31.

18. Kearney and Knopp, *Border Cuates*, 22.

19. Daniel D. Arreola, "Border-City Idée Fixe," *Geographical Review* 86, no. 3 (1996): 357–58.

20. Ladis K. D. Kristof, "The Nature of Frontiers and Boundaries," *Annals of the Association of American Geographers* 49, no. 3 (1959): 269–82.

21. Joseph Nevins, *Operation Gatekeeper: The Rise of the "Illegal Alien" and the Making of the U.S.-Mexico Boundary* (New York: Routledge, 2002), x.

22. Jorge A. Vela, "Laredoans Protest After Photos Show Poor Conditions at Animal Shelter," *Laredo Morning Times* online, June 23, 2021, https://www.lmt online.com/insider/article/Animal-shelter-pics-show-poor-conditions-1626 7763.php.

23. David J. Danelo, *The Border: Exploring the U.S.-Mexico Divide* (Mechanicsburg, Pa.: Stackpole Books, 2008), 46–47.

24. David Stea, Jamie Zech, and Melissa Gray, "Change and Non-change in the U.S.-Mexico Borderlands After NAFTA," in *Understanding Life in the Borderlands: Boundaries in Depth and Motion*, ed. William I. Zartman (Athens: University of Georgia Press, 2010), 105–30.

25. Nevins, *Operation Gatekeeper*, 5–6.

26. Danelo, *The Border*, 183.

27. Patricia Price, "Inscribing the Border: Schizophrenia and the Aesthetics of Aztlán," *Journal of Social and Cultural Geography* 1 (2000): 101–16.

28. Michael Peter Smith, "Postmodernism, Urban Ethnography, and the New Social Space of Ethnic Identity," *Theory and Society* 21 (1992): 493–531.

29. "President Richard Nixon on the Campaign Trail at Laredo Air Force Base," September 22, 1972, DocsTeach, https://www.docsteach.org/documents/docu ment/nixon-laredo-airforce-base.

30. Oscar J. Martínez, *Border People: Life and Society in the U.S.-Mexico Borderlands* (Tucson: University of Arizona Press, 1994), 5–10.

31. Daniel D. Arreola and James R. Curtis, *The Mexican Border Cities: Landscape Anatomy and Place Personality* (Tucson: University of Arizona Press, 1993), 188.

32. Nestor Rodriguez and Jacqueline Hagan, "Transborder Community Relations at the U.S.-Mexico Border: Laredo/Nuevo Laredo and El Paso/Ciudad Juárez," in *Caught in the Middle: Border Communities in an Era of Globalization*, ed. Demetrios G. Papademetriou and Deborah Waller Meyers (Washington, D.C.: Carnegie Endowment for International Peace, 2001), 97–101.

33. Chunghong Zhao, Jennifer Jensen, and Benjamin Zhan, "A Comparison of Urban Growth and Their Influencing Factors of Two Border Cities: Laredo in the U.S. and Nuevo Laredo in Mexico," *Applied Geography* 79 (February 2017): 230–33.

34. Néstor García Canclini, *Hybrid Cultures: Strategies for Entering and Leaving Modernity* (Minneapolis: University of Minnesota Press, 1995), 258–63.

35. Robert Lee Maril, *The Fence: National Security, Public Safety, and Illegal Immigration Along the U.S.-Mexico Border* (Lubbock: Texas Tech University Press, 2011), 268.

36. Lawrence A. Herzog, *Where North Meets South: Cities, Space, and Politics on the U.S.-Mexico Border* (London: Routledge, 1997), 138.

37. "Federal Surplus Commodities Corporation," Wikipedia, https://en.wikipedia .org/wiki/Federal_Surplus_Commodities_Corporation.

Chapter 2

1. Jerry E. Mueller, *Restless River: International Law and the Behavior of the Rio Grande* (El Paso: Texas Western Press, 1975), 41–42.

2. Oscar J. Martínez, *Border People: Life and Society in the U.S.-Mexico Borderlands* (Tucson: University of Arizona Press, 1994), 11–12.

3. Peter Andreas. "Politics on Edge: Managing the U.S.-Mexico Border," *Current History* 105, no. 688 (2006): 64–68.

4. Timothy J. Dunn, *The Militarization of the U.S.-Mexico Border, 1978–1992* (Austin, Tex.: CMAS Books, 1996), 68.

5. "Laredo Sector Texas," U.S. Customs and Border Protection, https://www.cbp.gov /border-security/along-us-borders/border-patrol-sectors/laredo-sector-texas.

6. Patricia Price, "Inscribing the Border: Schizophrenia and the Aesthetics of Aztlán," *Journal of Social and Cultural Geography* 1 (2000): 105.

7. Skip Hollandsworth, "The Hunt for the Serial Killer of Laredo," *Texas Monthly*, October 2019, https://www.texasmonthly.com/articles/serial-killer-border-patrol/.

8. http://www.borderregion.org/.

9. María Eugenia Guerra, "Attorney Ron Rodriguez Testifies Before Senate Committee on GEO Corporate Record of Abuse, Neglect, Prisoner Civil Rights Violations, and Cover-Up," *LareDOS*, October 2007.

10. Nicholas Hudson, *Ground Zero: The Laredo Superjail and the No Action Alternative* (Austin, Tex.: Grassroots Leadership, 2006), 1.

11. Dunn, *Militarization of the U.S.-Mexico Border*, 75.

12. Hudson, *Ground Zero*, 3–4.

13. Steve Horn, "Private Prison Operator Emerald Corrections Out of Business," *Prison Legal News*, September 3, 2018, https://www.prisonlegalnews.org/news /2018/sep/3/private-prison-operator-emerald-corrections-out-business/.

14. "CoreCivic," Wikipedia, https://en.wikipedia.org/wiki/CoreCivic.

15. "Temporary Checkpoints Popping Up Around Town," KGNS+, https://www .kgns.tv/content/news/Temporary-checkpoints-popping-up-around-town-5132 47121.html.

16. Guillermina Gina Nuñez and Georg M. Klamminger, "Centering the Margins: The Transformation of Community in Colonias on the U.S.-Mexico Border,"

in *Cities and Citizenship at the U.S.-Mexico Border: The Paso del Norte Metropolitan Region*, ed. Kathleen Staudt, César M. Fuentes, and Julia E. Monárrez Fragoso (New York: Palgrave Macmillan, 2010), 147–48.

17. Robert Lee Maril, *The Fence: National Security, Public Safety, and Illegal Immigration Along the U.S.-Mexico Border* (Lubbock: Texas Tech University Press, 2011), 202.

18. Sheila M. Olmstead, "Thirsty Colonias: Rate Regulation and the Provision of Water Service," *Land Economics* 80, no. 1 (2004): 136–50.

19. "Webb County Colonia," *Mapbook: Web County, Texas*, https://webbcountytx .gov/Planning/GISMaps/maps/2.2.pdf.

20. Robert H. Wilson and Miguel Guajardo, "Capacity Building and Governance in El Cenizo," *Cityscapes* 5, no. 1 (2000): 106, https://www.huduser.gov/Periodicals /CITYSCPE/VOL5NUM1/wilson.pdf.

21. Peter M. Ward, *Colonias and Public Policy in Texas and Mexico: Urbanization by Stealth* (Austin: University of Texas Press, 1999), 43–44.

22. Wilson and Guajardo, "Capacity Building," 109–11.

23. Wilson and Guajardo, 109–11.

24. Nunez and Klamminger, "Centering the Margins," 158–59.

25. Nunez and Klamminger, 168.

26. Claudia Kolker, "Border Town Adopts Spanish: Law Makes It Official Language," *SFGate*, August 13, 1999, https://www.sfgate.com/news/article/Border -Town-Adopts-Spanish-Law-makes-it-2913503.php.

27. Mehnaaz Momen, "Are You a *Citizen*? Insights from Borderlands," *Citizenship Studies* 9, no. 3 (2005): 323.

28. Momen, 327–29.

29. Dunn, *Militarization of the U.S.-Mexico Border*, 82.

30. Duncan Earle, "The Borderless Borderlands: Texas's Colonias as Displaced Settlements," in *Identities on the Move: Transnational Processes in North America and the Caribbean Basin*, ed. Liliana R. Goldin (Albany: Institute for Mesoamerican Studies, State University of New York, Albany, 1999), 169–83.

31. Nunez and Klamminger, "Centering the Margins," 157.

32. Taking advantage of the poor and passive population in the Rio Bravo and El Cenizo colonias, Texas governor Abbott has recently awarded a new contract for a small portion of the border wall (nine miles) limited to these areas. Justin Miller, "Texas Awards Biggest Border Wall Contract Yet to Trump-Tied Firm," *Texas Observer*, January 6, 2023, https://www.texasobserver.org/texas-awards -biggest-border-wall-contract-yet-to-trump-tied-firm/.

33. Edgar Saldivar, "'She Can't Be Forgotten': Family of Unarmed 20-Year-Old Killed by Border Patrol Seeks Justice," *ACLU Newsletter*, May 24, 2019, https:// www.aclutx.org/en/news/she-cant-be-forgotten-family-unarmed-20-year-old -killed-border-patrol-seeks-justice?fbclid=IwAR3_6dm0.

34. Mike Davis, *Magical Urbanism: Latinos Reinvent the U.S. City* (London: Verso, 2000), 27.

35. Peter Andreas, "Redrawing the Line: Borders and Security in the Twenty-First Century," *International Security* 28, no. 2 (Autumn, 2003): 80–81.

36. Josiah McC. Heyman, "Constructing a Virtual Wall: Race and Citizenship in U.S.-Mexico Border Policing," *Journal of the Southwest* 50, no. 3 (2008): 311.

37. Dunn, *Militarization of the U.S.-Mexico Border*, 132.

38. Andreas, "Redrawing the Line," 82–83.

39. Sylvia Longmire, *Border Insecurity: Why Big Money, Fences, and Drones Aren't Making Us Safer* (New York: Palgrave Macmillan, 2014), 54.

40. "Operation Linebacker," Bureau of Justice Assistance, U.S. Department of Justice, https://bja.ojp.gov/funding/awards/2008-dd-bx-0188.

41. David J. Danelo, *The Border: Exploring the U.S.-Mexico Divide* (Mechanicsburg, Pa.: Stackpole Books, 2008), 102.

42. Maril, *The Fence*, 234.

43. Maril, 281.

44. Longmire, *Border Insecurity*, 89–90.

45. Cari Lee Skogberg Eastman, *Shaping the Immigration Debate: Contending Civil Societies on the U.S.-Mexico Border* (Boulder, Colo.: FirstForumPress, 2012), 74.

46. "Presidential Proclamation on Declaring a National Emergency Concerning the Southern Border of the United States," February 15, 2019, https://trumpwhite house.archives.gov/presidential-actions/presidential-proclamation-declaring -national-emergency-concerning-southern-border-united-states/.

47. Ian Gordon and Camille Squires, "400 Tweets. 585 Miles. $9 Billion: Trump's Border Wall Boondogle," *Mother Jones* (May/June 2020), https://www.mother jones.com/politics/2020/06/trump-border-wall-cost-fisher-gravel-boondoggle /?fbclid=IwAR1kWjc6IjHqkNvcBbSRf9CY3KhQRPEZ91wE4nhrmEeP_g4xd kOTBszZj7Q.

48. Daniel van Schooten, "Bad Actors Among Border Wall Contractors," Project on Government Oversight, April 17, 2018, https://www.pogo.org/analysis/2018/04 /bad-actors-among-border-wall-contractors/.

49. Julia Wallace, "$275 Million Construction Contract Awarded to Build First Section of Border Wall in Webb County," *Laredo Morning Times* online, May 9, 2020, https://www.lmtonline.com/local/article/275-million-construction-contract -awarded-to-15258812.php.

50. Melissa del Bosque, "Border Wall Construction Set to Begin Near Historic Cemeteries in South Texas," *The Intercept*, August 23, 2020, https://theintercept .com/2020/08/23/border-wall-construction-historic-cemeteries-texas/.

51. "We Build the Wall," Wikipedia, https://en.wikipedia.org/wiki/We_Build_The _Wall.

52. Brian Kolefage, the founder of the group, wanted to donate money to the government, but the federal government has no mechanism to accept private donations. They evolved into a nonprofit with big-name supporters like Steve Bannon on their board and started constructing a wall in Mission, Texas, with-

out government permit. The National Butterfly Center and the International Boundary and Water Commission took them to court, and a judge in Hidalgo County halted the construction because the wall would cause flooding in the Rio Grande and harm the center. Legally, they have to take down the wall as they cannot connect with the section built by the federal government. Yet in January 2020, a federal judge lifted the injunction, allowing a construction firm to move forward with the three-mile project along the Rio Grande. This "steel fortress" is about to collapse at the Rio Grande, soon after its much hailed construction. Jeremy Schwartz and Perla Trevizo, "He Built a Privately Funded Border Wall: It's Already at Risk of Falling Down If Not Fixed," *Texas Tribune* and *Propublica*, July 2, 2020, https://www.texastribune.org/2020/07/02/texas -border-wall-private/.

53. Stefanie Herweck and Scott Nicol, *Death, Damage, and Failure: Past, Present, and Future Impacts of Walls on the U.S.-Mexico Border* (New York: American Civil Liberties Union, 2019), 69.

54. Heyman, "Constructing a Virtual Wall," 305–8.

55. Heyman, 314.

56. CRS Report for Congress, *Border Security: Inspection Practices, Policies, and Issues* (Congressional Research Services. January 2005), 19.

57. Maril, *The Fence*, 289.

58. Peter Andreas, "The Re-bordering of America after 11 September," *Brown Journal of World Affairs* 8, no. 2 (Winter 2002): 197.

59. Peter Andreas, *Border Games: Policing the U.S.-Mexico Divide* (Oxford: Oxford University Press, 2009), 11–12.

60. Longmire, *Border Insecurity*, 96.

61. Andreas, *Border Games*, 15–16.

Chapter 3

1. Saskia Sassen, "The Global City: Strategic Site/New Frontier," in *Readings in Urban Theory*, 3rd ed., ed. Susan S. Fainstein and Scott Campbell (Malden, Mass.: Wiley-Blackwell, 2011), 55–72.

2. John A. Adams Jr., *Conflict and Commerce on the Rio Grande: Laredo, 1775–1955* (College Station: Texas A&M University Press, 2008), 45–48.

3. Adams, 81.

4. Adams, 33.

5. Adams, 51–52.

6. Adams, 33.

7. Gilberto Miguel Hinojosa, *A Borderlands Town in Transition: Laredo, 1775–1870* (College Station: Texas A&M University Press, 1983), 87.

8. https://www.youtube.com/watch?v=hdxvHdKBpqo.

9. Peter Andreas, *Smuggler Nation: How Illicit Trade Made America* (Oxford: Oxford University Press, 2013), 157–67.

10. Samuel E. Bell and James M. Smallwood, "*Zona Libre*: Trade and Diplomacy on the Mexican Border 1858–1905," *Arizona and the West* 24, no. 2 (Summer 1982): 121–23.

11. Bell and Smallwood, 121.

12. Bell and Smallwood, 123–51.

13. Bell and Smallwood, 141–43.

14. Kathleen Da Camara, *Laredo on the Rio Grande* (San Antonio, Tex.: Naylor, 1949), 23–24.

15. Adams, *Conflict and Commerce*, 127–28.

16. Da Camara, *Laredo on the Rio Grande*, 23–29.

17. Da Camara, 23–24.

18. Adams, *Conflict and Commerce*, 107–12.

19. Adams, 80.

20. Milo Kearney and Anthony Knopp, *Border Cuates: A History of the U.S.-Mexican Twin Cities* (Austin, Tex.: Eakin Press, 1995), 125.

21. Kearney and Knopp, 37.

22. Da Camara, *Laredo on the Rio Grande*, 19.

23. Adams, *Conflict and Commerce*, 156.

24. Adams, 143–44.

25. Adams, 130.

26. Adams, 143.

27. Adams, 166.

28. Adams, 140.

29. Da Camara, *Laredo on the Rio Grande*, 35.

30. Da Camara, 35–36.

31. Da Camara, 36–37.

32. Da Camara, 38–39.

33. James R. Curtis, "Central Business Districts of the Two Laredos," *Geographical Review* 83, no. 1 (January 1993): 54–65.

34. Adams, *Conflict and Commerce*, 158.

35. Adams, 169.

36. James R. Giermanski, "NAFTA and the South Texas Border: Is the Border Fit to Compete?" *Journal of the Southwest* 39, no. 2 (Summer 1997): 291.

37. Timothy C. Brown, "The Fourth Member of NAFTA: The U.S.-Mexico Border," in "NAFTA Revisited: Expectations and Realities," special issue, *Annals of the American Academy of Political and Social Science* 550 (March 1997): 115.

38. Cleveland Historical, "Rock and Roll Hall of Fame," https://clevelandhistorical.org/items/show/704.

39. Mimi Swartz, "Green Acres," *Texas Monthly*, October 2015, https://www.texasmonthly.com/the-culture/green-acres-2/.

40. Ian Burton, "A Restatement of the Dispersed City Hypothesis," *Annals of the Association of American Geographers* 53, no. 3 (September 1963): 288.

41. Burton, 286.

42. Curtis, "Central Business Districts," 60–61.

43. Curtis, 62–63.

44. Lawrence A. Herzog, *Where North Meets South: Cities, Space, and Politics on the U.S.-Mexico Border* (London: Routledge, 1997), 53.

45. David E. Lorey, *The U.S.-Mexican Border in the Twentieth Century: A History of Economic and Social Transformation* (Wilmington, Del.: SR Books, 1999), 173.

46. Robert B. South, "Transnational 'Maquiladora' Location," *Annals of the Association of American Geographers* 80, No. 4 (December 1990): 549–70.

47. Isidro Morales, "NAFTA: The Institutionalisation of Economic Openness and the Configuration of Mexican Geo-economic Spaces," in "New Regionalisms in the New Millennium," special issue, *Third World Quarterly* 20, no. 5 (October 1999): 981.

48. Mike Davis, *Magical Urbanism: Latinos Reinvent the U.S. City* (London: Verso, 2000), 29–30.

49. Lorey, *U.S.-Mexican Border*, 175.

50. Peter Andreas, "U.S.-Mexico: Open Markets, Closed Border," *Foreign Policy* 103 (Summer 1996): 59.

51. Giermanski, "NAFTA and the South Texas Border," 290–93.

52. Andreas, "U.S.-Mexico," 58.

53. Herzog, *Where North Meets South*, 47.

54. Herzog, 62.

55. Andreas, "U.S.-Mexico," 58.

56. John Barkdull and John P. Tuman, "Texas and the International Economy," *State and Local Government Review* 31, no. 2 (Spring 1999): 106–22.

57. "Trump Migration Separation Policy: Children 'in Cages' in Texas," BBC News, June 18, 2018, https://www.bbc.com/news/world-us-canada-44518942.

58. Freddy Mariñez Navarro and Leonardo Vivas, "Violence, Governance, and Economic Development at the U.S.-Mexico Border: The Case of Nuevo Laredo and Its Lessons," *Mexican Studies/Estudios Mexicanos* 28, no. 2 (Summer 2012): 396.

59. James T. Peach and Richard V. Adkisson, "NAFTA and Economic Activity Along the U.S.-Mexico Border," *Journal of Economic Issues* 34, no. 2 (June 2000): 488.

60. Scarlett G. Hardesty, Malcolm D. Holmes, and James D. Williams, "Economic Segmentation and Worker Earnings in a U.S.-Mexico Border Enclave," *Sociological Perspectives* 31, no. 4 (October 1988): 466–89.

61. Giermanski, "NAFTA and the South Texas Border," 287–88.

62. Giermanski, 287.

63. Curtis, "Central Business Districts," 55.

64. James R. Curtis and Daniel D. Arreola, "Zonas de Tolerancia on the Northern Mexican Border," *Geographical Review* 81, no. 3 (July 1991): 333.

65. C. Boggs, "The Great Retreat: Decline of the Public Sphere in Late Twentieth-Century America," *Theory and Society* 26, no. 6 (1997): 749–50.

66. "Mall del Norte," Malls of America, January 22, 2007, http://mallsofamerica .blogspot.com/2007/01/mall-del-norte.html.

67. Curtis, "Central Business Districts," 55–56.
68. Curtis, 57.
69. Mehnaaz Momen, "Remembering Laredo: Spatial Reflections," *Space and Culture* 10, no. 1 (2007): 119.
70. David Bryne, *Understanding the Urban* (London: Palgrave, 2001), 51.
71. The 74th Texas legislature approved the expansion of four-year status to the existing Laredo State University, https://www.tamiu.edu/general.shtml.
72. Noi Mahoney, "Laredo, Texas, Becomes No. 1 U.S. Trade Hub," *FreightWaves*, June 6, 2019, https://www.freightwaves.com/news/laredo-texas-becomes-no-1-us-trade-hub.
73. *City of Laredo, Texas: Comprehensive Annual Financial Report for Fiscal Year Ended September 30, 2018* (Laredo: City of Laredo Financial Services Department, Accounting Division, 2018), v, https://www.cityoflaredo.com/Finance/CAFRs/2018_CAFR.pdf.
74. Michael Peter Smith, *Transnational Urbanism: Locating Globalization* (Malden, Mass.: Blackwell, 2001), 3–4.
75. Smith, 5.
76. Saskia Sassen, *Cities in the World Economy* (Thousand Oaks, Calif.: Pine Forge Press, 2006), 75–79.
77. M. Coleman, "U.S. Statecraft and the U.S.-Mexico Border as Security/Economy Nexus," *Political Geography* 24 (2005): 185–209.
78. Vincenzo Ruggiero and Nigel South, "The Late-Modern City as a Bazaar: Drug Markets, Illegal Enterprise and the 'Barricades,'" *British Journal of Sociology* 48, no. 1 (March 1997): 54–70.
79. Ruggiero and South, 62–66.
80. Texas Governor Abbott's attempt to do just that, namely to inspect all truck traffic, came to a disastrous end because of the horrendous traffic jams that predictably resulted. J. David Goodman, "Texas Governor Offers Deal to End Snarled Traffic at Border," *New York Times*, April 13, 2022, https://www.nytimes.com/2022/04/13/us/texas-border-abbott-trucks.html.

Chapter 4

1. Saskia Sassen, "Introduction: Whose City Is It? Globalization and the Formation of New Claims," in *The Blackwell City Reader*, ed. Gary Bridge and Sophie Watson (Malden, Mass.: Blackwell2002), 162.
2. The collection of decrees by the Spanish Crown that regulated public law spanning the social, political, religious, and economic aspects of life in the colonies during the sixteenth, seventeenth, and eighteenth centuries. Britannica online, s.v. "Laws of the Indies," https://www.britannica.com/event/Laws-of-the-Indies.
3. The 1890 city map of Laredo, designed by Mayor Samuel Jarvis, showed a town plan with twenty-three plazas and a "central park" at the four corners of LISD

(Martin High School, Leyendecker Elementary, the PAC, and sports facilities). Although he planned all of those plazas, many became school and other build-ing sites.

4. Raphael Longoria and Stephen Fox, "The Streets of Laredo: Reevaluating the Vernacular Urbanism of Old Nuevo Santander," in *Architecture, Material and Imagined: Proceedings of the 85th ACSA Annual Meeting and Technology Conference*, ed. Lawrence W. Speck and Dominique Bonnamour-Lloyd (Washington, D.C.: Association of Collegiate Schools of Architecture, 1997), 341–46.

5. The Spanish colonial architecture that centered on a town square and was used in the spatial design of Spanish settlements. The plan was influenced by Aztec as well as Italian and French planning, which the Spanish adopted for their colonies. See Setha M. Low, "Cultural Meaning of the Plaza: The History of the Spanish-American Gridplan-Plaza Urban Design," in *The Cultural Meaning of Urban Space*. ed. R. Rotenberg and G. McDonough (Westport, Conn.: Bergin and Garvey, 1992), 76–93. "Spanish Colonial architecture," Wikipedia, https://en.wikipedia.org/wiki/Spanish_Colonial_architecture.

6. The planning of residential zones away from the city center.

7. Michael S. Yoder and R. La Perriére de Gutiérrez, "Social Geography of Laredo, Texas, Neighborhoods: Distinctiveness and Diversity in a Majority-Hispanic Place," in *Hispanic Spaces, Latino Places: Community and Cultural Diversity in Contemporary America*, ed. Daniel D. Arreola (Austin: University of Texas Press, 2004), 62–65.

8. Neil Smith, *The New Urban Frontier: Gentrification and the Revanchist City* (London: Routledge: 1996), 13.

9. M. Christine Boyer, *Dreaming the Rational City: The Myth of American City Planning* (Cambridge, Mass.: MIT Press, 1983), 163–69.

10. Christina M. Jiménez, "From the Lettered City to the Seller's City: Vendor Politics and Public Space in Urban Mexico, 1880–1926," in *The Spaces of the Modern City: Imaginaries, Politics, and Everyday Life*, ed. Gyan Prakash and Kevin M. Kruse (Princeton, N.J.: Princeton University Press, 2008), 218–19.

11. https://historiclaredo.blogspot.com/.

12. JeriLynn Thorpe, "City of Laredo Calling on Artists for New Murals in Beautification Project," *Laredo Morning Times* online, February 21, 2018, https://www.lmtonline.com/local/article/City-of-Laredo-calling-on-artists-for-mural-12630780.php.

13. Selina Villarreal, "Murals in Laredo," Laredo, July 13, 2020, https://www.visitlaredo.com/p/things-to-do/murals-in-laredo.

14. JeriLynn Thorpe, "The Story Behind the Iconic 'I Love U Chingos' Sign, One of Laredo's Best Selfie Spots," *Laredo Morning Times* online, February 14, 2018, https://www.lmtonline.com/local/article/story-behind-I-Love-U-Chingos-sign-Laredo-s-selfie-12613631.php?ipid=artem#taboola-1.

15. *937 Gallery*, January 28–April 10, Other Border Wall Project, https://www.otherborderwallproject.com/.

16. https://laredotheaterguild.org/productions/icons-of-the-arts-gala/.

17. David Karas, "Highway to Inequity: The Disparate Impact of the Interstate Highway System on Poor and Minority Communities in American Cities," *New Visions for Public Affairs* 7 (April 2015): 9–21.

18. https://unitedwaylaredo.org/the-holding-institute/.

19. "Life Story: Jovita Idár Juárez (1885–1946)," Women and the American Story, New-York Historical Society, https://wams.nyhistory.org/modernizing-america /xenophobia-and-racism/jovita-idar-juarez/.

20. https://www.facebook.com/OurLaredo.

21. https://www.facebook.com/redwinglaredo/.

22. https://www.facebook.com/NoBorderWallCoalition/.

23. Sandra Sanchez, "Laredo Nonprofit Awarded Art Grant for Anti-border Wall Initiatives," *Border Report*, July 6, 2021, https://www.borderreport.com/hot -topics/the-border-wall/laredo-nonprofit-awarded-art-grant-for-anti-border -wall-initiatives/?fbclid=IwAR1w56A4AxGYZkLqXm1wUogSZ5LjTOYP2JE4 Q3G_wYadFw1DjnEKsz16fjk.

24. James Barragán, "Texas to Spend $25 Million on 2-Mile Concrete Barrier amid Gov. Greg Abbott's Push for a State-Funded Border Wall," *Texas Tribune*, August 13, 2021, https://www.texastribune.org/2021/08/13/texas-border-wall -greg-abbott/.

25. Boyer, *Dreaming the Rational City*, 288–89.

26. Leonie Sandercock, *Cosmopolis II: Mongrel Cities of the 21st Century* (London: Continuum, 2003), 186–97.

27. Dolores Hayden, *The Power of Place: Urban Landscapes as Public History* (Cambridge, Mass.: MIT Press, 1997), 46.

28. Viva Laredo, https://www.vivalaredo.org/the-process.

29. M. Christine Boyer, *Dreaming the Rational City*, 9–26.

30. Viva Laredo, https://www.vivalaredo.org/the-process.

31. Viva Laredo, https://www.vivalaredo.org/.

32. Boyer, *Dreaming the Rational City*, 69.

33. City of Laredo, *Viva Laredo Comprehensive Plan* (Laredo, Tex.: City of Laredo, 2017), i.1.

34. City of Laredo, 1.24–1.26.

35. https://laredoparksandrec.com/laredo-parks/aldo-tatangelo-walkway/.

36. City of Laredo, *Viva Laredo*, 2.48–2.54.

37. City of Laredo, 3.40–3.45.

38. City of Laredo, 4.77–4.85.

39. City of Laredo, 5.31–5.32.

40. City of Laredo, 6.22–6.25.

41. City of Laredo, 7.22–7.27.

42. City of Laredo, 8.14–8.17.

43. City of Laredo, 9.36–9.38.

44. City of Laredo, 10.14–10.15.

45. City of Laredo, 11.9–11.11.
46. City of Laredo, 12.4–12.54.
47. https://www.welfareinfo.org/poverty-rate/texas/laredo.
48. The Dakota Access Pipeline is a controversial underground oil pipeline that spans over 1,172 miles across North Dakota, South Dakota, Iowa, and Illinois. Indigenous tribes protested against its construction because of the environmental impact on their land and water. Drawing people from all over the nation, these protests were brutally curbed by the federal, state, and local governments. "Dakota Access Pipeline," Wikipedia, https://en.wikipedia.org/wiki/Dakota_Access_Pipeline.
49. "Uni-Trade Stadium," Wikipedia, https://en.wikipedia.org/wiki/Uni-Trade_Stadium.
50. John Hannigan, *Fantasy City: Pleasure and Profit in the Postmodern Metropolis* (London: Routledge, 1998), 56.
51. Hannigan, 57.
52. Julia Wallace, "Funding Secured for Multi-million Dollar Convention Center in Downtown Laredo," *Laredo Morning Times* online, July 12, 2017, https://www.lmtonline.com/local/politics/article/Funding-secured-for-multi-million-dollar-11282877.php.
53. https://trahanarchitects.com/work/laredo-convention-center/.
54. Julián Aguilar and Arya Sundaram, "Laredo Officials Want to Use Border Wall Money to Fund a Riverfront Project," *Texas Tribune*, March 20, 2019, https://www.texastribune.org/2019/03/20/laredo-border-wall-fund-municipal-project/.
55. "Fronteras: Two Nations, One River—Proposed Binational Park Will Connect Los Dos Laredos," Texas Public Radio, June 24, 2022, https://www.tpr.org/podcast/fronteras/2022-06-24/fronteras-two-nation-one-riveproposed-binational-river-park-will-connect-los-dos-laredos?fbclid=IwAR1NZwO6z05kutWV0dUwaMezNvSVSut-zsXswMPZViKi_eWmgSXO0fiiyxI&fs=e&s=cl.
56. https://www.golondrinafoodpark.com/.
57. https://www.facebook.com/LaredoUrbanAg/.
58. "Sames Auto Arena," https://en.wikipedia.org/wiki/Sames_Auto_Arena.
59. https://www.citymakery.com/.
60. https://www.facebook.com/lagordiloca956.
61. Anthony D'Alessandro, "George Robinson to Star in Feature Take of *Texas Monthly* Article 'Still Life': Kevin James and Jeff Sussman Producing," *Deadline*, March 9, 2022, https://deadline.com/2022/03/kevin-james-texas-monthly-still-life-movie-george-robinson-1234974438/.
62. Sharon Zukin, *The Culture of Cities* (Malden, Mass.: Blackwell, 1995), 288–89.
63. Mary Umberger, "The Perils of 'Privatopia': Taking a Second Look," *Chicago Tribune*, June 17, 2011, https://www.chicagotribune.com/real-estate/ct-xpm-2011-06-17-sc-cons-0616-umberger-privatopia-20110617-story.html.
64. Thomas F. Gieryn, "A Space for Place in Sociology," *Annual Review of Sociology* 26 (2000): 481.

65. Hayden, *The Power of Place*, 9–13.
66. Nisha A. Fernando, "Open-Ended Space," in *Loose Space: Possibility and Diversity in Urban Life*, ed. Karen A. Franck and Quentin Stevens (London: Routledge, 2007), 54–72.
67. Karen A. Franck and Quentin Stevens, "Tying Down Loose Space," in *Loose Space: Possibility and Diversity in Urban Life*, ed. Karen A. Franck and Quentin Stevens (London: Routledge, 2007), 1–34.

Chapter 5

1. Gloria E. Anzaldúa, *Borderlands/La Frontera: The New Mestiza* (San Francisco: Aunt Lute Books, 2007).
2. Mike Davis, *Magical Urbanism: Latinos Reinvent the U.S. City* (London: Verso, 2000).
3. Fernando Piñon, *Patron Democracy* (Mexico City: Ediciones Contraste, 1985), 51.
4. Webb County is divided into a number of districts, and each district elects its representative to give more power to voters, as opposed to at-large elections, where it is more difficult for a small group of voters to hold any of the multiple county commissioners accountable. "Single-member district," Wikipedia, https://en.wikipedia.org/wiki/Single-member_district.
5. A Municipal Utility District (MUD) is a political subdivision of the State of Texas that gets basic amenities like water, sewage, drainage, and other services within its boundaries through bonds authorized by the Texas Commission of Environmental Quality (TCEQ). https://www.jbgoodwin.com/buying/municipal-utility-districts.
6. https://www.masselec.com/our-work/industrial/water-related-infrastructure/el-pico-surface-water-treatment-plant/.
7. "TCEQ Gives Statement on City of Laredo Water Distribution System," KLTV, July 6, 2021. https://www.kltv.com/2021/07/06/tceq-gives-statement-city-laredo-water-distribution-system/.
8. Julia Wallace, "Records Detail Corruption Allegations Against Former City, County Officials," *Laredo Morning Times* online, October 20, 2018. https://www.lmtonline.com/local/politics/article/Records-detail-corruption-allegations-against-13322790.php.
9. Joseph Nevins, *Operation Gatekeeper: The Rise of the 'Illegal Alien' and the Making of the U.S.-Mexico Boundary* (New York: Routledge, 2002), 20–27.
10. Andrew Graybill, "Texas Rangers, Canadian Mounties, and the Policing of the Transnational Industrial Frontier, 1885–1910," *Western Historical Quarterly* 35, no. 2 (Summer 2004): 167–91.
11. David J. Danelo, *The Border: Exploring the U.S.-Mexico Divide* (Mechanicsburg, Pa.: Stackpole Books, 2008), 6.
12. Nevins, *Operation Gatekeeper*, 92.

13. Timothy J. Dunn, *The Militarization of the U.S.-Mexico Border, 1978–1992* (Austin, Tex.: CMAS Books, 1996), 51.

14. Robert Lee Maril, *The Fence: National Security, Public Safety, and Illegal Immigration Along the U.S.-Mexico Border* (Lubbock: Texas Tech University Press, 2011), 283.

15. Judith Warner, *U.S. Border Security: A Reference Handbook* (Santa Barbara, Calif.: ABC-Clio, 2010), 20.

16. Maril, *The Fence*, 283.

17. Charles C. Cumberland, "Border Raids in the Lower Rio Grande Valley, 1915," *Southwestern Historical Quarterly* 57, no. 3 (1954): 285–311.

18. Rebecca Onion, "America's Lost History of Border Violence," *Slate*, May 5, 2016.

19. Marlene Lenthang, "The Lone Star State's Bloody Shame: How Texas Rangers Murdered Thousands of Mexicans over 10 Years from 1910 and Were Hailed Heroes as State Representative Suggests History Is Repeating Itself," *Daily Mail*, August 8, 2019.

20. http://www.lynchingintexas.org/items/browse?tags=1882.

21. Peter Andreas, *Border Games: Policing the U.S.-Mexico Divide* (Oxford: Oxford University Press, 2009), 30.

22. Kelly Lytle Hernández, *La Migra! A History of the U.S. Border Patrol* (Berkeley: University of California Press, 2010), 219.

23. Hernández, 68.

24. Robert Lee Maril, *Patrolling Chaos: The U.S. Border Patrol in Deep South Texas* (Lubbock: Texas Tech University Press, 2004).

25. Maril, *The Fence*.

26. "Laredo's Concentrated Poverty Rate Is the Highest in All of Texas," The Center Square, January 12, 2021, https://www.thecentersquare.com/texas/laredo-s-concentrated-poverty-rate-is-the-highest-in-all-of-texas/article_895e918e-508d-11eb-bf66-776830dbff01.html.

27. Mr. South Texas is the designation regardless of the gender of the award recipient.

28. Julia Wallace, "After 20 Years, Tom Miller Retires from Science Center," *Laredo Morning Times* online, September 1, 2020, https://www.lmtonline.com/news/article/After-20-years-Tom-Miller-retires-from-science-15532158.php.

29. https://www.ibwc.gov/Organization/Operations/Field_Offices/Nuevo_Laredo.html.

30. Maril, *The Fence*, 202.

31. Jorge A. Vela, "Cigarroa Continues Family Tradition of Public Service," *Laredo Morning Times* online, January 19, 2021, https://www.lmtonline.com/insider/article/Cigarroa-continues-family-tradition-of-public-15881245.php.

32. "Robert Rodriquez," Wikipedia, https://en.wikipedia.org/wiki/Robert_Rodriguez.

33. Gabriela A. Treviño, "Indie Film to Be Shot in Laredo," *Laredo Morning Times* online, May 28, 2015. https://www.lmtonline.com/entertainment/article/Indie-film-to-be-shot-in-Laredo-9987931.php.

34. "Laredo Birding Festival Next Week," *Winter Texan Times*, October 18, 2022, https://www.wintertexantimes.com/news/around-town/3093-laredo-birding -festival-next-week.html.

35. https://laredobirdingfestival.org/about/.

36. https://www.inaturalist.org/projects/laredo-riverbend.

37. Christian Alejandro Ocampo, "Laredo Nature Preserve, Bird Sanctuary Approved by City Council," *Laredo Morning Times* online, May 21, 2021, https:// www.lmtonline.com/insider/article/Laredo-nature-preserve-bird-sanctuary -approved-16193120.php.

38. "Rio Grande International Study Center Receives $100K in Funding," MYSA, May 13, 2020, https://www.mysanantonio.com/news/article/Rio-Grande-Inter national-Study-Center-receives-15267642.php.

39. James Bird, *Centrality and Cities* (London: Routledge & Kegan Paul, 1977): 115–17.

40. https://www.facebook.com/watch/?v=2819663498072859.

41. *The Story of Plastic*, The Story of Stuff Project, https://www.storyofstuff.org /movies/the-story-of-plastic-documentary-film/.

42. *Rhapsody on the Rio Grande*, PBS, May 4, 2017, https://www.pbs.org/video /rhapsody-on-the-rio-grande-6lzukl/.

43. "Documentary Film, 'Rhapsody on the Rio Grande,' Bows, Wows at TAMIU," April 13, 2017, https://www.tamiu.edu/newsinfo/2017/04/TAMIURhapsody 41317.shtml.

44. John MacCormack, "Border Mayor Fights for His City's Image," *Houston Chronicle*, September 24, 2012, https://www.houstonchronicle.com/news/houston -texas/article/Border-mayor-fights-for-his-city-s-image-3888061.php.

Chapter 6

1. David Stea, Jamie Zech, and Melissa Gray, "Change and Non-change in the U.S.-Mexico Borderlands After NAFTA," in *Understanding Life in the Borderlands: Boundaries in Depth and Motion*, ed. William I. Zartman (Athens: University of Georgia Press, 2010), 108–9.

2. Nezar AlSayyad, "Hybrid Culture/Hybrid Urbanism: Pandora's Box of the 'Third Place,'" in *Hybrid Urbanism: On the Identity Discourse and the Built Environment*, ed. Nezar AlSayyad (Westport, Conn.: Praeger, 2001), 6–11.

3. Ananya Roy, "The Reverse Side of the World: Identity, Space and Power," in *Hybrid Urbanism: On the Identity Discourse and the Built Environment*, ed. Nezar AlSayyad (Westport, Conn.: Praeger, 2001), 229–45.

4. Gilberto Miguel Hinojosa, *A Borderlands Town in Transition: Laredo, 1775–1870* (College Station: Texas A&M University Press, 1983), xv.

5. Hinojosa, 32–33.

6. Hinojosa, 42.

7. Hinojosa, 76–79.

8. J. Fred Rippy, "Border Troubles Along the Rio Grande, 1848–1860," *Southwestern Historical Quarterly* 23, no. 2 (1919): 91–111.

9. Rippy, 100–104.

10. Robert D. Wood, *Life in Laredo: A Documentary History from the Laredo Archives* (Denton: University of North Texas Press, 2004), 112–13.

11. Milo Kearney and Anthony Knopp, *Border Cuates: A History of the U.S.-Mexican Twin Cities* (Austin, Tex.: Eakin Press, 1995), 43.

12. Hinojosa, *Borderlands Town in Transition*, 99.

13. Hinojosa, 101.

14. Hinojosa, 103.

15. Hinojosa, 66–68.

16. Joseph Nevins, *Operation Gatekeeper: The Rise of the "Illegal Alien" and the Making of the U.S.-Mexico Boundary* (New York: Routledge, 2002), 96–97.

17. Antonio N. Zavaleta, "Colored Death: The Tragedy of Black Troops on the Lower Rio Grande," in *Studies in Rio Grande Valley History*, ed. Milo Kearney, Anthony Knopp, and Antonio Zavaleta (Brownsville: University of Texas at Brownsville and Texas Southmost College, 2005), 343–60, https://drtony zavaleta.com/colored-death-the-tragedy-of-black-troops-on-the-lower-rio -grande-1864-1906/.

18. Carmina Danini, "The Ku Klux Klan Drew in Noted Civic Leaders and Sowed Terror in Texas," *San Antonio Express-News*, November 27, 2017, https://www .expressnews.com/sa300/article/The-Ku-Klux-Klan-drew-in-noted-civic -leaders-and-12387412.php.

19. Oscar J. Martínez, *Troublesome Border* (Tucson: University of Arizona Press, 1988), 81–98.

20. Oscar J. Martínez, *Border People: Life and Society in the U.S.-Mexico Borderlands* (Tucson: University of Arizona Press, 1994), 252–53.

21. Martínez, *Border People*, 277–280.

22. The five most influential families in Laredo have surnames like Cigarroa or Bruni, suggesting the prevalence of intermarriage between Anglos and Hispanics.

23. Matt Young, "'Bad Hombres' Tells Story of Texas-Mexico Border Through Baseball," *Chron.com*, October 15, 2020, https://www.chron.com/sports/astros /article/Showtime-Bad-Hombres-Tecolotes-Laredo-Luis-Flores-15650596.php.

24. Elaine A. Peña, "More Than a Dead American Hero: Washington, the Improved Order of Red Men, and the Limits of Civil Religion," *American Literary History* 26, no. 1 (Spring 2014): 61–62.

25. Peña, 63.

26. Peña, 75.

27. Mimi Swartz, "Once upon a Time in Laredo," *National Geographic*, November 2006, 92–106.

28. Peña, "More than a Dead American Hero," 64–65.

29. Peña, 71.

30. Peña, 71.
31. Elliot Young, "Red Men, Princess Pocahontas, and George Washington: Harmonizing Race Relations in Laredo at the Turn of the Century," *Western Historical Quarterly* 29, no. 1 (Spring 1998): 83–84.
32. Young, 48–50.
33. "Improved Order of Red Men," Wikipedia, https://en.wikipedia.org/wiki/Improved _Order_of_Red_Men.
34. Young, "Red Men," 53–57.
35. Young, 59.
36. Young, 64–67.
37. Young, 55.
38. Young, 79–80.
39. Elaine A. Peña, *¡Viva George!: Celebrating Washington's Birthday at the US-Mexico Border* (Austin: University of Texas Press, 2020), 65–70.
40. Valentine J. Belfiglio, "Bruni, Antonio Mateo (1856–1931)," Texas State Historical Association, May 1, 1995, https://www.tshaonline.org/handbook/entries /bruni-antonio-mateo.
41. Martínez, *Border People*, 274–75.
42. Martínez, 273–74.
43. Martínez, 277–78.
44. Martínez, 278–79.
45. Karen Olsson, "All the News That Fits Laredo," *Texas Observer*, February 18, 2000, https://www.texasobserver.org/129-all-the-news-that-fits-laredo-meet -meg-guerra-of-laredos-debutante-scholar-student-activist-and-crusading -hometown-publisher/.
46. Elaine A. Peña, *¡Viva George!*, 35–37.
47. Peña, 48–52.
48. Ritual dancing that originated in Spain and was adopted by North and South American native tribes, especially in Mexico and Peru.
49. The pilgrimage of Mary and Joseph to Bethlehem is acted out with songs and ends with finding a safe haven in an inn where people come together to party. https://www.learnreligions.com/christmas-posadas-tradition-in-mexico -1588744.
50. https://www.facebook.com/gsagroupllc/.
51. Fernando Piñón, *Searching for America in the Streets of Laredo: The Mexican-American Experience in the Anglo-American Narrative* (Mexico City: Centro de Estudios Sociales Antonio Gramsci A.C., 2015), 37.
52. Piñón, 204–5.
53. Piñón, 221–23.
54. "Port of Entry: Laredo; Impact to the Texas Economy, 2018," Comptroller.Texas .gov, https://comptroller.texas.gov/economy/economic-data/ports/laredo.php.
55. Martínez. *Border People*, 53.
56. Stea and Gray, "Change and Non-change," 109.

Conclusion

1. Gloria E. Anzaldúa, *Borderlands/La Frontera: The New Mestiza* (San Francisco: Aunt Lute Books, 2007), 25.

2. Edward W. Soja, *Thirdspace: Journeys to Los Angeles and Other Real-and-Imagined Places* (Oxford: Blackwell, 1996), 127–29.

3. Saskia Sassen, "Old Borders and New Bordering Capabilities: Cities as Frontier Zones." *Scienza & politica* 27, no. 53 (2015): 295–306.

4. Ben Masters, dir., *The River and the Wall* (Gravitas Ventures, 2019), https://the riverandthewall.com/.

5. Edward W. Soja, *Postmetropolis: Critical Studies of Cities and Regions* (Oxford: Blackwell, 2000), 189–232.

6. Soja, 298–322.

7. Saskia Sassen, "The Global City: Strategic Site/New Frontier," in *Readings in Urban Theory*, 3rd. ed., ed. Susan S. Fainstein and Scott Campbell (Malden, Mass.: Wiley-Blackwell, 2011), 55–72.

8. Soja, *Postmetropolis*, 264–97.

9. Sharon Zukin, *Naked City: The Death and Life of Authentic Urban Places* (Oxford: Oxford University Press, 2010), 220.

10. Zukin, 220–23.

11. https://noborderwallcoalition.com/2020/08/18/defund-the-wall-fund-our-future -massive-street-mural-completed/.

12. Kate McGee, "Two Texas Universities That Serve Students of Color Receive Multimillion-Dollar Donations from Philanthropist MacKenzie Scott," *Texas Tribune*, December 15, 2020, https://www.texastribune.org/2020/12/15/prairie -view-donation-mackenzie-scott/.

13. Saskia Sassen, "When the Center No Longer Holds: Cities as Frontier Zones," *Cities* (2012): 1–4.

14. Erik Swyngedouw, "Globalisation or 'Glocalisation'? Networks, Territories and Rescaling," *Cambridge Review of International Affairs* 17, no. 1 (2004): 25–48.

15. Anssi Paasi, "Boundaries as Social Processes: Territoriality in the World of Flows," *Geopolitics* 3, no. 1 (1998): 69–88.

Bibliography

Adams, John A., Jr. *Conflict and Commerce on the Rio Grande: Laredo, 1775–1955.* College Station: Texas A&M University Press, 2008.

AlSayyad, Nezar. "Hybrid Culture/Hybrid Urbanism: Pandora's Box of the 'Third Place.'" In *Hybrid Urbanism: On the Identity Discourse and the Built Environment,* edited by Nezar AlSayyad, 1–18. Westport, Conn.: Praeger, 2001.

Anderson, James, and Liam O'Dowd. "Borders, Border Regions and Territoriality: Contradictory Meanings, Changing Significance." *Regional Studies* 33, no. 7 (1999): 593–604.

Andreas, Peter. *Border Games: Policing the U.S.-Mexico Divide.* Oxford: Oxford University Press, 2009.

Andreas, Peter. "Politics on Edge: Managing the U.S.-Mexico Border." *Current History* 105, no. 688 (2006): 64–68.

Andreas, Peter. "The Re-bordering of America after 11 September." *Brown Journal of World Affairs* 8, no. 2 (Winter 2002): 195–202.

Andreas, Peter. "Redrawing the Line: Borders and Security in the Twenty-First Century." *International Security* 28, no. 2 (Autumn 2003): 78–111.

Andreas, Peter. *Smuggler Nation: How Illicit Trade Made America.* Oxford: Oxford University Press, 2013.

Andreas, Peter. "U.S.-Mexico: Open Markets, Closed Border." *Foreign Policy* 103 (Summer 1996): 51–69.

Andreas, Peter, and Timothy Snyder. *The Wall Around the West: State Borders and Immigration Controls in North America and Europe.* Lanham, Md.: Rowman & Littlefield, 2000.

Anzaldúa, Gloria E. *Borderlands/La Frontera: The New Mestiza.* San Francisco: Aunt Lute Books, 2007.

Arreola, Daniel D. "Border-City Idée Fixe." *Geographical Review* 86, no. 3 (1996): 356–69.

Arreola, Daniel D. "Plaza Towns of South Texas." *Geographical Review* 8, no. 21 (1992): 18–47.

Arreola, Daniel D. *Postcards from the Río Bravo Border: Picturing the Place, Placing the Picture, 1900s–1950s.* Austin: University of Texas Press, 2013.

Arreola, Daniel D. *Tejano South Texas: A Mexican American Cultural Province.* Austin: University of Texas Press, 2002.

Arreola, Daniel D. "Urban Ethnic Landscape Identity," *Geographical Review* 85, no. 4 (1995): 524–28.

Arreola, Daniel D., and James R. Curtis. *The Mexican Border Cities: Landscape Anatomy and Place Personality.* Tucson: University of Arizona Press, 1993.

Barkdull, John, and John P. Tuman. "Texas and the International Economy." *State and Local Government Review* 31, no. 2 (Spring 1999): 106–22.

Bell, Samuel E., and James M. Smallwood. "*Zona Libre*: Trade and Diplomacy on the Mexican Border 1858–1905." *Arizona and the West* 24, no. 2 (Summer 1982): 119–52.

Bird, James. *Centrality and Cities.* London: Routledge & Kegan Paul, 1977.

Body-Gendrot, Sophie. *Globalization, Fear and Insecurity: The Challenges for Cities North and South.* London: Palgrave Macmillan, 2012.

Boggs, C. "The Great Retreat: Decline of the Public Sphere in Late Twentieth-Century America." *Theory and Society* 26, no. 6 (1997): 741–80.

Boyer, M. Christine. *Dreaming the Rational City: The Myth of American City Planning.* Cambridge, Mass.: MIT Press, 1983.

Brown, Timothy C. "The Fourth Member of NAFTA: The U.S.-Mexico Border." In "NAFTA Revisited: Expectations and Realities." Special issue, *Annals of the American Academy of Political and Social Science* 550 (March 1997): 105–21.

Broyles, Bill, and Mark Haynes. *Desert Duty: On the Line with the U.S. Border Patrol.* Austin: University of Texas Press, 2010.

Brunet-Jailly, Emmanuel. "Toward a Model of Border Studies: What Do We Learn from the Study of the Canadian-American Border?" *Journal of Borderlands Studies* 19, no.1 (2004): 1–12.

Burton, Ian. "A Restatement of the Dispersed City Hypothesis." *Annals of the Association of American Geographers* 53, no. 3 (September 1963): 285–89.

Byrne, David. *Understanding the Urban.* London: Palgrave, 2001.

Canclini, Néstor García. *Hybrid Cultures: Strategies for Entering and Leaving Modernity.* Minneapolis: University of Minnesota Press, 1995.

Cantú, Norma Elia. *Canícula: Snapshots of a Girlhood en La Frontera.* Albuquerque: University of New Mexico Press, 1995.

City of Laredo. *Viva Laredo: City of Laredo, TX, Comprehensive Plan.* Laredo, Tex.: City of Laredo, 2017. https://s3.amazonaws.com/wix-anyfile/oTSmhV8bSNiGxXB 9ayc5_Plan%20VIVA%20Laredo_%20First%20Edition_Second%20Revision.pdf.

Coleman, M. "U.S. Statecraft and the U.S.-Mexico Border as Security/Economy Nexus." *Political Geography* 24 (2005): 185–209.

CRS Report for Congress. *Border Security: Inspection Practices, Policies, and Issues.* Congressional Research Services. January 19, 2005. https://www.everycrsreport .com/files/20050119_RL32399_a04e9f1fa3bf3164c08074d1298234138dbc5e80.pdf.

Cruz, Gilbert R. *Let There Be Towns: Spanish Municipal Origins in the American Southwest, 1610–1810*. College Station: Texas A&M University Press, 1988.

Cumberland, Charles C. "Border Raids in the Lower Rio Grande Valley, 1915." *Southwestern Historical Quarterly* 57, no. 3 (1954): 285–311.

Curtis, James R. "Central Business Districts of the Two Laredos." *Geographical Review* 83, no. 1 (January 1993): 54–65.

Curtis, James R., and Daniel D. Arreola. "Zonas de Tolerancia on the Northern Mexican Border." *Geographical Review* 81, no. 3 (July 1991): 333–46.

Da Camara, Kathleen. *Laredo on the Rio Grande*. San Antonio, Tex.: Naylor, 1949.

Danelo, David J. *The Border: Exploring the U.S.-Mexican Divide*. Mechanicsburg, Pa.: Stackpole Books, 2008.

Davis, Mike. *Magical Urbanism: Latinos Reinvent the U.S. City*. London: Verso, 2000.

Dunn, Timothy J. *The Militarization of the U.S.-Mexico Border, 1978–1992*. Austin, Tex.: CMAS Books, 1996.

Earle, Duncan. "The Borderless Borderlands: Texas's Colonias as Displaced Settlements." In *Identities on the Move: Transnational Processes in North America and the Caribbean Basin*, edited by Liliana R. Goldin, 169–83. Albany: Institute for Mesoamerican Studies, State University of New York, Albany, 1999.

Eastman, Cari Lee Skogberg. *Shaping the Immigration Debate: Contending Civil Societies on the U.S.-Mexico Border*. Boulder, Colo.: FirstForumPress, 2012.

Fernando, Nisha A. "Open-Ended Space." In *Loose Space: Possibility and Diversity in Urban Life*, edited by Karen A. Franck and Quentin Stevens, 54–72. London: Routledge, 2007.

Franck, Karen A., and Quentin Stevens. "Tying Down Loose Space." In *Loose Space: Possibility and Diversity in Urban Life*, edited by Karen A. Franck and Quentin Stevens, 1–34. London: Routledge, 2007.

Giermanski, James R. "NAFTA and the South Texas Border: Is the Border Fit to Compete?" *Journal of the Southwest* 39, no. 2 (Summer 1997): 287–302.

Gieryn, Thomas F. "A Space for Place in Sociology." *Annual Review of Sociology* 26 (2000): 463–96.

Graybill, Andrew. "Texas Rangers, Canadian Mounties, and the Policing of the Transnational Industrial Frontier, 1885–1910." *Western Historical Quarterly* 35, no. 2 (Summer 2004): 167–91.

Grodach, Carl, and Daniel Silver, eds. *The Politics of Urban Cultural Policies: Global Perspectives*. London: Routledge, 2013.

Guerra, María Eugenia. "Attorney Ron Rodriguez Testifies Before Senate Committee on GEO Corporate Record of Abuse, Neglect, Prisoner Civil Rights Violations, and Cover-Up." *LareDOS*, October 2007.

Hannigan, John. *Fantasy City: Pleasure and Profit in the Postmodern Metropolis*. London: Routledge, 1998.

Hardesty, Scarlett G., Malcolm D. Holmes, and James D. Williams. "Economic Segmentation and Worker Earnings in a U.S.-Mexico Border Enclave." *Sociological Perspectives* 31, no. 4 (October 1988): 466–89.

Hayden, Dolores. *The Power of Place: Urban Landscapes as Public History*. Cambridge, Mass.: MIT Press, 1997.

Hernández, Kelly Lytle. *La Migra! A History of the U.S. Border Patrol*. Berkeley: University of California Press, 2010.

Herweck, Stefanie, and Scott Nicol. *Death, Damage, and Failure: Past, Present, and Future Impacts of Walls on the U.S.-Mexico Border*. New York: American Civil Liberties Union, 2019.

Herzog, Lawrence A. *Where North Meets South: Cities, Space, and Politics on the U.S.-Mexico Border*. London: Routledge, 1997.

Heyman, Josiah McC. "Constructing a Virtual Wall: Race and Citizenship in U.S.-Mexico Border Policing." *Journal of the Southwest* 50, no. 3 (2008): 305–33.

Hinojosa, Gilberto Miguel. *A Borderlands Town in Transition: Laredo, 1775–1870*. College Station: Texas A&M University Press, 1983.

Hudson, Nicholas. *Ground Zero: The Laredo Superjail and the No Action Alternative*. Austin, Tex.: Grassroots Leadership, 2006.

Jiménez, Christina M. "From the Lettered City to the Sellers' City: Vendor Politics and Public Space in Urban Mexico, 1880–1926." In *The Spaces of the Modern City: Imaginaries, Politics, and Everyday Life*, edited by Gyan Prakash and Kevin M. Kruse, 214–46. Princeton, N.J.: Princeton University Press, 2008.

Karas, David. "Highway to Inequity: The Disparate Impact of the Interstate Highway System on Poor and Minority Communities in American Cities." *New Visions for Public Affairs* 7 (April 2015): 9–21.

Kearney, Milo, and Anthony Knopp. *Border Cuates: A History of the U.S.-Mexican Twin Cities*. Austin, Tex.: Eakin Press, 1995.

Klein, Alan. *Baseball on the Border: A Tale of Two Laredos*. Princeton, N.J.: Princeton University Press, 1997.

Kolossov, Vladimir. "Border Studies: Changing Perspectives and Theoretical Perspectives." *Geopolitics* 10 (2005): 606–32.

Krabbendam, Hans, Marja Roholl, and Tity de Vries, eds. *The American Metropolis: Image and Inspiration*. Amsterdam: VU University Press, 2001.

Kristof, Ladis K. D. "The Nature of Frontiers and Boundaries." *Annals of the Association of American Geographers* 49, no. 3 (1959): 269–82.

Lenthang, Marlene. "The Lone Star State's Bloody Shame: How Texas Rangers Murdered Thousands of Mexicans over 10 Years from 1910 and Were Hailed Heroes as State Representative Suggests History Is Repeating Itself." *Daily Mail*, August 8, 2019.

Longmire, Sylvia. *Border Insecurity: Why Big Money, Fences, and Drones Aren't Making Us Safer*. New York: Palgrave Macmillan, 2014.

Longoria, Raphael, and Stephen Fox. "The Streets of Laredo: Reevaluating the Vernacular Urbanism of Old Nuevo Santander." In *Architecture, Material and Imagined: Proceedings of the 85th ACSA Annual Meeting and Technology Conference*, edited by Lawrence W. Speck and Dominique Bonnamour-Lloyd, 341–46. Washington, D.C.: Association of Collegiate Schools of Architecture, 1997.

Lorey, David E. *The U.S.-Mexican Border in the Twentieth Century: A History of Economic and Social Transformation.* Wilmington, Del.: SR Books, 1999.

Low, Setha M. "Cultural Meaning of the Plaza: The History of the Spanish-American Gridplan-Plaza Urban Design." In *The Cultural Meaning of Urban Space,* edited by R. Rotenberg and G. McDonough, 76–93. Westport, Conn.: Bergin and Garvey, 1992.

Maldonado, Ray Ybarra. *Born on the Border: Minutemen Vigilantes, Origins of Arizona's Anti-Immigrant Movement, and a Call for Increased Civil Disobedience.* Phoenix, Ariz.: Hispanic Institute of Social Issues, 2013.

Maril, Robert Lee. *The Fence: National Security, Public Safety, and Illegal Immigration Along the U.S.-Mexico Border.* Lubbock: Texas Tech University Press, 2011.

Maril, Robert Lee. *Patrolling Chaos: The U.S. Border Patrol in Deep South Texas.* Lubbock: Texas Tech University Press, 2004.

Martínez, Oscar J. *Border People: Life and Society in the U.S.-Mexico Borderlands.* Tucson: University of Arizona Press, 1994.

Martínez, Oscar J. *Troublesome Border.* Tucson: University of Arizona Press, 1988.

Momen, Mehnaaz. "Are You a *Citizen*? Insights from Borderlands." *Citizenship Studies* 9, no. 3 (2005): 323–34.

Momen, Mehnaaz. "Remembering Laredo: Spatial Reflections." *Space and Culture* 10, no. 1 (2007): 115–28.

Morales, Isidro. "NAFTA: The Institutionalisation of Economic Openness and the Configuration of Mexican Geo-economic Spaces." In "New Regionalisms in the New Millennium." Special issue, *Third World Quarterly* 20, no. 5 (Oct., 1999): 971–993.

Mueller, Jerry E. *Restless River: International Law and the Behavior of the Rio Grande.* El Paso: Texas Western Press, 1975.

Navarro, Freddy Mariñez, and Leonardo Vivas. "Violence, Governance, and Economic Development at the U.S.-Mexico Border: The Case of Nuevo Laredo and Its Lessons." *Mexican Studies/Estudios Mexicanos* 28, no. 2 (Summer 2012): 377–416.

Nevins, Joseph. *Operation Gatekeeper: The Rise of the "Illegal Alien" and the Making of the U.S.-Mexico Boundary.* New York: Routledge, 2002.

Newman, David. "The Lines That Continue to Separate Us: Borders in Our 'Borderless' World." *Progress in Human Geography* 30, no. 2 (2006): 143–61.

Nickell, Pat Smith. "Postmodern Aspects in Larry McMurtry's *Lonesome Dove, Streets of Laredo, Dead Man's Walk,* and *Comanche Moon.*" PhD diss., Texas Tech University, 1999.

Nuñez, Guillermina Gina, and Georg M. Klamminger. "Centering the Margins: The Transformation of Community in Colonias on the U.S.-Mexico Border." In *Cities and Citizenship at the U.S.-Mexico Border: The Paso del Norte Metropolitan Region,* edited by Kathleen Staudt, César M. Fuentes, and Julia E. Monárrez Fragoso, 147–72. New York: Palgrave Macmillan, 2010.

Olmstead, Sheila M. "Thirsty Colonias: Rate Regulation and the Provision of Water Service." *Land Economics* 80, no. 1 (2004): 136–50.

Onion, Rebecca. "America's Lost History of Border Violence." *Slate*, May 5, 2016.

Paasi, Anssi. "Boundaries as Social Processes: Territoriality in the World of Flows." *Geopolitics* 3, no. 1 (1998): 69–88.

Paasi, Anssi, and Kaj Zimmerbauer. "Penumbral Borders and Planning Paradoxes: Relational Thinking and the Question of Borders in Spatial Planning." *Environment and Planning A* 48, no. 1 (2006): 75–93.

Peach, James T., and Richard V. Adkisson. "NAFTA and Economic Activity Along the U.S.-Mexico Border." *Journal of Economic Issues* 34, no. 2 (June 2000): 481–89.

Peña, Elaine A. "More Than a Dead American Hero: Washington, the Improved Order of Red Men, and the Limits of Civil Religion." *American Literary History* 26, no. 1 (Spring 2014): 61–82.

Peña, Elaine A. *¡Viva George! Celebrating Washington's Birthday at the US-Mexico Border*. Austin: University of Texas Press, 2020.

Piñon, Fernando. *Patron Democracy*. Mexico City: Ediciones Contraste, 1985.

Piñon, Fernando. *Searching for America in the Streets of Laredo: The Mexican-American Experience in the Anglo-American Narrative*. Mexico City: Centro de Estudios Sociales Antonio Gramsci A.C., 2015.

Price, Patricia. "Inscribing the Border: Schizophrenia and the Aesthetics of Aztlán." *Journal of Social and Cultural Geography* 1 (2000): 101–16.

Rippy, J. Fred. "Border Troubles Along the Rio Grande, 1848–1860." *Southwestern Historical Quarterly* 23, no. 2 (1919): 91–111.

Rodriguez, Nestor, and Jacqueline Hagan. "Transborder Community Relations at the U.S.-Mexico Border: Laredo/Nuevo Laredo and El Paso/Ciudad Juárez." In *Caught in the Middle: Border Communities in the Era of Globalization*, edited by Demetrios G. Papademetriou and Deborah Waller Meyers, 88–116. Washington, D.C.: Carnegie Endowment for International Peace, 2001.

Romero, Fernando, and Laboratory of Architecture staff. *Hyper-Border: The Contemporary U.S.-Mexico Border and Its Future*. New York: Princeton Architectural Press, 2008.

Roy, Ananya. "The Reverse Side of the World: Identity, Space and Power." In *Hybrid Urbanism: On the Identity Discourse and the Built Environment*, edited by Nezar AlSayyad, 229–45. Westport, Conn.: Praeger, 2001.

Ruggiero, Vincenzo, and Nigel South. "The Late-Modern City as a Bazaar: Drug Markets, Illegal Enterprise and the 'Barricades.'" *British Journal of Sociology* 48, no. 1 (March 1997): 54–70.

Saldivar, Edgar. "'She Can't Be Forgotten': Family of Unarmed 20-Year-Old Killed by Border Patrol Seeks Justice." *ACLU Newsletter*, May 24, 2019. https://www.aclutx.org/en/news/she-cant-be-forgotten-family-unarmed-20-year-old-killed-border-patrol-seeks-justice?fbclid=IwAR3_6dm0.

Sandercock, Leonie. *Cosmopolis II: Mongrel Cities of the 21st Century*. London: Continuum, 2003.

Sassen, Saskia. *Cities in the World Economy*. Thousand Oaks, Calif.: Pine Forge Press, 2006.

Sassen, Saskia. "The Global City: Strategic Site/New Frontier." In *Readings in Urban Theory*, 3rd ed., edited by Susan S. Fainstein and Scott Campbell, 55–72. Malden, Mass.: Wiley-Blackwell, 2011.

Sassen, Saskia. "Introduction: Whose City Is It? Globalization and the Formation of New Claims." In *The Blackwell City Reader*, edited by Gary Bridge and Sophie Watson, 161–70. Malden, Mass.: Blackwell, 2002.

Sassen, Saskia. "Old Borders and New Bordering Capabilities: Cities as Frontier Zones." *Scienza & politica* 27, no. 53 (2015): 295–306.

Sassen, Saskia. "When the Center No Longer Holds: Cities as Frontier Zones." *Cities* 34 (2013): 67–70.

Sites, William. "Primitive Globalization? State and Locale in Neoliberal Global Engagement." *Sociological Theory* 18, no. 1 (2000): 121–44.

Smith, Michael Peter. "Postmodernism, Urban Ethnography, and the New Social Space of Ethnic Identity." *Theory and Society* 21 (1992): 493–531.

Smith, Michael Peter. *Transnational Urbanism: Locating Globalization*. Malden, Mass.: Blackwell, 2001.

Smith, Neil. *The New Urban Frontier: Gentrification and the Revanchist City*. London: Routledge, 1996.

Soja, Edward W. *Postmetropolis: Critical Studies of Cities and Regions*. Oxford: Blackwell, 2000.

Soja, Edward W. *Thirdspace: Journeys to Los Angeles and Other Real-and-Imagined Places*. Oxford: Blackwell, 1996.

South, Robert B. "Transnational 'Maquiladora' Location." *Annals of the Association of American Geographers* 80, no. 4 (December 1990), 549–70.

Squint, Dale. *My Border Patrol Diary: Laredo, Texas*. Bloomington, Ind.: Authorhouse, 2007.

Stea, David, Jamie Zech, and Melissa Gray. "Change and Non-change in the U.S.-Mexico Borderlands After NAFTA." In *Understanding Life in the Borderlands: Boundaries in Depth and Motion*, edited by William I. Zartman, 105–30. Athens: University of Georgia Press, 2010.

Swartz, Mimi. "Once upon a Time in Laredo." *National Geographic*, November 2006, 92–106.

Swyngedouw, Erik. "Globalisation or 'Glocalisation'? Networks, Territories and Rescaling." *Cambridge Review of International Affairs*, 17, no. 1 (2004): 25–48.

Ward, Peter M. *Colonias and Public Policy in Texas and Mexico: Urbanization by Stealth*. Austin: University of Texas Press, 1999.

Warner, Judith A. *U.S. Border Security: A Reference Handbook*. Santa Barbara, Calif.: ABC-Clio, 2010.

Wilcox, Seb. S. "Laredo During the Texas Republic." *Southwestern Historical Quarterly* 42, no. 2 (1938): 83–107.

Wilson, Robert H., and Miguel Guajardo. "Capacity Building and Governance in El Cenizo." *Cityscapes* 5, no. 1 (2000): 101–23. https://citeseerx.ist.psu.edu/viewdoc/download?doi=10.1.1.569.9047&rep=rep1&type=pdf.

Wood, Robert D. *Life in Laredo: A Documentary History from the Laredo Archives.* Denton: University of North Texas Press, 2004.

Yoder, Michael. S., and R. La Perriére de Gutiérrez. "Social Geography of Laredo, Texas, Neighborhoods: Distinctiveness and Diversity in a Majority-Hispanic Place." In *Hispanic Spaces, Latino Places: Community and Cultural Diversity in Contemporary America,* edited by Daniel D. Arreola, 55–76. Austin: University of Texas Press, 2004.

Young, Elliot. "Red Men, Princess Pocahontas, and George Washington: Harmonizing Race Relations in Laredo at the Turn of the Century." *Western Historical Quarterly* 29, no. 1 (Spring 1998): 48–85.

Zhao, Chunghong, Jennifer Jensen, and Benjamin Zhan. "A Comparison of Urban Growth and Their Influencing Factors of Two Border Cities: Laredo in the U.S. and Nuevo Laredo in Mexico." *Applied Geography* 79 (February 2017): 223–34.

Zukin, Sharon. *The Culture of Cities.* Malden, Mass.: Blackwell, 1995.

Zukin, Sharon. *Naked City: The Death and Life of Authentic Urban Places.* Oxford: Oxford University Press, 2010.

Index

About the Author

Dr. Mehnaaz Momen teaches political science and public administration courses in the Department of Social Sciences at Texas A&M International University (TAMIU). She worked at a nonprofit organization in Bangladesh and completed higher education in Halifax, Canada, and Cleveland, Ohio. She is the author of *The Paradox of Citizenship in American Politics: Ideals and Reality* (Palgrave Macmillan, 2017) and *Political Satire, Postmodern Reality, and the Trump Presidency: Who Are We Laughing At?* (Lexington Books, 2019).